THE SOCIAL MESSAGE OF THE GITA SYMBOLIZED AS LOKASAṀGRAHA

SELF-COMPOSED SANSKRIT ŚLOKAS WITH ENGLISH COMMENTARY

THE SOCIAL MESSAGE OF THE GITA SYMBOLIZED AS LOKASAṀGRAHA

SELF-COMPOSED SANSKRIT ŚLOKAS WITH
ENGLISH COMMENTARY

SATYA P. AGARWAL
Ph.D. (UC, Berkeley)
Center for South Asia Studies
University of California
Berkeley, California,
U.S.A

Publisher:
URMILA AGARWAL
11293 Ridermark Row
Columbia, Maryland 21044
U.S.A

First Edition : Columbia, MD 1995

Published by:

URMILA AGARWAL
11293 RIDERMARK ROW
COLUMBIA, MARYLAND 21044
U.S.A.

Also available at:

URMILA AGARWAL
C-157, Anand Vihar
Delhi 110 092
INDIA

MOTILAL BANARSIDASS
41 U.A. Bungalow Road
Delhi 110 007
INDIA

ISBN: 81-208-1319-7

TYPESET AND PRINTED IN INDIA AT

SHRI JAINENDRA PRESS,
A-45 NARAINA, PHASE I, NEW DELHI 110 028

To
My elder brother
the late Shri Krishna Chandra Agarwal
Gita scholar and social worker

लोकसंग्रहसन्देशः

LOKASAṀGRAHA SANDEŚAḤ

THE SOCIAL MESSAGE OF THE GITA SYMBOLIZED AS LOKASAṀGRAHA

PART ONE

गीतायां लोकपक्षप्रतिपादनम्

Gītāyāṁ Lokapakṣapratipādanam

AFFIRMATION OF THE SOCIAL CONCERNS OF THE GITA

PART TWO

लोकहिते गीताप्रयोगकथाचयनम्

Lokahite Gītāprayogakathācayanam

GITA APPLICATIONS FOR SOCIAL CAUSES: A SELECTIVE NARRATION

PART THREE

रेखाङ्कनं नवरूपाणां लोकसंग्रहस्य

Rekhāṁkanaṁ Navarūpāṇāṁ Lokasaṁgrahasya

OUTLINE OF NEW FORMS OF LOKASAṀGRAHA

CONTENTS

PART TWO

लोकहिते गीताप्रयोगकथाचयनम्
Lokahite Gītāprayogakathācayanam
GITA APPLICATIONS FOR SOCIAL CAUSES: A SELECTIVE NARRATION

PART THREE

रेखाङ्कनं नवरूपाणां लोकसंग्रहस्य
Rekhāṁkanaṁ Navarūpāṇāṁ Lokasaṁgrahasya
OUTLINE OF NEW FORMS OF LOKASAṀGRAHA

PREFACE

by

Professor Madhav M. Deshpande

I am delighted to present to the readers Dr. Satya Prakash Agarwal's new book *The Social Message of the Gītā Symbolized as Lokasaṁgraha*. Dr. Agarwal comes from a family which cherished the classical texts of the *Gītā* and the *Rāmāyaṇa* and transmitted this treasure to him since his childhood. His father, Shri Ram Swarup Agarwal, was a social worker and a scholar specializing in the *Gītā* and the *Rāmāyaṇa*. This unique combination has been especially significant for the modern evolution of India and Indian nationalism, where, for more than a hundred years, the active social workers, reformers, and patriots have sought inspiration and confirmation of their ideas and idealisms in the classical traditions. Whatever the original intent of these classical texts, it is clear that until the emergence of the modern period, the classical texts were interpreted more in the context of the devotional tradition of Bhakti and the ascetic-meditative traditions of Vedanta. Rarely does one find an activist interpretation of these classical texts. Thus, the activist interpretation of these texts needs to be understood as a relatively modern phenomenon, and one needs to study its contents, its textual and contextual sources, and its impact on its environment. Dr. Satya P. Agarwal has been busy expounding this activist interpretation for many years. He is not only a scholar of Sanskrit, but he also taught courses on Indian social problems, and his interpretation of the *Gītā* now represents a synthesis of his manifold interests. While he had been giving lectures on the *Gītā* for many years, his specific focus on the social role of the *Gītā* has resulted in several recent publications. Among these, I should like to particularly mention his 1993 book: *The Social Role of the Gītā: How and Why*.

His present book is unique for a number of reasons. Indeed, it continues his previous approach. However, it significantly adds to this particular view by succinctly putting its conclusions in the form of Sanskrit verses. Just as the tradition of Bhakti originated in vernaculars and then was ultimately Sanskritized, similarly the activist and the social interpretation of the *Gītā* began with the writings of Aurobindo Ghose and Lokamanya Tilak and is now being transported back to Sanskrit in the verses composed by Dr. Agarwal.

I am especially pleased to introduce this book because I have myself been advocating a somewhat similar interpretation of the *Gītā*, though indeed for very different reasons. In my article "The Epic Context of the Bhagavad Gītā," (in *Essays on the Mahābhārata*, edited by Arvind Sharma, E.J. Brill, Leiden, 1991, pp. 334-348), I have shown that the *Gītā* must be interpreted within its epic context and that the epic context of the *Gītā* significantly shapes its philosophical arguments. Here is a conversation between two Kṣatriyas on the battlefield. The starting point of the text is the resignation of Arjuna from the battle, and the conclusion of the text is his decision to join the battle once again. Whatever happens in the middle must be viewed as something that takes Arjuna from his resignation to his engagement in the battle. Any interpretation of the *Gītā* which does injustice to this intrinsic directionality of the text has little chance of being close to the intended original message. In another article,"The Kṣatriya Core of the Bhagavad Gītā," which should appear shortly in the Professor R.K. Sharma Felicitation Volume (Nag Publishers, Delhi), I have discussed the internal evidence in the text of the *Gītā* and the *Mahābhārata* to suggest that the textual layer advocating the doctrine of Karmayoga must have been historically the earliest layer in the text, and the Vedāntic and the devotional layers in the text are probably later accretions. However, even in the Vedāntic and the devotional layers, the *Gītā* continues to maintain its insistence on being active in the world. In this sense, the *Gītā* is a truly unique text advocating a middle ground between the rampant self-indulgent ritualism on the one hand and the escapist path of renunciation from the world on the other. It advocates selfless action for the betterment of the world as the essential factor of any and every path. It is clearly opposed to renunciation of the involvement in the world, but it incorporates the renunciation of the fruit of action. Even in the layer advocating the doctrine of Bhakti, the *Gītā* is different from the devotional paths seen in the *Bhaktisūtras* of Nārada, the *Bhāgavata-Purāṇa*, or the devotional writings of the medieval saints like Mīrābāī and Sūrdās. The *Gītā* advocates action and involvement in the world, with devotion and surrender to God. One is advised in the *Gītā* to carry on selfless action in the world with devotion in one's heart, and not just to be busy in acts or rituals of devotion with little attention to the fate of the society. In this sense, the modern activist interpretation of the *Gītā* is, in my view, somewhat closer to the original intent of the text and its historical core, as compared to the interpretations one finds in the traditional commentaries of Śaṅkara, Rāmānuja, and Madhva.

I congratulate Dr. Agarwal on his significant accomplishment. His Sanskrit verses are divided into eighteen chapters like the chapters of the *Gītā* itself, and in these chapters he provides to us in full his understanding of the social role of the *Gītā*. He not only offers us his personal understanding of the message of the *Gītā*, he also gives an account of how the *Gītā* was understood in the last two hundred years by the leaders of the Indian nationalist movement. Thus, this is a presentation of the history of modern interpretation of the *Gītā*. This interpretation is of interest not only as a different interpretation, but for its impact on the entire nationalist movement.

The Sanskrit text of Dr. Agarwal's verses is of great interest to me as a student of the linguistic features of modern Sanskrit. Modern Sanskrit often represents a conceptual and linguistic Sanskritization of the vernacular material. In the process of modernization of Hindi, numerous Sanskrit words were taken over, newly coined, and used in specific modern meanings. Modern Sanskrit compositions, Dr. Agarwal's verses included, indicate the process of using these Sanskritized Hindi expressions again in Sanskrit. Here one must keep in mind that the outer surface of many expressions is in Sanskrit, but their meaning must be understood not from their classical use, but from their use in modern Hindi. Such modern Sanskrit expressions are found side by side with purely classical and epic expressions in Dr. Agarwal's work. This is indeed inevitable, if one is to be able to express the concerns of the modern environment in Sanskrit.

If one restricts oneself purely to the classical expressions and meanings, one cannot use Sanskrit to express the concerns of the present age. Thus, I would encourage the readers to keep in mind the modernity of Dr. Agarwal's Sanskrit while reading these verses.

I have been impressed by the synthesis of ideas presented by Dr. Agarwal in this work. The *Gītā* is a text of the highest importance, not only for the Orientalists and Indologists who may analyze it from their academic ivory towers, but for the millions of people in modern India, who seek inspiration and guidance from it. As Vivekananda, Tilak, and Gandhi discovered and preached, the *Gītā* has the message of selfless action for social upliftment that India and the world needs today. On behalf of all the readers, I take this opportunity to thank Dr. Agarwal for his continuing efforts to expound this message.

Professor Madhav M. Deshpande
Professor of Sanskrit and Linguistics
Department of Asian Languages & Cultures
The University of Michigan
Ann Arbor, Michigan 48109, USA

ACKNOWLEDGEMENTS

How and from where came to me the inspiration to compose Sanskrit ślokas to convey the Lokasaṁgraha-message of the Gita? The search for an answer takes me to the early years of my life when the Gita-based non-violent struggle to achieve India's independence deeply influenced millions of families. Even children learnt by heart some of the Gita-ślokas in Sanskrit as well as Hindi songs based thereon. Because of my parents' active participation in social work and educational activities, Sanskrit-learning within our family tended to incorporate an element of creativity also. For example, the way I was brought up by my parents and elder brothers helped cultivate naturally an aptitude to express ideas in the form of Sanskrit verses. Frequent visits of well-known Sanskrit scholars like the late Shri Hanuman Prasad Poddar, Editor of Gita Press Gorakhpur strengthened the process of creative development of which the seeds were sown in the family atmosphere. These are the primary sources to whom I owe the most and whose contribution to the present publication I want to acknowledge first. Of course, formal education received later from Sanskrit teachers like Pandit Vidyadhar Shastri also played a significant role, and to all of them too I want to express my indebtedness and gratitude.

During my graduate study, research and initial employment in the United States, spread over the period 1948-1956, although I taught Sanskrit, Hindi and a social problem-oriented course, the subject which brought to me some of my best life-long friends was Sanskrit. It was a thrilling experience for me as well as my wife Urmila—who attended courses in Asian Studies—to watch American students trying to apply their knowledge of Sanskrit grammar to certain texts from the Mahabharata. Subsequently, during the seventies and the eighties, when employment with the United Nations took us to Asia, Africa and Europe, my wife and I found how keenly interested Indian families living in the various countries were, in listening to Gita-ślokas recited by me in the original Sanskrit, followed by an explanation in Hindi or English.

After my retirement from the United Nations, the Indian community in Cairo, Egypt, led by Dr. R.S.S. Sarma and Dr. M. Sivamurthy, who organised so many socio-religious activities, enabled me, during 1988-89, to share my views on the Gita, on a weekly basis, with members of an active Study Group.

The drafting of Sanskrit ślokas for the present publication began slowly in 1992 when Professor Goldman approved my research associateship with the Center for South Asia Studies at the University of California, Berkelely—the same university where I had studied from 1948 onward. Close collaboration with Professor van Nooten at the same university was particularly helpful, not only for my earlier book "The Social Role of the Gita: How and Why", but it also paved the way for the drafting of the Sanskrit manuscript for "The Social Message of the Gita Symbolized as Lokasaṁgraha". While the research-oriented Berkeley-support has continued over the last three years, it has been supplemented with valuable advice that I received from Professor Vishnu Raj Atreya of Mahendra Sanskrit University, Nepal and Dr. Brahma Nand Sharma, Ex-Director, Rajasthan Oriental Research Institute, Jaipur. To all the above-named Sanskrit scholars, I want to convey my heart-felt thanks.

Moving next, from the Sanskrit ślokas to the English commentary thereon, the choice of ideas to be highlighted was facilitated by the feedback that I received from the audiences, in India, USA and UK, where I had the opportunity to speak on the Gita during the last two years. In this connection, special mention needs to be made of meetings organised by M.S. University, Baroda, Gita-interest group brought together by Arun Kumar Gupta, New Delhi, Gita Mandal of Indianapolis, Indian cultural get-together of Raleigh, North Carolina, Orland Park, Illinois, Fremont, San Jose and Sunnyvale, California, India Club of the World Bank, Washington, D.C., and National and International Gita conferences presided over by Swami Hari Harji Maharaj. I am grateful to all the persons who organised these meetings. Furthermore, since Swami Hari Harji Maharaj—who has set up hundreds of Gita centers all over the world—constitutes a special category by himself, the impact of his blessings and highly appreciative words about my book "The Social Role of the Gita" cannot be over-estimated. The feedback that I received from the meetings of these Gita centers in Chicago, Illinois, Springfield, Illinois, St. Louis, Missouri, and London, UK was nothing short of an inspiration to write the Gita message in words that can carry a truly universal appeal.

There are many others—including political and administrative leaders, academicians and social workers—who welcomed my earlier book and thus provided encouragement for the present one. Governor Schaefer of the State of Maryland awarded the Governor's Citation, recognizing the value of my contribution not only professionally but also as a service to society. Shri Bhajan Lal, Chief Minister of Haryana State—the State which takes pride in having within its borders Kurukṣetra where the message of the Gita was first given—released my book at a function in Haryana Bhawan organised by his Principal Secretary, Shri Dhanendra Kumar. Shri Gajanan Wakankar, who is not only a senior member of the Indian Foreign Service but is also a Gita scholar himself, generously characterized my contribution as a living example of Lokasaṁgraha-oriented Karmayoga. I want to express my thanks to all of them for their appreciation and support.

As a research worker, I have derived professional satisfaction from the kind words conveyed to me by educationists and academicians. My formulation of the Lokasaṁgraha message has received warm applause from Professors M.V. Mathur, Karl H. Potter, P.S. Sangal, R.S. Dwivedi, R.R. Gupta, Satish C. Goyal and Linda Hess—to mention only a few—and to all of them I am indebted for their support.

Socio-cultural and religious leaders, who are trying to ensure the preservation of the right values in the society, have also welcomed my contribution. Again I have to be content with only a selective listing, for example, Swami Prabuddhananda of the Ramakrishna Mission, San Francisco, Swami Dayatmananda of the R.K. Vedanta Centre, Bourne End, UK, Shri Mathour Krishnamurti of the Bharatiya Vidya Bhawan, UK, Dr. P. Jayaraman of the Bharatiya Vidya Bhawan, New York, Pandit Damodar Dutt Shastri, Dr. Natwerlal S. Jani, Shri Hardev S. Palta, Dr. Piyush Agrawal, Dr. Jagdish Rustagi, Shri Pradeep Joshi, Shri N.S. Choudhry and Matra Mashruwala. I am grateful for the help that they gave to enable me to expound the

Lokasaṁgraha message of the Gita and thus to get the feedback which has been of immense use to me in preparing the present publication.

I want to thank Prof. Robert P. Goldman, Chairman, and Dr. Steven M. Poulos,Vice-Chairman, Center for South Asia Studies, Berkeley for continuing my university-linked identity, namely, as an Honorary Research Associate. Similarly, I am indebted to Prof. Madhav M. Deshpande, Professor of Sanskrit and Linguistics, University of Michigan, who has written the Preface to this book, in spite of heavy pressure of work.

Within my own family or svajanam, in the language of the Gita, my wife Urmila's role as an active research partner and publisher deserves to be particularly highlighted. We have worked and travelled together extensively, and she not only provided constant companionship and encouragement but also valuable feedback, based on a thorough reading of all the drafts, conference notes and related literature. Nishkam and Kokila, and similarly, Seema and David Harding—that is, the next generation and their spouses—provided technical skills, time and energy needed to convert a hand-written draft into a computer-processed manuscript, containing so many references and footnotes. Besides them, there was an extended family support group that included Purnima Gupta, Savita Choudhry, Rajiv Bhushan, Aveesh Kumar, Neena Kumar and Vivek Mital—to name only a few. Valuable feedback and technical help also came from Shri Harish Kashyap, Shri I.C. Gupta, Shri S.N. Goyal, Shri Arya Bhushan, Dr. Krishna Mohan and Renu Mital, Girish and Rashmi Gupta, Abhay and Judith Bhushan, and M.M. Agarwal. Even grandchildren—Isha, Kiran, Priya and Maya—helped keep alive the spirit of devotion to the cause of book-writing, by asking what I was writing and by listening attentively to stories connected with the Gita.

It is a happy coincidence that the date of completion of this book marks the Diamond Jubilee of the English translation of Lokamanya Tilak's Gita-rahasya. Although the process of highlighting Karmayoga under modern social conditions was started by Raja Rammohun Roy in 1818 and elaborated further, from 1893 onward, by Swami Vivekananda, a full-length Gita-commentary challenging non-activist interpretations became available for the first time through Gita-rahasya only in the twentieth century. In respect of that pioneering book too, only the Marathi version was published in 1915, while translations in some of the other Indian languages—Hindi, Gujarati, Bengali, Tamil, Telugu and Kannada—appeared during the years 1917-1924. The English translation of Gita-rahasya (from the original Marathi text) took twenty years and was completed on 12th June 1935. I hope my humble contribution, made with gratitude to all pioneers—Roy, Vivekananda, Tilak, Aurobindo, Gandhi and others—will help maintain as well as rejuvenate the process of continuation of the selfless effort which sought to make available to readers all over the world a detailed, scholarly commentary on the half-forgotten Karmayoga message of the Gita, founded on Lokasaṁgraha. The importance of restating this message from time to time has been highlighted by Śrī Kṛṣṇa Himself in the Gita, and this is the basis of the historical-cum-empirical approach which I have adopted and which has prompted me to structure this book in the form of the following three parts:

Part One: Affirmation of the Social Concerns of the Gita
Part Two: Gita Applications for Social Causes: A Selective Narration
Part Three: Outline of New Forms of Lokasaṁgraha.

The topic of Lokasaṁgraha is undoubtedly vast and complex, and it is only through the generosity and blessings of Gita-scholars and others—some of whom have been specified above—that I have arrived at the present stage of research and writing. While reiterating my deep sense of gratitude to all of them, I express the hope that similar support will be forthcoming when I continue study and research on Lokasaṁgraha. Finally, to clarify the limitations of my institutional relationship with the University of California, I must add that responsibility for the ideas expressed in the book is entirely mine, and not that of the Center for South Asia Studies.

Center for South Asia Studies
University of California
Berkeley, California, USA
12 June, 1995

Satya P. Agarwal

PART ONE

गीतायां लोकपक्षप्रतिपादनम्

Gītāyāṁ Lokapakṣapratipādanam

AFFIRMATION OF THE SOCIAL CONCERNS OF THE GITA

CHAPTER ONE

नवयुगारम्भः
NAVAYUGĀRAMBHAḤ

BEGINNING OF A NEW ERA

This chapter takes the reader to a time period approximately two hundred years ago, that is to the early years of the nineteenth century, and more specifically to the years 1811-18. At that time, the Indian society in general, and the Hindu society in particular, had degenerated to such an extent that, if no serious effort were made to lift it up, a complete social disintegration would have taken place. Christian missionaries from Europe—irrespective of whether their general approach to the Indian society was hostile, indifferent or sympathetic—felt that Hinduism would "die of degeneration within a century".[1] But such a catastrophe did not occur because a strong social reform movement aimed at protecting some of the oppressed people was set in motion by Raja Rammohun Roy, and the arguments which he used to convince the orthodox section of the society were based mainly on the Bhagavad-Gita. While details about the reform movement and its use of the Gita will be given in Part Two of this book, and particularly in chapter seven, the point to be stressed at this stage is that, the Gita helped Rammohun Roy to stop the process of social degeneration and to begin a new era or Navayuga as it is called in this chapter. With this brief introduction, the self-composed Sanskrit ślokas, together with an English commentary, are now presented.

१.१. द्विशताब्दपूर्वमहो शृण्वन्तु हितकामिनः ।
गीताप्रयोगस्यारम्भः त्रस्तजनवर्गहिते ।।

dviśatābdapūrvamaho śṛṇvantu hitakāminaḥ
gītāprayogasyārambhaḥ trastajanavargahite

Listen, O well-wishers of humanity, it was nearly two hundred years ago that those who wanted to help the oppressed sections of the society started taking the help of the Gita for their social causes. We do not mean to say that such uses of the Gita were not made prior to that; however, written and dated records of such uses are not readily available. Also, since the time period that we are referring to marks a turning point in the socio-religious history of modern India, its significance and relevance in the context of present-day society can be easily appreciated.

We feel that the two criteria—availability of written and dated records, and relatively shorter distance in terms of time from the present age—provide adequate justification for restricting the scope of this book to what is commonly called the modern era. Ramesh Betai, author of the book "Gita and Gandhiji", also lends an indirect support to our approach when he says that the types of problems that have appealed to the "moderns" are qualitatively different from those in which the "ancients" were primarily interested:

With the moderns, we come to quite a different approach. . . . Naturally it has happened that the problems that have appealed to the modern writers have not appealed to the ancients, in fact such an outlook was not conceivable for them . . . As the modern critical method and research methods are applied to the Gita, so many problems in which the ancients had no interest or which they could not conceive of as problems altogether, are discussed today by the moderns. . . It cannot be denied that the moderns have given to us a new vision and approach towards the interpretation of the Gita and we have definitely come to a better understanding of the secret of the doctrine of the Gita.[2]

By addressing the opening verse of this book to well-wishers of humanity, we want to make it clear that the social message of the Gita is not for Hindus alone, nor for Indians alone, but for all those in the world who want to bring about peace, prosperity and happiness for everyone, without any distinction of race, creed, sex, nationality, etc.

१.२. परिस्थितिः सामाजिकी बाहुल्येन कुरीतीनाम् ।
वर्णिता ह्यतिदुःखदा नारीभ्यस्तु विशेषतः ॥

paristhitiḥ sāmājikī bāhulyena kurītīnām
varṇitā hyatiduḥkhadā nārībhyastu viśeṣataḥ

At that time, social conditions in India had deteriorated because of too many of the evil customs. Large sections of the society, and particularly the women, felt extremely miserable. Evil customs prevalent at that time included child marriages, burning of widows—even if they were quite young—with the dead body of their husband, discriminatory attitudes that adversely affected the bringing up of girls, and even the practice of offering small babies to the river Ganga—or Ganges, as it was called in English in those days. Two of these—widow-burning and child-sacrifice—are particularly referred to in the next verse because these were visible examples of what can be characterized as "murder".

१.३. विधवानां देहदाहो निम्नतमकोटिपापम् ।
अंधविश्वासजनिता बालहत्या जले त्यक्त्वा ॥
vidhavānāṁ dehadāho nimnatamakoṭipāpam
andhaviśvāsajanitā bālahatyā jale tyaktvā

The worst imaginable criminal act was the practice of burning widows with the body of their dead husband. Similarly, misguided by superstition, several families used to offer their small babies as a sacrifice to the River.

The practice of widow-burning—or Suttee, as it was called—was not only prevalent in Bengal at that time but was even defended by orthodox elements in the Hindu society as being beneficial to the widows and their families. However, regarding the practice of throwing children into the mouth of the river Ganges near Calcutta, Nirad C. Chaudhuri has explained that, although "everybody (including myself as a child) knew it as a fact", some people expressed "impulsive disbelief".[3]

A significant turning point came—or a new era began nearly two hundred years ago—because at the darkest hour, the Gita message or Mantra of protection reappeared, this time to a social reformer—reminiscent of the original Gita message that was given to Arjuna at Kurukṣetra long ago. The next verse, drawing attention to this, can be called "Gita-mantra's Reappearance Declaration".

गीतामंत्रप्राकट्यघोषणा
GĪTĀMANTRAPRĀKAṬYAGHOṢAṆĀ

१.४. एतस्मिन् काले कराले रक्षामंत्रः श्रीगीतोक्तः ।
प्रकटोऽभवद्धि पुनः यथा पूर्वं कुरुक्षेत्रे ॥

etasmin kāle karāle rakṣāmantraḥ śrīgītoktaḥ
prakaṭo'bhavaddhi punaḥ yathā pūrvaṁ kurukṣetre

At such a critical juncture, social activists thought of taking the help of the teachings of the Gita to save human lives. It was as if the protective message of the Gita, which was first heard long ago at Kurukṣetra was heard again during the new era.

The reference here is to social activists led by Rammohun Roy whose pioneering work of social reform based on the Gita is described in chapter seven. Roy's movement focussed attention on widow-burning, because, as Nirad Chaudhuri says, the practice of throwing children into the River was, in the mean time, prohibited by a legislative order of the Governor-General.[4] There is no evidence to suggest, however, that a similar prohibition by the British administration against widow-burning would have occurred if Roy had not created public opinion against this evil custom.

The time period, when the use of the Gita for social reform began in India, was notable also for another important development concerning the spread of the Gita to Europe and America. Rammohun Roy's knowledge of Sanskrit enabled him to read the original version of the Gita. However, the process of making the Gita available to those who only knew European languages began when Roy was still a boy. With the approval and support of Sanskrit scholars in India—and carrying also an enthusiastic advocacy from Warren Hastings, the Governor of Bengal—the first book to be translated into English by Charles Wilkins in 1785 was the Gita. Although Gita translations into Latin and other European languages appeared from 1825 onwards, it was Wilkins' translation, offered on sale in England from 1785 onwards, that reached Emerson and other American thinkers during the first half of the nineteenth century. Thus, when we speak of the reappearance of the Gita-message to social reformers in India, nearly two hundred years ago, the parallel spread of the Gita to readers in Europe and America can also be viewed as significant. In fact, Wilkins' translation of the Gita into English in 1785 is considered so significant by Eric Sharpe of Australia that in 1985 he published a book entitled "The Universal Gita: Western Images of the Bhagavad Gita, A Bicentenary Survey".[5]

१.५. गीताप्रयोगकथानां लोकहिते नवयुगे ।
वर्णनं समासतोऽत्र कृतं मंगलेच्छया हि ॥
gītāprayogakathānāṁ lokahite navayuge
varṇanaṁ samāsato'tra kṛtaṁ maṁgalecchayā hi

We are attempting, in this book, to describe briefly how a new era began when practical applications of the Gita were made to help oppressed people. We hope this attempt of ours will contribute to the well-being of mankind—for example, by encouraging those who want to help the weaker sections of the human society.

१.६. न तु लेखके विद्वत्ता रचयितुं काव्यपदम् ।
अन्तः प्रेरितः प्रयासः श्रीगीताश्रोतृभ्योऽर्पितः ॥
na tu lekhake vidvattā racayituṁ kāvyapadam
antaḥ preritaḥ prayāsaḥ śrīgītāśrotṛbhyo'rpitaḥ

Although this book is written in the form of self-composed Sanskrit ślokas, we must admit that the author does not have the qualifications of a poet. The author feels as if Sanskrit verses are coming out of his inner self as a natural inspiration, and we offer them, with all humility, to Gita-listeners.

The use of self-composed Sanskrit verses to convey the social message of the Gita can be considered a special feature of this book. The earlier book by the author on practically the same subject—but in greater detail—is entirely in English, and carries the title "The Social Role of the Gita: How and Why".[6]

१.७. लोकसंग्रहसंदेशो जनहिते गीताशिक्षा ।
नवयुगकथासारो ग्रन्थस्य नाम कायश्च ॥
lokasaṁgrahasaṁdeśo janahite gītāśikṣā
navayugakathāsāro granthasya nāma kāyaśca

What is the real essence of the social applications of the teachings of the Gita made in the new era? Since such applications were made for the good of humanity, they brought to the forefront the Gita teaching of Lokasaṁgraha—holding the society and the world together on the right path. An appropriate title of this book is therefore Lokasaṁgraha-Sandeśaḥ—The Social Message of the Gita symbolized as Lokasaṁgraha. And an integrated account of how this message has been given during the last two hundred years, why it was possible to derive this message from the Gita and what new forms it could possibly assume in the context of the modern society, constitutes the body of this book.

Rammohun Roy's initial use of the Gita for a social cause was followed, in due course of time, with even bigger uses by other leaders of social, religious and political movements. Details about four other uses, selected from those pertaining to the post-Rammohun Roy period, are given in chapters eight to eleven of Part Two of this book. The Gita-word "Lokasaṁgraha"—interpreted in several ways but all of them denoting essentially 'the good of the society'—provides the common link between Roy and others who came after him. In order to explain why it was possible to derive the social message from the Gita, an in-depth study of "Lokasaṁgraha" is given in chapters two to six of Part One. Furthermore, the term "Lokasaṁgraha" being non-sectarian, secular, comprehensive, and wide enough to be able to include even modern concepts, possibilities of associating therewith some new forms of socially beneficial ideas and work-programmes are discussed in chapters twelve to eighteen of Part Three of this book.

१.८. द्विशतश्लोकमाध्यमात् द्विशतवर्षकथानाम् ।
सारांशोऽत्र प्रतिष्ठितो लोकसंग्रहसंदेशः ॥
dviśataślokamādhyamāt dviśatavarṣakathānām
sārāṁśo'tra pratiṣṭhito lokasaṁgrahasaṁdeśaḥ

Only a brief history is narrated in this book as to how the Lokasaṁgraha teaching of the Gita has been applied during the last two hundred years. This narration is contained in two hundred Sanskrit verses in this book. Even though briefly narrated, the social message of the Gita, we hope, will arouse feelings of awe and respect for the Gita as well as for those who applied its teachings for the good of humanity.

A forward-looking wish underlying the use of the same number of Sanskrit ślokas as the number of years covered by the Gita applications included in this book, is that, with the passage of time, longer and more detailed books on Lokasaṁgraha may hopefully appear, in Sanskrit as well as in other languages of the world.

CHAPTER TWO

देशे काले योगविशेषः
DEŚE KĀLE YOGAVIŚEṢAḤ

YOGA TO SUIT TIME AND PLACE

This chapter puts forth the argument that, although the Gita contains several Yogas—the main Yogas being Karmayoga, Bhaktiyoga, Jñānayoga—the focus needs to be shifted from one Yoga to another according to the changing needs of the society. The words "deśe kāle" occur in the Gita itself (XVII.20), to emphasize the importance of time and place. Kashi Nath Upadhyaya has stated that the three Yogas "are meant for people of different temperaments to start with. . .".[1] This is one aspect of how the choice of a particular Yoga can be related to the practitioner's temperament. But this is essentially an individual-centered approach. What is sought to be highlighted in the present chapter is a society-centered approach, namely that, at any particular time and place, a movement aimed at tackling urgent social problems needs to focus attention on a specific Yoga that can provide the maximum possible support.

Śrī Aurobindo, in his "Essays on the Gita", speaks of the world as a 'theatre' on which two 'struggles' are continuously going on—the inner struggle and the outer struggle:

> In the inner struggle the enemies are within, in the individual, and the slaying of desire, ignorance, egoism, is the victory. . .
>
> But there is an outer struggle between the powers of the Dharma and the Adharma in the human collectivity. . . This outer struggle too the Avatāra comes to aid, directly or indirectly, to destroy the reign of the Asuras, the evil-doers, and in them depress the power they represent and to restore the oppressed ideals of the Dharma.[2]

Although the Gita could be invoked to tackle both types of struggles, problems or crises—at the individual level as well as at the social level—the emphasis in this book is on the latter, that is, on social problems, the actual nature and form of which change from time to time, and from place to place—deśe kāle, to use Gita's words. How Gita-interpreters assessed the changing needs of the society and how they shifted the emphasis from one yoga to another—this is brought out in the verses of this chapter.

२.१. **गीताग्रन्थो योगशास्त्रः परं तु देशे काले च ।**
रूपविशेषो योगस्य बुद्धिप्रयोगात् संज्ञितः ॥
gītāgrantho yogaśāstraḥ paraṁ tu deśe kāle ċa
rūpaviśeṣo yogasya buddhiprayogāt saṁjñitaḥ

The Bhagavad-Gita, as a scripture, is described, in the colophon that occurs at the end of each chapter, as Yoga-Śāstra. Is any particular Yoga to be considered as the central one? Perhaps not for all times and places, because the specific form of the Yoga relevant to each time and place has to be identified through proper reasoning and analysis or Buddhiyoga, in the language of the Gita.

The colophon at the end of each chapter uses the expression "Brahmavidyāyāṁ Yogaśāstre" which has been explained by S. Radhakrishnan in the following words:

> To help us to understand the nature of reality is the purpose of brahmavidyā . . . Yoga-śāstra literally means the scripture of Yoga . . .[3] The Bhagavad-Gita gives us not only a metaphysics (brahmavidyā) but also a discipline (yogaśāstra) . . . The different yogas are special applications of the inner discipline which leads to the liberation of the soul and a new understanding of the unity and meaning of mankind . . .[4] Marx's criticism, that philosophers interpret the world while the real task is to change it, does not apply to the author of the Gita, who gives us not only a philosophical interpretation, brahmavidyā, but also a practical programme, Yogaśāstra . . .[5]

The importance of Buddhiyoga is stressed in the Gita not only in the beginning (II.49), but also in the middle (X.10) and again at the end (XVIII.57). Verse 2.1 of this chapter visualizes that the act of choosing any particular yoga relevant to the needs of the society can and should be facilitated with the help of buddhiyoga. This idea is strongly supported by the explanation that D.S. Sarma has given about the role of buddhiyoga in the Gita:

> Buddhi-yoga implies equanimity or evenness of mind, an attitude of detachment, freedom from error or delusion, and ability to rise above the mere letter of the books. In short, it is the preliminary discipline of the mind indispensable to every kind of spiritual life—whether it is karma-yoga, bhakti-yoga, dhyāna-yoga or jñāna-yoga . . .
>
> The Gita is aware that without a disciplined mind, karma-yoga would result only in rash action, bhakti-yoga in superstitious worship, and jñāna-yoga in vague abstractions. Though the Gita is a theistic gospel, its object is not to bring to the feet of God a rash or a sentimental or an anaemic soul, but a fully developed, well integrated, dynamic soul.[6]

One of the uses of buddhiyoga highlighted by D.S. Sarma is "to rise above the mere letter of the books". This is further explained in the following verse:

२.२. शब्दार्थमात्रं गीतायाः न ददाति पूर्णभावम् ।
स्वानुभवाद्गूढभावं पश्याशब्दं श्रुतौ यथा ॥

śabdārthamātraṁ gītāyāḥ na dadāti pūrṇabhāvam
svānubhavādgūḍhabhāvaṁ paśyāśabdaṁ śrutau yathā

If one goes merely by the literal meaning of Gita's words, one cannot hope to understand fully what those words should mean to us in the present context. It is important, therefore, that the real message of the Gita should be understood in the light of the experience gained while trying to implement the teachings in the context of the life's problems. In the śruti (Maitrāyaṇī Upaniṣad) also, the importance of going beyond śabda—to aśabda—has been stressed.

Vinoba Bhave, in his selective study of eighteen upaniṣads, entitled "Aṣṭādaśī", has explained that, following the Maitrāyaṇī Upaniṣad, we should initially take the help of words—śabda—but eventually the stage of aśabda will be reached when actual experience or realization will be more important than words.[7]

The important difference between śabda and aśabda became clear when Mahatma Gandhi derived the message of Ahiṁsā—

non-violence—from the Gita, although scholars interpreting the Gita literally did not quite agree with him. Obviously, the Mahatma placed more reliance on "forty years' unremitting endeavour" than on the literal meaning of Gita's words:

> Let it be granted that according to the letter of the Gita it is possible to say that warfare is consistent with renunciation of fruit. But after forty years' unremitting endeavour fully to enforce the teaching of the Gita in my own life, I have in all humility, felt that perfect renunciation is impossible without perfect observance of ahiṁsā in every shape and form . . . I am not aware of the claim made by (other) translators of enforcing their meaning of the Gita in their own lives.[8]

२.३. ज्ञानयोगः शंकरेण भक्तिः रामानुजेन च ।
बोधितस्तथैवाधुना कर्मयोगस्तिलकेन ॥

jñānayogaḥ śaṁkareṇa bhaktiḥ rāmānujena ca
bodhitastathaivādhunā karmayogastilakena

In his Gita-commentary, Śaṁkara emphasized Jñānayoga, while Rāmānuja emphasized Bhaktiyoga. In modern times, however, Tilak emphasized Karmayoga.

Although a large number of Gita-commentaries are available, the contributions of Śaṁkara, Rāmājuna and Tilak are particularly referred to because each of them took the lead in explaining why a specific Yoga—namely, Jñāna, Bhakti, Karma, respectively—represents the essence of the Gita. For example, K.N. Upadhyaya too mentions these three commentaries before speaking of the views of others:

> Śaṁkara, the well-known champion of the path of knowledge, makes an unambiguous declaration: 'Salvation is to be attained by knowledge alone—this indeed is the definite purport of the Gita, as also of all the Upaniṣads'. . . Rāmānuja, on the other hand, points out that 'under the cover of encouraging Arjuna for battle, the Lord indeed has propounded his own subject, the path of devotion, as the means of salvation. . . The path of action is highlighted by B.G. Tilak who says: 'The doctrine of action is the principal theme of the Gita and all other things have been stated to support the same . . . '[9]

२.४. समयस्थानानुकूलो निःश्रेयसकरो योगः ।
युगधर्माद्यथाशक्यं प्राणिनामप्यभ्युदयः ॥
samayasthānānukūlo niḥśreyasakaro yogaḥ
yugadharmādyathāśakyaṁ prāṇināmapyabhyudayaḥ

Salvation of the self is best achieved by the yoga which is in tune with the times; such a yoga can appropriately be called yugadharma, that is, dharma suitable to that time. Well-being of all living beings, too, is attainable, as far as possible, through yugadharma.

The two goals—niḥśreyasa and abhyudaya—are together referred to by Śaṁkara in the opening paragraph of his Gita-commentary. According to Swami Ranganathananda, both the goals are attainable by a suitable combination of pravṛtti (outward-directed action) and nivṛtti (inward-directed action), and he further says that two alternative terms—dharma and amṛta—are used in the Gita (XII.20) to convey the same meaning:

> Dharma (outward-directed action) gives abhyudaya (social welfare), while amṛta (inward-directed action) ensures niḥśreyasa (spiritual freedom) . . .[10] Śrī Kṛṣṇa's message is both dharma and amṛta, capable of ensuring collective social welfare and the realization by the individual of his immortal divine nature, as defined by Himself in the Gita (XII.20) . . .[11]

Since suitable solutions to social problems have been put forward by Gita-followers from time to time, and even implemented in the face of serious challenges, the next verse drawing attention to this can be called "Lokasaṁgraha Confidence Affirmation Declaration."

लोकसंग्रहविश्वासघोषणा
LOKASAṀGRAHAVIŚVĀSAGHOṢAṆĀ

२.५. यदा यदा जनवर्गाः भेदत्रस्ताः निराश्रयाः ।
तदागमन्गीताभक्ताः रक्षार्थं तेषामन्यायात् ॥
yadā yadā janavargāḥ bhedatrastāḥ nirāśrayāḥ
tadāgamangītābhaktāḥ rakṣārthaṁ teṣāmanyāyāt

Whenever certain sections of society have become victims of discriminatory oppression and have felt helpless, then Gita-followers have come forward to protect them from such injustice.

This verse can be viewed as having the same place in the social message of the Gita as śloka IV.7 has in the Bhagavad-Gita. The words "yadā yadā" used in this verse are intended to bring to mind śloka IV.7 of the Gita which is reproduced here for ready reference:

यदा यदा हि धर्मस्य ग्लानिर्भवति भारत ।
अभ्युत्थानमधर्मस्य तदात्मानं सृजाम्यहम् ॥
yadā yadā hi dharmasya glānirbhavati bhārata
abhyutthānamadharmasya tadātmānaṁ sṛjāmyaham

Whenever there is a decline of righteousness and rise of unrighteousness, O Arjuna, then I send forth (create, incarnate) Myself. (IV.7)

२.६. एवं तु गीतायोगिभिः अवतारेण वा पुनः ।
न हि नीतिरक्षणं चेत् कः तदा श्रीगीतां पठेत् ॥
evaṁ tu gītāyogibhiḥ avatāreṇa vā punaḥ
na hi nītirakṣaṇam cet kaḥ tadā śrīgītāṁ paṭhet

It is crucial to have such an assurance, namely, that either God's Avatāra or Gita-followers would come forward to protect innocent sufferers; if such an assurance of protection from gross injustice were not there, then what will inspire people to read the Gita and to follow its teachings ?

२.७. अन्यधर्मप्रचारकाः अवदन् कटुवाक्यं हि ।
क्रूरताविरोधाद्विना गीताधर्मः कथं जीवेत् ॥
anyadharmapracārakāḥ avadan kaṭuvākyaṃ hi
krūratāvirodhādvinā gītādharmaḥ kathaṁ jīvet

We all know that missionaries of other religions—particularly in the early years of the nineteenth century—spoke harsh words against Hinduism. Under those difficult circumstances, the dharma of the Gita was able to survive only because Gita-followers opposed those who were committing acts of cruelty against weaker sections of the society. If Gita-followers had not stood up in opposition to cruelty, Hinduism would have died because of deep social degeneration—as was widely believed by missionaries at that time.

For verifying the gloomy forecast about Hinduism, made by the missionaries during the early years of the nineteenth century, please see the opening paragraph in chapter one of this book.

२.८. न किंचित् नवीनमस्मिन् अध्यात्मवादसंघर्षे ।
विषमा स्थितिरेव हि गीतोपदेशप्रेरिका ॥
na kiṁcit navīnamasmin adhyātmavādasaṁgharṣe
viṣamā sthitireva hi gītopadeśaprerikā

To be exposed to harsh words was nothing new in the long history of Hinduism and the Gita—in fact, during debates on philosophic and spiritual matters, from time to time, it was quite common to face challenges and difficult situations. The Gita is particularly capable of facing critical situations, because the delivery of the Gita-message on the battlefield of Kurukṣetra was itself inspired because of the crisis situation.

The word "viṣama" meaning "crisis" occurs in śloka II.2 of the Gita. In fact, Śrī Kṛṣṇa begins His statement in this śloka by asking Arjuna why his frame of mind was inappropriate to face the crisis situation. The Gita's approach can therefore be described as essentially crisis-oriented or problem-oriented. Klaus K. Klostermaier envisages the 'need' to turn to the Gita, especially in times of crises and confusion:

> Many Indians, and increasingly many non-Indians, too, have considered the Gita not only a book to be read and studied but a guide to living. A need for such guidance is felt, especially in times of crises and confusion like ours, when the institutions are no longer able to provide orientation and when there are no longer commonly accepted values and standards. Clearly, the Gita is a book of crisis.[12]

२.९. विषमे समुपस्थितमर्जुनं प्राह श्रीकृष्णः ।
क्षुद्रं हृदयदौर्बल्यं त्यक्त्वोत्तिष्ठ परन्तप ॥

viṣame samupasthitamarjunaṁ prāha śrīkṛṣṇaḥ
kṣudraṁ hṛdayadaurbalyaṁ tyaktvottiṣṭha parantapa

Reminding Arjuna that he was in the midst of a crisis situation, Śrī Kṛṣṇa told him that with dejected spirits, he could not possibly handle the crisis. Therefore, said Śrī Kṛṣṇa, cast off this petty faintheartedness and arise.

The second line of this verse is the same as that of śloka II.3 of the Gita. This is reproduced here in the original because, according to Swami Vivekananda, "If one reads this one śloka, that is II.3, one gets all the merits of reading the entire Gita; for in this one śloka lies embodied the whole Message of The Gita."[13]

२.१०. स्वार्थेच्छया ह्यविद्वांसो यथा कुर्वन्ति सक्ताश्च ।
कुर्याद्विद्वांस्तथाऽसक्तश्चिकीर्षुर्लोकसंग्रहम् ॥
svārthecchayā hyavidvāṁso yathā kurvanti saktāśca
kuryādvidvāṁstathā'saktaścikīrṣurlokasaṁgraham

The unwise engage themselves in action—and that (to be engaged in action) is a good thing to do—but there are two deficiencies in their approach, namely, one that they are prompted by the desire for selfish gains, and secondly, that they are attached to the fruits of their actions. Śrī Kṛṣṇa's teaching in the Gita is that the wise people are those who also engage themselves in action but only after removing the two deficiencies from which the unwise suffer. In other words, the wise are prompted not by the desire for selfish gains—svārtha—but by the desire for the good of the society—Lokasaṁgraha—and secondly, they are not attached to the fruits of their actions.

Verse 2.10 is a modified form of śloka III.25 of the Gita. The second line is the same in both; it specifies that Lokasaṁgraha and Anāsakti are the two main noteworthy features of the actions of the wise. The first line in verse 2.10 seeks to reinforce this message by saying that the two main deficiencies of the actions of the unwise are Svārtha and Āsakti. From the social point of view, it was felt that Svārtha as the opposite of Lokasaṁgraha should be specifically mentioned in verse 2.10.

२.११. लोकसंग्रहभावेन रक्षिता: निर्बला: वर्गा: ।
संघर्ष: कर्मयोगिभि: यथा नारीरक्षणाय ॥

lokasaṁgrahabhāvena rakṣitāḥ nirbalāḥ vargāḥ
saṁgharṣaḥ karmayogibhiḥ yathā nārīrakṣaṇāya

When the modern era began, since weaker sections of the society were being killed, under one pretext or the other, the obvious task for engaging in Lokasaṁgraha—the good of the society—was to try to protect the weak and the oppressed. Since women were the worst sufferers in the early years of the nineteenth century; a movement to protect them was the first major Lokasaṁgraha-activity of the Karmayogins.

The reference here is to the social movement started by Rommohun Roy in the year 1818—after having made up his mind in 1811 to do so—to create public opinion against the burning of widows with the dead body of their husband. More details will be given in chapter seven.

२.१२. संघर्षेषु प्रयुक्तानि साधनानि नवान्येव ।
देशकालपात्रोचिता वर्णिता हि गीताशिक्षा ॥
saṁgharṣeṣu prayuktāni sādhanāni navānyeva
deśakālapātrocitā varṇitā hi gītāśikṣā

During the Lokasaṁgraha-struggles for social justice, the actual means adopted had to be thought out afresh so as to be able to meet each new challenge. This is what Śrī Kṛṣṇa had in mind when He said in the Gita that considerations of time and place are very important.

While using the basic teaching of the Gita, leaders of social movements during the last two hundred years did not all follow any set pattern. Since the challenges they faced over time were different, practical ways and means for meeting those challenges had to be worked out afresh on every occasion. Details will be given in chapters seven to eleven, the five leaders covered therein being: Raja Rammohun Roy, Swami Vivekananda, Lokamanya Bal Gangadhar Tilak, Śrī Aurobindo, and Mahatma Gandhi.

२.१३. निश्चितः किं तु संदेशो लोकसंग्रहदायकः ।
आर्तजनवर्गहितं प्राप्तव्यं गीतायोगिभिः ॥

niścitaḥ kiṁ tu saṁdeśo loksaṁgrahadāyakaḥ
ārtajanavargahitaṁ prāptavyaṁ gītāyogibhiḥ

Underlying all these adjustments that had to be made in regard to practical ways and means, there was continuity from one social movement to another because the guiding spirit for each movement was clearly the Lokasaṁgraha message of the Gita. The goal of all the Gita-followers was the good of the society in general, and the good of the oppressed sections of the society in particular.

CHAPTER THREE

अवतारः प्राणिवर्गो लोकसंग्रहहेतवः
AVATĀRAḤ PRĀṆIVARGO LOKASAṀGRAHAHETAVAḤ

LOKASAṀGRAHA—THE COMMON GOAL OF AVATĀRA AND HUMAN BEINGS

The Lokasaṁgraha teaching of the Gita is introduced by Śrī Kṛṣṇa in the third chapter, and the Avatāra declaration is made in the fourth chapter. The purpose underlying the present chapter in this book is to clarify that the Lokasaṁgraha-function, expressed by terms that convey the same meaning, runs throughout the Gita—be it the Avatāra declaration, or the characteristics of one who has attained perfection, through Karmayoga or Bhaktiyoga or Jñānayoga or Dhyānayoga. A conclusion commonly accepted by practically all Gita-scholars and activists (and particularly the modern ones) is that, like the Avatāra—God's incarnation—human beings too, when they achieve perfection, work for Lokasaṁgraha, irrespective of the Yoga or yogas which helped them achieve perfection. But the statement that we make in this chapter, drawing inspiration from Tilak, for example, goes a step further, namely, that one need not wait for the attainment of perfection before starting to work for Lokasaṁgraha. This extension of the commonly agreed idea will be presented as part of the commentary on verse 3.7. To start with, we study the linkage between the Avatāra Declaration of the Gita and the Lokasaṁgraha ślokas thereof.

३.१. सम्भवामि युगे युगे सद्घोषणा श्रीकृष्णस्य ।
तत्कर्म नीतिरक्षणं प्रोक्तं च लोकसंग्रहः ॥

sambhavāmi yuge yuge sadghoṣaṇā śrīkṛṣṇasya
tatkarma nītirakṣaṇaṁ proktaṁ ca lokasaṁgrahaḥ

Śrī Kṛṣṇa declares in verse IV.8 of the Gita: I come into being from age to age—for the protection of the good, for the destruction of the wicked, and for the establishment of Dharma. But the purpose of the Avatāra has been indicated in other ślokas of the Gita also, namely, preservation of the moral order and Lokasaṁgraha.

The word "Dharma" occurring in śloka IV.8 obviously refers to its universal aspect, as distinguished from the individual aspect. Earlier, in śloka II.7, Arjuna had confessed that, since his own mind was confused about his dharma, he was seeking light and guidance from Śrī Kṛṣṇa, as a pupil seeks from his teacher. Arjuna as an ordinary human being, engrossed in narrow personal and family problems, had used the word "dharma" in its individual aspect. His goal also was rather limited—individual salvation or Śreyas, as it is called in the Gita. Śrī Kṛṣṇa, in His reply, initially shows to Arjuna how his limited goal—śreyas—can be achieved by observing dharma at the individual level. However, Śrī Kṛṣṇa did not stop there; He went further, on His own initiative, and stressed also the social and universal aspect of dharma which was closely linked with Lokasaṁgraha. P.M. Thomas draws attention to the two aspects of Dharma in the Gita:

> The concept of dharma has two distinct aspects, namely individual or particular, and social or universal. . .
>
> The very context in which the discourses are given is the confusion of Arjuna about his dharma (II. 7). This is the individual aspect of dharma. . .
>
> The universal aspect (of dharma) is taken up most directly when Kṛṣṇa argues that the purpose of avatāra (incarnation) is to protect dharma (IV.8).[1]

The identity between the Avatāra declaration of the Gita-śloka IV.8 and the Lokasaṁgraha-function referred to in the earlier śloka III.20 has been explicitly stated by Tilak:

> Lokasaṁgraha (III.20) is only another name for the work which the Blessed Lord does by being incarnated in this manner (IV. 8).[2]

Regarding the preservation of the moral order as a purpose of the Avatāra, a specific mention is made in śloka XVIII. 78, that is, the last śloka of the Gita. This is taken up in the next verse.

३.२. प्रभावो हरिकर्मणो वर्णितः संजयेन हि ।
तत्र श्रीर्विजयो भूतिर्ध्रुवा नीतिर्मतिर्मम ॥

prabhāvo harikarmaṇo varṇitaḥ saṁjayena hi
tatra śrīrvijayo bhūtirdhruvā nītirmatirmama

Sanjaya, after narrating to Dhritarashtra the entire Gita-dialogue between Śrī Kṛṣṇa and Arjuna, has summarized in the end as to what wonderful results follow when the yoga taught by the Avatāra is implemented whole-heartedly and with full energy by human beings like Arjuna. In Sanjaya's opinion, the results will be: good fortune, victory, welfare, and a stable moral order.

S. Radhakrishnan has explained that this summarization includes the double purpose of human life, personal perfection and social efficiency;

The tremendous facts of life divine are: yoga, the realization of God through worship and entire submission to His will, and dhanuḥ or active participation in the furtherance of the cosmic plan. Spiritual vision and social service should go together. The double purpose of human life, personal perfection and social efficiency, is indicated here.[3]

What a stable moral order implies for a modern society is specifically taken up in the next verse.

३.३. ध्रुवानीत्याः सत्प्रभावादभावः क्रूरकर्मणः ।
आर्द्रभावो व्यवहारे न्यायभावनाप्रेरितः ॥
dhruvānītyāḥ satprabhāvādabhāvaḥ krūrakarmaṇaḥ
ārdrabhāvo vyavahāre nyāyabhāvanāpreritaḥ

In a modern society, cruel and unjust behaviour towards the weaker sections is a crucial issue, and therefore tackling this problem is a pre-requisite for the establishment of a stable moral order. The social goal should be a state of mutually sympathetic behaviour, free from injustice, cruelty and discrimination.

Wicked behaviour towards the poor and the weak was identified by Swami Vivekananda as an important criterion of lack of purity of heart. He knew that many of the orthodox scholars who knew Vedantic scriptures by heart were as much guilty of unkind treatment towards the low-caste, poor countrymen as other high-caste Hindus who were not scholars. He therefore put as much emphasis on getting rid of "wickedness" as of "ignorance":

If there is dirt and dust on a mirror, we cannot see our image. So ignorance and wickedness are the dirt and dust that are on the mirror of our hearts . . . [4]

The nation is sinking, the curse of unnumbered millions is on our heads—the unnumbered millions to whom we have talked of Vedanta and whom we have hated with all our strength, to whom we have talked theoretically that we are all the same and all are one with the same Lord, without even an ounce of practice . . . [5]

३.४. उत्सीदेयुरिमे लोका न कुर्यां कर्म चेदहम् ।
एवं वर्णितं कृष्णेन रूपं लोकसंग्रहस्य ॥
utsīdeyurime lokā na kuryāṁ karma cedaham
evaṁ varṇitaṁ kṛṣṇena rūpaṁ lokasaṁgrahasya

After telling Arjuna in śloka III.20 that he should go beyond narrow considerations of personal and family interests, and work for Lokasaṁgraha, Śrī Kṛṣṇa explained in śloka III.24 what practical form Lokasaṁgraha should take, by indicating what would happen if He did not work for Lokasaṁgraha. He said "If I should cease to work for Lokasaṁgraha, the human society and all these worlds would fall in ruin."

The first line of verse 3.4 is the same as that of śloka III.24 in the Gita. This is a very forceful statement of Śrī Kṛṣṇa's role as the preserver and protector of the universe, and the moral order on which the human society is based. That the Lokasaṁgraha-function of the Avatāra is not different from what is mentioned in the Avatāra declaration of śloka IV.8 is explicitly stated in the next verse.

३.५. उक्तमवतारकर्म धर्मसंस्थापनादि च ।
न भिन्नं लोकसंग्रहात् विमृष्टं यद्यशेषेण ॥
uktamavatārakarma dharmasaṁsthāpanādi ca
na bhinnaṁ lokasaṁgrahāt vimṛṣṭaṁ yadyaśeṣeṇa

The Avatāra declaration of śloka IV.8 mentions three broad functions which an Avatāra performs, namely, protection of the good, destruction of the wicked, and the establishment of Dharma. These functions are not different from Lokasaṁgraha, and a careful and in-depth study of the matter will confirm this.

Mahatma Gandhi says that Śrī Kṛṣṇa's functions as preserver of the universe include the unceasing movement of the sun, the moon, the earth, etc. as also nature's processes and laws which are guided by divine intelligence and will. In addition, says Gandhi, even the actions of the Avatāra narrated in Hindu scriptures present a great ideal of serving the people:

> Kṛṣṇa served the people all his life, a real servant of the people. He could have led the hosts at Kurukṣetra, but he preferred to be Arjuna's charioteer. His whole life was an unbroken Gita of karma. . . As a child he was a cowherd and we still know him by the name of Gopāla, cowherd . . . Kṛṣṇa knew no sleep nor idleness. He kept a sleepless vigil over the world.[6]

Writing in a similar vein, Vinoba Bhave presents further details of what Śrī Kṛṣṇa did as a karmayogin:

> In Mahabharata war, everybody at sunset leaves the field for evening prayer, but Lord Kṛṣṇa unyokes the horses from the chariot, gives them water, rubs them, removes the burrs from their bodies, and feeds them from his yellow garment which he has filled with grain . . .
>
> At the Pandavas' Rājasūya sacrifice, Śrī Kṛṣṇa clears the leaf-plates after the feast . . .
>
> So the saints have pictured a karmayogi God who rubs horses, takes cows out to graze, drives a chariot, cleans dishes and mops up floors.[7]

Swami Vivekananda also, speaking about Śrī Kṛṣṇa and the Gita, described Śrī Kṛṣṇa as 'the most rounded man' he knew of, wonderfully developed equally in brain and heart and hand.[8] Every moment of Śrī Kṛṣṇa, said Vivekananda, was alive with activity, either as a gentleman, as a scholar, as a poet. This all-rounded and wonderful activity and combination of brain and heart, Vivekananda saw in the Gita—"and nothing can approach it anywhere",[9] as he declared emphatically. . . This tremendous activity of the man (Śrī Kṛṣṇa), said Swami Vivekananda, and then that heart! Vivekananda recognized Śrī Kṛṣṇa as "the first man, way before Buddha, to open the door of religion to every caste".[10] . . .Moreover, said Vivekananda, Kṛṣṇa preached in the midst of the battlefield. . . It means nothing to this man—the flying of missiles about him. Calm and sedate he goes on discussing the problems of life and death. He practised what he preached in the Gita: He who in the midst of intense activity finds himself in the greatest calmness, and in the greatest peace finds intense activity, that is the greatest Yogi as well as the wisest man.[11]

Lokasaṁgraha as the purpose of the Avatāra—this was the case not only at the time of Śrī Kṛṣṇa, but Śrī Rāma as well—the only difference being that the word "Mangalam", meaning the good of the people, has been used instead of Lokasaṁgraha, in Rāmcharitmānas of Tulsidas. The next verse, drawing attention to this, can be called "In Rāmāyaṇa too Lokamangala Declaration".

रामायणेऽपि लोकमंगलघोषणा
RĀMĀYAṆE'PI LOKAMANGALAGHOṢAṆĀ

३.६. गीतायां लोकसंग्रहो रामायणे तु मंगलम् ।
यथा सर्वभूतहितं तथैव लोकमंगलम् ॥

gītāyāṁ lokasaṁgraho rāmāyaṇe tu maṁgalam
yathā sarvabhūtahitaṁ tathaiva lokamaṁgalam

It is not that Lokasaṁgraha was the function of the Avatāra only when He appeared as Śrī Kṛṣṇa; the same was true when He appeared as Śrī Rāma. What the Gita conveys by the word Lokasaṁgraha, the Rāmāyaṇa conveys by the word Mangalam. In the Gita, we have Sarvabhūtahitam, and in the Rāmāyaṇa we have Lokamangalam, but both these expressions convey the same idea—the good of all beings.

The word "Mangalam"—meaning 'the good of all'—occurs in the opening verse of Rāmcharitmānas (written by Tulsidas) and also in many other verses of this Hindi rendering of the Rāmāyaṇa, which can be considered as the most widely read version of the ancient epic composed by Vālmīki.[12] The term "sarvabhūtahitam" occurs twice in the Gita—ślokas V.25 and XII.4—as part of the phrase "sarvabhūtahite ratāḥ" which has been translated by Radhakrishnan as "persons who rejoice in doing good to all creatures".

Although it might appear from the Avatāra declarations of the

Gita and the Rāmāyaṇa that, after an Avatāra has established Dharma, the wicked wait for some time and then reassert themselves till the next Avatāra puts them down, ślokas III.23-24 of the Gita make it clear that there is no such discontinuity in the functioning of God for Lokasaṁgraha. Whether or not a popularly recognized Avatāra is visible, the divine process of preservation and protection of the universe and the Dharma is continuously in operation.

A question is often raised, 'If God himself is continuously working for Lokasaṁgraha, why do we see so much destruction and unrighteousness?' Mahatma Gandhi's replies to such questions spring from his faith in the existence of an invisible law:

> I have found that life persists in the midst of destruction and, therefore, there must be a higher law than that of destruction. . .
>
> Superficially we are surrounded in life by strife and bloodshed, life living upon life. But some great seer, who ages ago penetrated the centre of Truth, said: It is not through strife and violence, but through non-violence that man can fulfil his destiny and his duty to his fellow-creatures. It is a force which is more positive than electricity and more powerful than even ether. At the centre of non-violence is a force which is self-acting.[13]

३.७. मत्कर्म कुरु संदेशः पार्थहिते श्रीकृष्णस्य ।
अवतारः प्राणिवर्गो लोकसंग्रहहेतवः ॥

matkarma kuru saṁdeśaḥ pārthahite śrī kṛṣṇasya
avatāraḥ prāṇivargo lokasaṁgrahahetavaḥ

God works for Lokasaṁgraha not only through the Avatāras and the unceasing natural processes and laws, but He also wants human beings to make their contribution to the same cause to the extent they can. That is why Śrī Kṛṣṇa tells Arjuna in the Gita "matkarma kuru", that is, do the same work as I am doing. Therefore Lokasaṁgraha should be understood as the common goal and function of the Avatāra as well as all human beings.

Lokamanya Tilak says that some of the followers of sannyāsa school try to justify their escapist attitude by arguing that since Parameśvara has created the world and is busy maintaining it also, why should they worry about Lokasaṁgraha? Although the hollowness of such arguments can be exposed in many ways, we quote below how Tilak finds the escapist attitude inconsistent with knowledge:

> If a man of knowledge becomes uniform with Parameśvara as a result of jñāna, how will he escape the necessity of performing that action which is performed by the Parameśvara? Besides, whatever the Parameśvara has to do, has to be done by Him through the medium of jñānins. Therefore, active noble sentiments full of sympathy towards all created beings must arise in the mind of the man who has had the direct realization of the form of the Parameśvara in the shape of the feeling that there is only one ātman in all created beings; and the trend of his mind must naturally be towards Lokasaṁgraha.[14]

As we mentioned in the opening paragraph of this chapter, this seems to be the right place to refer to Tilak's idea that, not only after achieving perfection but also during the Sādhanā stage, all human beings should work for Lokasaṁgraha according to their capacity:

> Although the essential basis of proper conduct (sadācaraṇa) is the equable Reason (samatvabuddhi), I must repeat here that, one cannot from that fact draw the inference that the man who performs Action, must wait for performing action until his Reason has reached that stage. It is the highest ideal of everybody to make his mind like that of a Sthitaprajña. But it is stated already in the commencement of the Gita, that because this is the highest ideal, one need not wait for performing Action until that ideal has been reached; that one should in the meantime perform all Actions with as much unselfishness as possible, so that thereby the reason will become purer and purer, and the highest state of perfection will ultimately be reached; and that one must not waste time by insisting on not performing any Action until the perfect state of the Reason has been reached.[15]

३.८. गीतोपदेशः कृष्णस्य न केवलं पार्थाय हि ।
ये ये तु सेवासंलग्नाः तेभ्यो मंगलकामेभ्यः ॥
gītopadeśaḥ kṛṣṇasya na kevalaṁ pārthāya hi
ye ye tu sevāsaṁlagnāḥ tebhyo maṁgalakāmebhyaḥ

From the above it is clear that the Lokasaṁgraha-teaching of

Śrī Kṛṣṇa is not only addressed to Arjuna but to all human beings. In particular, this teaching provides inspiration and guidance to those who are well-wishers of humanity and who are therefore engaged in doing acts of service to society.

Tilak warned common people not to be under a wrong impression that Lokasaṁgraha can be done only by important people:

> Every human being. . .acquires by birth, the high or low qualification of maintaining and uplifting society according to his or her own powers, and proportionately with whatever intellectual capacity, authoritative capacity, financial capacity, or physical capacity is either naturally possessed by him, or can be acquired by him having regard to his status in life. Just as extremely small wheels are necessary along with large wheels in order that any machine should work properly, so also is it necessary that the authority of common-place persons should be exercised properly and fully in the same way as the authority of superior persons like Vyāsa and others, in order that the immense and ponderous activity or mechanism of the Cosmos should continue to work in a properly regulated manner. . . If the potters do not manufacture pots or weavers do not weave cloth, the maintenance of society (Lokasaṁgraha) cannot be satisfactorily carried out, even if the king protects the society properly. . .[16]

३.९. **तत्रैवं सति पार्थस्य दृष्टव्या विषमा स्थितिः ।**
मोहजनितश्च शोकः श्रोतव्यो ज्ञातुं गीतार्थम् ॥

tatraivaṁ sati pārthasya dṛṣṭavyā viṣamā sthitiḥ
mohajanitaśca śokaḥ śrotavyo jñātuṁ gītārtham

Even after we recognize that the Lokasaṁgraha-teaching is for all people, an in-depth study of Arjuna is essential to understand the real meaning of the Gita. What sort of crisis Arjuna was facing and how his grief was connected with his ignorance and narrow vision and what practical lessons we can derive therefrom—these aspects will be taken up in the next chapter.

In the opinion of Ramesh Betai, one of the differences between the "ancients" and the "moderns" is that the former "do not take any serious notice of the viṣāda—depression—by which Arjuna is overcome" in the beginning of the Gita.[17] Radhakrishnan's comments on Arjuna's viṣāda, as described in chapter one of the Gita, link it with his detachment from social obligations:

> Chapter One ends in dejection and sorrow and this is also called Yoga as this darkness of the soul is an essential step in the progress to spiritual life. . . Arjuna passes through a great spiritual tension. When he detaches himself from his social obligations and asks why he should carry out the duty expected of him by society, he gets behind his socialized self and has full awareness of himself as an individual, alone and isolated. He faces the world as a stranger thrown into a threatening chaos, . . . feeling . . . anxiety, aloneness, doubt and insecurity. If he is to function successfully, these feelings must be overcome.[18]

CHAPTER FOUR

स्वलाभात्परं स्वजनहितादपि परम्
SVALĀBHĀTPARAṀ SVAJANAHITĀDAPI PARAM

BEYOND SELFISH INTERESTS AND BEYOND NARROW GROUP INTERESTS TOO

In this chapter, an in-depth study of the first three chapters of the Gita is made in order to discover how and at what stage the Lokasaṁgraha teaching is introduced by Śrī Kṛṣṇa. Arjuna himself does not ask for it. He, as an ordinary human being, is initially depicted as too much engrossed in narrow personal and family problems. The first point in Arjuna's initial question is—admitting that the Kauravas have committed crimes and are determined to fight, why should not the Pāṇḍavas, realizing the huge loss involved in the destruction of the family, think of a unilateral solution, like 'refusing to fight' (I.38-47 and II.9). This is accompanied with Arjuna's suggestion that he better run away from the battlefield and live on bhaikṣyam or charity.

In reply, Śrī Kṛṣṇa rules out escapism and emphasizes that Karma is unavoidable, and that even the minimum goal of life, śarīrayātrā or maintenance of physical life, cannot be achieved without karma (III.8). Śrī Kṛṣṇa then takes up the next point in Arjuna's question, namely his desire for obtaining śreyas or 'good', and release from sin and grief. Śrī Kṛṣṇa explains that the root cause of grief and bondage is not karma but attachment to the fruits thereof, and that, therefore, Arjuna must act without attachment (III.19). Śrī Kṛṣṇa's assurance that everything which Arjuna was looking for—freedom from sin, release from grief, and even the ultimate goal of śreyas—can be achieved by performing Niṣkāma Karma, could be considered as marking the completion of the first stage of the Karmayoga teaching.

An obvious question that arises is: "Why then does the conversation proceed to the next stage?" The answer to that is provided by Śrī Kṛṣṇa himself when he tells Arjuna (in part, explicitly, and to some extent, implicitly): "Your vision is narrow because you do not look beyond your own good or that of your near and dear ones, svajanam. But you have to take into account the society and the world, the Loka (III.20). By all means strive for your limited personal goals, but also keep in mind the larger social and world goals, of preserving dharma and order, and of achieving harmony, unity and universal welfare, Lokasaṁgraha."

It is important to keep in mind that the Gita, being a synthesis of Brahmavidyā and Yogásāstra—i.e. metaphysics and ethics—sets forth the essential principles of a spiritual religion. All the ideas are presented here as a 'saṁvāda', that is, in the form of conversation between Śrī Kṛṣṇa and Arjuna. The conversational style, being different from that of a systematic monologue, puts forth the various elements of the teaching as answers to questions—say, in instalments—rather than in a pre-arranged 'lump sum' fashion.

On most of the occasions in the Gita, Arjuna asks a question to which Śrī Kṛṣṇa gives a reply. But not so for the teaching on Lokasaṁgraha which is conveyed by Śrī Kṛṣṇa almost entirely on His own initiative. We can interpret this as an indirect evidence that the subject of Lokasaṁgraha is so important that, even without Arjuna's asking, Śrī Kṛṣṇa includes it in his teaching, and he cites his own practical example of working for Lokasaṁgraha and warning of a grave crisis in the world if he did not do so. A practical distinction between Niṣkāma Karma and Lokasaṁgraha is that, while the former provides the technique of work, the latter provides the content of work and its goal.

With this introduction, it is hoped that the significance of the ideas contained in this chapter will be better appreciated. Now we take up the verses one by one.

४.१. अर्जुनः स्वधर्मं त्यक्त्वा स्वजनासक्तिमोहितः ।
भैक्ष्यमपि श्रेयो भोक्तुमित्याह श्रीभगवन्तः ॥

arjunaḥ svadharmaṁ tyaktvā svajanāsaktimohitaḥ
bhaikṣyamapi śreyo bhoktumityāha śrībhagavantaḥ

Arjuna got confused about his dharma because of his attachment to his own people—svajanam. He placed loyalty to his family as ahead of his duty to fight. He thought it would be better for him to run away from the battlefield and live on bhaikṣyam or charity. He conveyed this to Śrī Kṛṣṇa, adding that he was afraid of incurring sin—pāpam—if he killed his own people.

What lay behind Arjuna's plea that he would incur sin (pāpam) if he killed Droṇa, Bhīṣma and the Kauravas? Radhakrishnan argues that Arjuna's plea for escapism was a product of tamas and rajas guṇas which prompted him to give up his duty due to ignorance and fear of physical suffering:

> Arjuna takes up a pacifist attitude and declines to participate in a fight for truth and justice. . . He does not raise the question of right or wrong of war. He has faced many battles and fought many enemies. He declares against war and its horror because he has to destroy his own friends and relations (svajanam). It is not a question of violence or non-violence but of using violence against one's own friends now turned enemies. His reluctance to fight is not the outcome of spiritual development or the preponderance of sattvaguṇa but is the product of tamas and rajas guṇas.[1]

Linking ignorance or confusion about one's duty to tāmasika or rājasī buddhi is one way of diagnosing Arjuna's problem. Another, related way is to link it with the concept of attachment which is used extensively in the Gita. Attachment clouds one's vision and shakes one's determination to stick to one's duty. Vinoba Bhave links Arjuna's confusion about his dharma with his attachment to his own people (svajanam):

> Was Arjuna moved by the spirit of non-violence, as Aśoka was to be later? No, this was only attachment to his own people. Arjuna's attachment confused him and overshadowed his devotion to duty. It was then that he thought of philosophy. When a man with a sense of duty is caught in illusion, even then he cannot bear to face the naked fact of his lapse from his duty. He usually covers it up with an inquiry into principles. Arjuna was just in this plight. He wanted to evade his duty because his vision was clouded by illusion, moha.[2]

४.२. अनिवार्यं तु कर्मेति मुख्यादेशो भगवतः ।
शरीरयात्राऽपि च ते न प्रसिद्ध्येदकर्मणः ॥
anivāryaṁ tu karmeti mukhyādeśo bhagavataḥ

śarīrayātrā'pi ca te na prasiddhyedakarmaṇaḥ

Śrī Kṛṣṇa wanted to make it absolutely clear to Arjuna that the very idea of running away from the battlefield was ridiculous. His main teaching on this point was: Don't think of escapism because action is inevitable and unavoidable for those who want to live in this world. Even the minimum goal of life, śarīrayātrā or maintenance of physical life, cannot be achieved without karma.

The second line of this verse is the same as that of śloka III.8 of the Gita. By emphasizing the idea of unavoidability of karma, modern interpreters of the Gita, starting primarily from Swami Vivekananda, were able to bring to the forefront the activist message of Karmayoga. Swami Vivekananda picked up the social service component of Karmayoga to revolutionize the concept and practice of Saṁnyāsa—details will be presented in chapter eight.

Tilak explained that the manner in which the Prasthāna-traya doctrine was traditionally interpreted was responsible for pushing Karmayoga in the background. In this connection, it is useful to recall that the three authoritative scriptures—the Upaniṣads, the Brahmasūtras, and the Gita—were collectively called Prasthāna-traya, and attempts were made to prove that their philosophical views are the same. Tilak argued that it was wrong to ignore Lokasaṁgraha on the ground that this term occurs only in the Gita but not in the Upaniṣads and the Brahmasūtras:

> Some people think that, as the Upāniṣads are generally in support of Sannyāsa, there will arise a mutual opposition between the three parts of the Prasthāna-traya, if the Gita is explained as being in support of Action; and the authoritativeness of the three parts will be endangered . . .
>
> As the Upaniṣads support the path of Sannyāsa, and the Gita supports the path of Karmayoga, these two parts of the Prasthāna-traya can be seen to be mutually cooperative like two hands, instead of being mutually antagonistic. . .
>
> If the Gita did not contain anything more than the Upaniṣads and the Brahmasūtras, there would be no point in including the Gita in the Prasthāna-traya.[3]

४.३. अनुचिता भिक्षावृत्तिः तया परावलम्बनम् ।
स्वावलम्बनं दानं वा सम्भवमेव कर्मणा ॥

anucitā bhikṣāvṛttiḥ tayā parāvalambanam
svāvalambanaṁ dānaṁ vā sambhavameva karmaṇā

Śrī Kṛṣṇa did not approve of Arjuna's suggestion that he could maintain himself by begging. Among the various arguments that can be advanced against the practice of begging in the modern age, one of the important ones is that a beggar cannot maintain his independence. Those who would like to be independent, to have enough for their own maintenance, and perhaps a little extra to contribute to social causes as dānam or charity, have to work and face the world.

One of the main reasons why the approaches of Arjuna and Śrī Kṛṣṇa were so different as to how to face the crisis, was that, while Arjuna viewed it as a personal crisis, Śrī Kṛṣṇa viewed it as a social crisis. The importance of distinguishing between two types of crisis is brought out in the next verse.

४.४. अर्जुनं प्राह श्रीकृष्णो विषमे समुपस्थितम् ।
द्विविधरूपं वैषम्यं वैयक्तिकं सामाजिकम् ।।
arjunaṁ prāha śrīkṛṣṇo viṣame samupasthitam
dvividharūpaṁ vaiṣamyaṁ vaiyaktikaṁ sāmājikam

Among the first words spoken by Śrī Kṛṣṇa in the Gita, while addressing Arjuna, were the following: "Engulfed in a crisis (viṣame samupasthitam) (II.2), give up faint-heartedness and stand up to fight".

But, is there only one type of crisis? Although not explicitly stated in the Gita, a careful reading thereof makes it clear that the crisis could be either 'personal' or 'social'—or rather, the same crisis situation could be viewed from these two angles. The following verses 4.5-9 try to explain how the crisis situation at Kurukṣetra was viewed by Arjuna and Śrī Kṛṣṇa from two different angles.

४.५. अर्जुनस्य दृष्टिकोणं सीमितमिति दर्शितम् ।
तस्मिन् स्वलाभः प्रमुखः तथा स्वजनरक्षणम् ।।
arjunasya dṛṣṭikoṇaṁ sīmitamiti darśitam
tasmin svalābhaḥ pramukhaḥ tathā svajanarakṣaṇam

The priorities which Arjuna has, in the beginning of the Gita, are basically two, namely, one's own benefit—svalābhaḥ—and protection of his own people—svajanam. Since Arjuna did not express any serious concern about the society at large, his vision can be described as narrow.

४.६. पार्थमते कुरुक्षेत्रे क्रूरः स्वजनसंग्रामः ।
स्यामः कथं हि सुखिनो हत्वा स्वजनं तद्वचः ॥
pārthamate kurukṣetre krūraḥ svajanasaṁgrāmaḥ
syāmaḥ kathaṁ hi sukhino hatvā svajanaṁ tadvacaḥ

Arjuna viewed the battle of Kurukṣetra as mainly a fight between two cousins—and not so much as a fight between right and wrong. He wanted to derive personal happiness as a result of this battle, and he was afraid that, if he kills his own people, then even the victory in the battle would not make him happy. He therefore told Śrī Kṛṣṇa: "By killing our own people—svajanam—how can we be happy?"

The second line of verse 4.6 is practically the same as the second line of the Gita śloka I.37.

४.७. कोऽर्थो वाञ्छितः पार्थेन स्वलाभः स्वजनाय च ।
तन्मते विषमा स्थितिः मुख्यतो हि वैयक्तिका ॥
ko'rtho vāñchitaḥ pārthena svalābhaḥ svajanāya ca
tanmate viṣamā sthitiḥ mukhyato hi vaiyaktikā

The two elements that constituted Arjuna's approach to the crisis situation and the battle and what could be expected therefrom, were: first, that it was mainly a personal crisis for him, and secondly, that he would be happy if he could derive benefits in such a way as to share them between himself and his own people.

After describing Arjuna's narrow vision in verses 4.5-7, the wider vision of Śrī Kṛṣṇa is described in verses 4.8-11.

४.८. कृष्णमते कुरुक्षेत्रे संघर्षः साधुदुष्कृताम् ।
साधूनां रक्षणं ध्येयः तथैव लोकसंग्रहः ॥
kṛṣṇamate kurukṣetre saṁgharṣah sādhuduṣkṛtām

sādhūnāṁ rakṣaṇaṁ dhyeyaḥ tathaiva lokasaṁgrahaḥ

Śrī Kṛṣṇa viewed the battle of Kurukṣetra as mainly a fight between the good and the evil—and not so much as a fight between two cousins. Similarly, the objective of the fight was essentially to ensure that the good wins over the evil so that the society as a whole would benefit—not giving prominence to personal and family benefits.

The idea that the main concern of the Avatāra is social crisis—rather than individual crisis—is specifically stated in the next verse, which can therefore be called "Avatāra for Social Crisis Declaration".

सामाजिकवैषम्याय अवतारघोषणा
SĀMĀJIKAVAIṢAMYĀYA AVATĀRAGHOṢAṆĀ

४.९. सामाजिकं वैषम्यं हि मुख्याधारोऽवतारस्य ।
तेन धर्मसंस्थापनं ध्रुवानीत्यास्तु सूचकम् ॥
sāmājikaṁ vaiṣamyaṁ hi mukhyādhāro'vatārasya
tena dharmasaṁsthāpanaṁ dhruvānītyāstu sūcakam

God's Avatāra appears on this earth mainly when there is a social crisis, and establishment of Dharma by the Avatāra means victory of the good over the evil and the preservation of a stable moral order founded on ethical, social values.

४.१०. ध्रुवानीतिसंस्थापने नियंत्रितः स्वार्थभावः ।
स्वजना अप्यपर्याप्ताः सर्वहितं हि वाञ्छितम् ॥
dhruvānītisaṁsthāpane niyaṁtritaḥ svārthabhāvaḥ
svajanā apyaparyāptāḥ sarvahitaṃ hi vāñchitam

Practical implications of a stable moral order founded on social values are that people keep under control their desire for selfish gains, and they do not confine their attention to what is beneficial to their own people, because their goal is to do good to all.

४.११. न केवलं स्वलाभश्च स्वजनहितं वा पुनः ।
अपि तु लोकसंग्रहो ध्येयो जनकस्य यथा ॥

na kevalaṁ svalābhaśca svajanahitaṁ vā punaḥ
api tu lokasaṁgraho dhyeyo janakasya yathā

To accept the Gita-ideal of Lokasaṁgraha means that one's vision is widened, and to appreciate the social significance of this process of the widening of the vision, it is helpful to recognize three levels. The narrowest vision is represented by utter selfishness, that is, to care for one's own benefit only. The next wider vision makes one pay attention to those whom one considers to be own people. However, under the widest vision, there is no distinction between "own people" and "other people", and therefore one works for the good of all—Lokasaṁgraha. In order that Arjuna, to whom this ideal is presented by Śrī Kṛṣṇa in the Gita, may understand it clearly, the concrete example of Janaka is given in śloka III.20. Five case studies that are presented in Part Two of this book are intended to serve the same purpose.

King Janaka of Mithilā is referred to in the Gita śloka III.20 as an ideal Karmayogin who worked for Lokasaṁgraha without any attachment. The Gita itself gives no further details, but they are provided by the Mahabharata. The most commonly quoted statement of Janaka, as a concrete proof of his non-attachment, is: "mithilāyāṁ pradīptāyāṁ na me dahyati kiñcana", that is, even if Mithilā, the capital of the kingdom is burnt, there is nothing in it that is mine that is burnt. According to Tilak, this famous statement, though significant, tells only half the story; because the second half of the story, as narrated in the Mahabharata, explains how Janaka's activities as a king were directed towards Lokasaṁgraha and not towards narrow goals. This is how Tilak completes Janaka's story:

> From the point of view of Lokasaṁgraha, the main question is why Janaka was still carrying on the activities of ruling, though he had no selfish interest or advantage and had become perfectly non-attached to his kingdom. Janaka himself says: 'all these activities are for the benefit of the gods, the ancestors, all creatures, but not for myself'.[4]

४.१२. प्रायो गीतोपदेशस्य पठितमर्धमात्रं हि ।
कर्मयोगे फलत्यागं तथा भक्तिं च ज्ञानं च ॥

prāyo gītopadeśasya paṭhitamardhamātraṁ hi
karmayoge phalatyāgaṁ tathā bhaktiṁ ca jñānaṁ ca

Since several Gita-readers do not highlight the Lokasaṁgraha-teaching, it can be said that such readers have grasped only half of the Gita. They do speak of the need not to hanker after results while they are engaged in Karmayoga, and they similarly speak of Bhaktiyoga and Jñānayoga. However, such an understanding of the Gita is still incomplete, as explained in the next verse.

४.१३. अपूर्णास्तु मार्गमात्राः विना हि लक्ष्यविस्तारात् ।
लक्ष्ये च तेषां पूर्णत्वं प्राप्तव्यं लोकसंग्रहे ॥
apūrṇāstu mārgamātrāḥ vinā hi lakṣyavistārāt
lakṣye ca teṣāṁ pūrṇatvaṁ prāptavyaṁ lokasaṁgrahe

Kramayoga, Bhaktiyoga, Jñānayoga—these are Mārga's or paths, and so long as the widest social goal is not associated with these paths, they will remain incomplete. Śloka III.20 of the Gita makes it clear that one needs to have a "double aim", namely, Lokasaṁgraha and individual salvation, as P.T. Raju has explained:

The teaching (of the Bhagavad-Gita) involves a double aim:

1. The process of the human world must be kept going. They should not be hindered, but furthered. When evil prevails and the good suffers, the Brahman takes on the appropriate incarnation, destroys evil, and protects the good. But why should the Brahman, which is eternally perfect and for which there is nothing to be desired, take the trouble of incarnating itself as a mundane being, go through the stages of birth, growth, and death? Why should the incarnation, that knows that it is the same as the eternal brahman, take the trouble of acting in this world? If it does not act, the world does not survive. . . Sustaining the world (is) Lokasaṁgraha. . .

2. The second aim of the teaching is salvation. It is through action without any self-centered motive that one attains salvation. . .[5]

The Gita śloka III.20 which introduces Lokasaṁgraha for the first time occurs in the Karmayoga section of the Gita. The question as to how Lokasaṁgraha is shown in the Gita to be essential for achieving perfection through Bhaktiyoga and Jñānayoga as well is taken up in chapter six of this book.

४.१४. लोकहितं यथाशक्यं संपश्यन् निजपौरुषम् ।
तदेव ज्ञेयं गन्तव्यं स्वलाभात् स्वजनहितात् ॥
lokahitaṁ yathāśakyaṁ saṁpaśyan nijapauruṣam
tadeva jñeyaṁ gantavyaṁ svalābhāt svajanahitāt

This verse summarizes the ideas contained in this chapter. The goal of one's life should be to go beyond personal gains, and also to go beyond what benefits narrow groups of those whom one calls own people. Ideally, the goal should be to work for the good of all, but to make it practicable, a proviso has been suggested in the Gita śloka XVIII.25 to the effect that one should take into account one's capability—pauruṣam. Also, Śrī Kṛṣṇa does not want any act for Lokasaṁgraha to be done unwillingly, therefore He says in śloka XVIII.63: yathecchasi tathā kuru, that is, do what you think best and you are willing to do.

CHAPTER FIVE

श्रेयोऽर्थं समत्वबुद्धिः साम्यदृष्टिस्तु लोकसंग्रहाय
ŚREYO'RTHAṀ SAMATVABUDDHIḤ SĀMYADṚṢṬISTU LOKASAṀGRAHĀYA

SAMATVABUDDHI FOR ŚREYAS AND SĀMYADṚṢṬI FOR LOKASAṀGRAHA

An indicator of the importance of the Lokasaṁgraha-teaching in the Gita is that it is reinforced by the use of several other terms or phrases which convey the same social message. To start with, the term 'Lokasaṁgraha' itself occurs twice in the Gita, in ślokas III.20 and III.25. Another closely related term is 'sarvabhūtahite ratāh' (persons who rejoice in doing good to all creatures) which occurs in chapters five and twelve of the Gita (ślokas V.25 and XII.4). But these two terms taken together still do not exhaust the coverage of Lokasaṁgraha in the Gita. There are several other terms that implicitly refer to Lokasaṁgraha, and they occur throughout the Gita, and in conjunction with not only karmayoga but bhaktiyoga and jñānayoga as well. We have already been looking at some of these terms, which are closely associated with Lokasaṁgraha, for example, 'sarvabhūtahitam' was referred to in chapter three. In this chapter, particular attention is devoted to "samatva" or even-mindedness, or rather to a variant thereof, namely, "sāmya" which, in the Gita, stands for equal vision. There are indications in the Gita which help us make a fine distinction between "even-mindedness in success or failure", on the one hand, and "equal vision towards all human beings", on the other. We then argue that the former of these two is mainly linked to "Śreyas" or individual salvation, while the latter is linked to "Lokasaṁgraha". How we arrive at this conclusion will be clear as we proceed verse-by-verse.

५.१. अर्जुनो धर्मसम्मूढ़ः सीमिता तस्य वन्दना ।
तदेकं वद निश्चित्य येन श्रेयोऽहमाप्नुयाम् ॥

arjuno dharmasammūḍhaḥ sīmitā tasya vandanā
tadekaṁ vada niścitya yena śreyo'hamāpnuyām

Arjuna is depicted in the beginning of the Gita as confused about his duty (śloka II.7). His vision about the goal that he should aim at is also narrow, confined to what might be good for himself and to his own people. In śloka III.2, he requests Śrī Kṛṣṇa: "Please tell me clearly one path which in your opinion will certainly enable me to attain Śreyas, that is, personal salvation". Since Arjuna is aiming at personal salvation, without thinking at the same time of the good of the society, his request can be characterized as narrow, having a limited horizon.

५.२. **श्रेयः कठोपनिषदि पुनश्च हरिगीतके ।**
पर्यायवाची मोक्षस्य तथा भिन्नं च प्रेयसः ॥
śreyaḥ kaṭhopaniṣadi punaśca harigītake
paryāyavācī mokṣasya tathā bhinnaṁ ca preyasaḥ

The word "Śreyas" occurs in Kaṭhopaniṣad, and as we already observed, in the Bhagavad-Gita also, in śloka III.2, for example, to denote personal salvation or Mokṣa. In Kaṭhopaniṣad, the word "Preyas"—meaning 'pleasant'—also occurs, to denote things which are spiritually inferior to Śreyas. The word Preyas does not as such occur in the Gita, but its two components—Artha and Kāma—are referred to.

The terms "preyas" and "śreyas" owe their popularity to the conversation between Yama and Nachiketa in Kaṭhopaniṣad. Some scholars interpret the Upaniṣadic text as presenting a choice between the two, and as asking one to strive for śreyas to the exclusion of preyas. However, according to Tilak, even Yama, in spite of giving priority to śreyas over preyas, by granting three blessings, enabled Nachiketa to obtain both:

In the phrase used for blessing, one says: śāntiḥ puṣṭis tuṣṭis cāstu, that is, may there be peace along with material happiness and contentedness (in proper proportions). The same is the moral of the Kaṭhopaniṣad. . . When Yama asked Nachiketa to ask for (three) blessings, Nachiketa did not in the first place ask for the blessing of Brahmajñāna, but first said: My father has got angry with me; may he become propitious to me. Secondly teach me the science of agni, that is, of all sacrificial ritual which will give me material opulence. When he had acquired these (two) blessings, he asked for the third one, saying: teach me the knowledge of the Ātman. But when Yama suggested that he would give him additional happiness instead of the third blessing, Nachiketa insisted: now explain to me that Brahmajñāna which will lead to śreyas, instead of aspiring for more of the knowledge of sacrificial ritual than was necessary for obtaining preyas. In short, as stated in the last mantra of this Upaniṣad, Nachiketa obtained both.[1]

In spite of the harmonizing interpretation given by Tilak to the last mantra of the Kaṭhopaniṣad, it can be argued that some of the other mantras of this Upaniṣad present Śreyas as the choice of the wise and Preyas as the choice of the unwise.[2] The Gita took a more balanced view. Although it did not use the term 'preyas', it recognized the importance of its two components—artha and kāma—i.e. wealth and pleasure—provided they are in conformity with Dharma—moral value. This can be called a conditional acceptance of the significant role of Preyas for an individual—representing a sort of modification of the Upaniṣadic view.[3]

५.३. आदौ कथितो हरिणा योगो निःश्रेयसकरः ।
ततो लोकसंग्रहस्य महिमाऽपि सुवर्णिता ॥
ādau kathito hariṇā yogo niḥśreyasakaraḥ
tato lokasaṁgrahasya mahimā'pi suvarṇitā

In the Bhagavad-Gita, since Arjuna specifically asked for instruction on Śreyas, Śrī Kṛṣṇa initially told him about the method by which he could achieve Śreyas. Thereafter, on His own initiative, Śrī Kṛṣṇa told Arjuna how important it was to go beyond personal and family goals and to work for Lokasaṁgraha—the good of the society.

५.४. श्रेयोऽर्थं भगवान् प्राह कर्मयोगं समाचर ।
कर्मसु कौशलार्थं तु फलत्यागो निर्धारितः ॥
śreyo'rthaṁ bhagavān prāha karmayogaṁ samācara
karmasu kauśalārthaṁ tu phalatyāgo nirdhāritaḥ

Śrī Kṛṣṇa told Arjuna: "To attain Śreyas, you should act in accordance with the Karmayoga teaching". He then explained that a successful implementation of Karmayoga is possible only if one can act without hankering after the fruit of one's action. This is called Niṣkāma Karma, for short.

५.५. कर्मण्येवाधिकारस्ते मा फलेषु कदाचन ।
मा कर्मफलहेतुर्भूर्मा ते सङ्गोऽस्त्वकर्मणि ॥
karmaṇyevādhikāraste mā phaleṣu kadācana
mā karmaphalaheturbhūrmā te saṁgo'stvakarmaṇi

Verse 5.5 is the same as the famous śloka II.47 of the Gita which has been translated by S. Radhakrishnan as follows:

"To action alone hast thou a right and never at all to its fruits; let not the fruits of action be thy motive; neither let there be in thee any attachment to inaction".[4]

५.६. सात्त्विकं कर्म निष्पापं निःस्वार्थभावनाश्रितम् ।
तस्मात् नारायणः प्राह तत्कुरुष्व मदर्पणम् ॥
sāttvikaṁ karma niṣpāpaṁ niḥsvārthabhāvanāśritam
tasmāt nārāyaṇaḥ prāha tatkuruṣva madarpaṇam

When one attempts to apply the teaching about not hankering after the fruits of one's action, one will find that only sāttvika actions are possible—that is, neither tāmasika nor rājasī. Sāttvika actions are pure, virtuous and ethical, and are founded on unselfish motives. Śrī Kṛṣṇa's advice "Dedicate all your acts to Me" encourages us to perform only sāttvika actions because only such actions are fit to be offered to God.

५.७. कर्मयोगी फलं त्यक्त्वा समाचरति साधनम् ।
तस्मात्तत्कर्म सफलं योगः कर्मसु कौशलम् ॥
karmayogī phalaṁ tyaktvā samācarati sādhanam
tasmāttatkarma saphalaṁ yogaḥ karmasu kauśalam

Since a Karmayogin does not hanker after the fruits of one's actions, he or she devotes all attention to the means and the effort to be put in. Therefore, the chances of success are relatively greater than if a part of the effort were wasted in worrying about results. That is why one of the definitions of yoga given in the Gita (śloka II.50) is that yoga means efficiency or skill in actions.

Mahatma Gandhi has explained, on the basis of his own experience, how the Gita's approach is both "unique" and "convincing":

> All activity, whether mental or physical, is to be included in the term 'action'. While on the one hand it is beyond dispute that all action binds, on the other hand it is equally true that all living beings have to do some work, whether they like it or not. Then how is one to be free from the bondage of action, even though he may be acting? The manner in which the Gita has solved the problem is to my knowledge unique. The Gita says: 'Do your allotted work but renounce its fruit—be detached and work—have no desire for reward and work'.
>
> This is the unmistakable teaching of the Gita. He who gives up action falls. He who gives up only the reward rises. But renunciation of fruit in no way means indifference to the result. In regard to every action one must know the result that is expected to follow, the means thereto, and the capacity for it. He, who, being thus equipped, is without desire for the result and is yet wholly engrossed in the due fulfilment of the task before him is said to have renounced the fruits of his action.
>
> Again let no one consider renunciation to mean want of fruit for the renouncer. The Gita reading does not warrant such a meaning. Renunciation means absence of hankering after fruit. As a matter of fact, he who renounces reaps a thousandfold. . .[5]

५.८. पुनश्च भगवान् प्राह योगस्य कुशलां विधिम् ।
सिद्ध्यसिद्ध्योः समो भूत्वा समत्वं योग उच्यते ॥
punaśca bhagavān prāha yogasya kuśalāṁ vidhim
siddhyasiddhyoḥ samo bhūtvā samatvaṁ yoga ucyate

In the previous verse, one of the definitions of yoga, namely, efficiency or skill in actions, was given. A practical approach, which not only helps achieve efficiency but also helps maintain peace of mind, has also been specified in the Gita (śloka II.48), namely, "Once you have put in your best effort in your action, don't let success or failure shake you from your mental equilibrium; treat success or failure as alike." This is another definition of yoga in the Gita, namely, even-mindedness in success or failure.

The Gita attaches so much importance to samatva or even-mindedness that its usefulness is stressed in several places. The first reference to samatva occurs in ślokas II.14-15, in the context of metaphysical knowledge. The next reference occurs in the context of svadharma, in ślokas II.31-38, where Śrī Kṛṣṇa recommends the samatva technique as an improvement of the traditional approach. To achieve this effect, a two-step argument is used. First, Arjuna is reminded that customary tradition associates social honour, earthly sovereignty, heavenly bliss, and śreyas, with the performance of svadharma. Secondly, Arjuna is told by Śrī Kṛṣṇa that if he could perform his traditional svadharma according to the (new) Gita-technique of samatva, then he need not have the fear of incurring sin (even if he killed his svajanam). Śloka II.48, which is substantially quoted in verse 5.8, thus marks the third reference to samatva in the Gita. Here, by coming to samatva through the defining characteristic of Karmayoga (namely, non-attachment to the fruit of action), the Gita elevates samatva to be synonymous with yoga.

Although samatva—even-mindedness—is thus assigned a high place in the Gita, we would like to mention that from the viewpoint of Lokasaṁgraha, a variant of samatva, called Sāmyadṛṣṭi—or equal vision—or Sāmya for short—is assigned a still higher place. The next verse which begins to put forward this idea can therefore be called "Lokasaṁgraha through Equal Vision Declaration".

साम्यात् लोकसंग्रहघोषणा
SĀMYĀT LOKASAṀGRAHAGHOṢAṆĀ

५.९. ततो लोकसंग्रहाय साम्यदृष्टिः सुवर्णिता ।
आत्मौपम्येन भावेन सहानुभूतिः सर्वेषु ॥
tato lokasaṁgrahāya sāmyadṛṣṭiḥ suvarṇitā
ātmaupamyena bhāvena sahānubhūtiḥ sarveṣu

Samatva or even-mindedness in success or failure can lead one to Śreyas or Personal salvation—this can be considered as a summary of the reply which Śrī Kṛṣṇa gave to Arjuna's question. Thereafter, Śrī Kṛṣṇa spoke of Lokasaṁgraha, the wider social goal, which calls for an attitude of sympathy and compassion—say, a warm heart—the climax of which, according to Gita, is "even-mindedness towards all people", or samaḥ sarveṣu bhūteṣu (śloka XVIII.54). Although the Sanskrit word "samatva" can denote even-mindedness of both types (first, in success or failure, and secondly, towards all people), the Gita also uses the word "sāmya" to denote even-mindedness towards all people (ślokas V.19 and VI.33). Those who have sāmya are also called in the Gita "samadarśinaḥ" (śloka V.18). The foundation of such equal vision (samadṛṣṭi) is, of course, the Vedantic philosophy that the same ātman resides in each being. The philosophical term used in the Gita (śloka VI.32) is "ātmaupamya" meaning equality of others with oneself, but in practice, equal vision is reflected in an attitude of sympathy towards all.

५.१०. आत्मौपम्यभावः सदा घोषितो दर्शनज्ञाने ।
सर्वेषां सुखदुःखेषु साम्यदृष्टिः व्यवहारे ॥
ātmaupamyabhāvaḥ sadā ghoṣito darśanajñāne
sarveṣāṁ sukhaduḥkheṣu sāmyadṛṣṭiḥ vyavahāre

The concept of ātmaupamya is part of the ancient declaration of Indian philosophy, but the Gita also insists that this should be expressed in practice by viewing the joys and sorrows of others as if they are one's own.

The term 'ātmaupamya' meaning 'equality of others with oneself' occurs in śloka VI.32 of the Gita which says: "He, O Arjuna, who sees with equality everything, in the image of his own self, whether in pleasure or in pain, he is considered a perfect yogi".

In Śaṁkara's words, "he sees that whatever is pleasant to himself is pleasant to all creatures, and that whatever is painful to himself is painful to all beings".[6] Even as he desires good to himself, he desires good to all.

The concept of ātmaupamya ultimately comes from the Upaniṣads, for example, Īśā Upaniṣad verse 6 says:

> The wise man who realizes all beings as not distinct from his own self, and his own self as the self of all beings, does not, by virtue of that perception, hate any one. (Īśā verse 6)

Swami Ranganathananda comments on the attitude and behaviour of such a person:

Narrow-mindedness, secretiveness, and hatred spring always from a sense of separateness. The sense of separateness gives rise to all kinds of selfish desires; the desire to hide one's thoughts and possessions from others, the desire to exploit or overcome somebody else, and so on. But when this sense of separateness vanishes, such calculations also vanish, leaving in their place a feeling of universal friendship and benevolence towards other beings. . .

All morality, all ethics and spirituality tell us that we are one, basically one. Jesus says, Love thy neighbour as thyself. The Upaniṣads add: For you are your neighbour.[7]

५.११. द्विविधरूपा वर्णिता समत्वबुद्धिः कृष्णेन ।
प्रथमा हि सिद्ध्यसिद्ध्योः द्वितीया सर्वभूतेषु ॥

dvividharūpā varṇitā samatvabuddhiḥ kṛṣṇena
prathamā hi siddhyasiddhyoḥ dvitīyā sarvabhūteṣu

In this way, Śrī Kṛṣṇa has described samatva or even-mindedness of two types, the first being in success or failure, and the second being towards all people.

"Even-mindedness in success or failure" occurs in the Gita śloka II.48, while the second type of even-mindedness—"samaḥ sarveṣu bhūteṣu"—is mentioned in śloka XVIII.54.

As the most obvious example of how the Gita has highlighted separately the two categories of samatva—that is, in two successive ślokas—we give below the translation of ślokas VI.8 and VI.9. In the former, samatva towards situations is called yoga, but in the latter, samatva towards people is called "excellent":

The yogi whose soul is satisfied with wisdom and knowledge, who is unchanging and master of his senses, to whom a clod, a stone and a piece of gold are the same, is said to be firm in yoga. (Gita śloka VI.8)

He who is equal-minded among friends, companions and foes, among those who are neutral and impartial, among those who are hateful and related, among saints and sinners, he excels. (Gita śloka VI.9)

The samatva-attitude towards a clod, a stone and a piece of gold which occurs in śloka VI.8 is repeated in the Gita śloka XIV.24 which forms part of the description of one who has risen above the three guṇas. In fact, the Gita account of the characteristics of those who have attained perfection by different means is broadly similar. Radhakrishnan comments on the yogi who has samatva of the first category: "He is unperturbed by things and happenings of the world and is therefore said to be equal-minded to the events of this changing world".[8] And about the second category of samatva, he writes (in another place): "This view makes us look upon our fellow beings with kindliness and compassion. The wise see the one God in all beings and develop the quality of equal-mindedness which is characteristic of the Divine".[9] The Gita śloka V.19 says: God is the same in all, and this is repeated in śloka IX.29 also.

Swami Chidbhavananda also compares the two categories of samatva and while admiring both, stresses the supreme importance of the latter for the conflict-ridden humanity (or Lokasaṁgraha, as we can call it):

> Inert things are all viewed with an equal eye by the yogi. . . The achievement of the yogi is that he is the conqueror of the senses. . .
> He stands supreme who has equal regard for people of varying status. His supremely benevolent attitude is the greatest gift made by him to the conflict-ridden humanity.[10]

५.१२. श्रेयोऽर्थं महत्त्वपूर्णा समबुद्धिः सिद्ध्यसिद्ध्योः ।
तथा लोकसंग्रहाय साम्यं तु सर्वभूतेषु ॥
śreyo'rthaṁ mahattvapūrṇā samabuddhiḥ siddhya-siddhyoḥ
tathā lokasaṁgrahāya sāmyaṁ tu sarvabhūteṣu

Two goals are important in life—Śreyas or personal salvation, and Lokasaṁgraha or the good of the society. Even-mindedness in success or failure can lead one to Śreyas. Similarly, equal vision towards all people can help achieve Lokasaṁgraha.

५.१३. एवं कृतः समन्वयो लोकसंग्रहश्रेयसाम् ।
समत्वबुद्ध्याः हि श्रेयः साम्यात्तु लोकसंग्रहः ॥

evaṁ kṛtaḥ samanvayo lokasaṁgrahaśreyasām
samatvabuddhyāḥ hi śreyaḥ sāmyāttu lokasaṁgrahaḥ

The two goals, Śreyas and Lokasaṁgraha, have been harmonized in the Gita, by linking the former with samatva of the first category, and by linking the latter with samatva of the second category.

Harmonization of the two goals—Śreyas and Lokasaṁgraha—is a special feature of the Gita. Both these goals are mentioned together in the Gita śloka III.20: "It was even by karma that Janaka and others attained to perfection (or śreyas). Thou shouldst do karma also, keeping an eye to Lokasaṁgraha". (III.20)

In the second line of the Gita śloka III.11, a linkage between Lokasaṁgraha and śreyas is brought about: "Fostering each other you shall attain to śreyas". This is similar to the first principle of sarvodaya (uplift of all) enunciated by Mahatma Gandhi: "The good of the individual is contained in the good of all".[11]

Vinoba Bhave harmonizes Lokasaṁgraha and śreyas by saying that service to society and personal salvation can be achieved simultaneously from the same action if performed in accordance with the teaching of the Gita:

> The service that is being rendered to the world through my external actions can itself, viewed from within, be described as spiritual exercise. The service of creation and the development of the spirit do not demand two different courses of action; service and spiritual growth are not different things. For both, the effort made, and the action performed is the same.[12]

Swami Vivekananda conveys the same idea by the phrase "ātmano mokṣārthaṁ jagaddhitāya ca" which means that individual salvation and universal welfare can be achieved simultaneously by the followers of Śrī Ramakrishna.[13] Details about Swami Vivekananda are given in chapter eight.

CHAPTER SIX

भक्त्याः ज्ञानस्यापि पूर्णत्वं लोकसंग्रहे

BHAKTYĀḤ JÑĀNASYĀPI PŪRṆATVAṀ LOKASAṀGRAHE

LOKASAṀGRAHA—ESSENTIAL FOR PERFECTION OF BHAKTI AND JÑĀNA AS WELL

In the preceding chapters, attention was devoted to three of the terms used in the Gita to convey the same social message as Lokasaṁgraha, the terms in Sanskrit being the following:

(i) sarvabhūtahitam
(ii) samaḥ sarveṣu bhūteṣu or sāmya
(iii) ātmaupamya

In this chapter, one more term (or rather, phrase) is highlighted as being closely linked with Lokasaṁgraha. The phrase "nirmamo nirahaṁkāraḥ" literally meaning "giving up mine-ness and egotism" has been identified by Vinoba Bhave as being indicative of Lokasaṁgraha in the Gita. Vinoba's argument (specifically given with reference to the Gita śloka II.71 which forms part of the description of a sthitaprajña) runs like this:

Nirmamo means that a sthitaprajña karmayogin has no selfish desires. Nirahaṁkāraḥ means that he has dedicated all his actions to Īśvara and does not regard himself as the doer. But still he puts in his best effort in whatever he does. What can he do other than Lokasaṁgraha? In fact, he lives only in order to benefit humanity.[1]

The close linkage between the phrase "nirmamo nirahaṁkāraḥ" and Lokasaṁgraha, as established by Vinoba Bhave, is utilized in this chapter to show that perfection in Bhaktiyoga or Jñānayoga cannot be achieved without Lokasaṁgraha. Of course, there are other ways of arriving at this conclusion, but the simplest way is to apply the criterion of "nirmamo nirahaṁkāraḥ", as we do in this chapter.

६.१. लक्षणं स्थितप्रज्ञस्य भक्तस्य ज्ञानिनस्तथा ।
उक्तं भिन्ने भिन्ने स्थाने किं तु लक्ष्यसमागतिः ॥
lakṣaṇaṁ sthitaprajñasya bhaktasya jñāninastathā
uktaṁ bhinne bhinne sthāne kiṁ tu lakṣyasamāgatiḥ

The Gita has described in detail, in different chapters, the characteristics of one who has attained perfection. For example, chapter II ślokas 54-72 describe a sthitaprajña karmayogin, chapter XII ślokas 13-20 describe a bhakta, and chapter XVIII ślokas 50-54 describe the state of perfection of a jñānin. Although perfect persons are given different titles, depending on which yoga they primarily followed to attain perfection, their characteristics are similar because all the yogas become unified in the state of perfection. In particular, they are all engaged in Lokasaṁgraha, and this fact is brought out by means of terms or phrases which are indicative of Lokasaṁgraha.

६.२. समत्वबुद्धिः प्रत्येके योगे तथैव साम्यं च ।
उक्तश्च योगी प्रत्येको निर्ममो निरहंकारः ॥
samatvabuddhiḥ pratyeke yoge tathaiva sāmyaṁ ca
uktaśca yogī pratyeko nirmamo nirahaṁkāraḥ

The similarity between the various yogas is established in the Gita by saying that, in the state of perfection attained by each yoga, one is even-minded in success or failure, and similarly one is even-minded towards all people. Another common characteristic of all these yogis who have achieved perfection is that each of them has been described in the Gita as "nirmamo nirahaṁkāraḥ", that is, free from mine-ness and egotism.

६.३. विहाय कामान्यः स्वार्थान् पुमांश्चरति निःस्पृहः ।
निर्ममो निरहंकारः स शान्तिमधिगच्छति ॥
vihāya kāmānyaḥ svārthān pumāṁścarati niḥspṛhaḥ
nirmamo nirahaṁkāraḥ sa śāntimadhigacchati

The first time the phrase "nirmamo nirahaṁkāraḥ" occurs in the Gita is in describing a sthitaprajña karmayogin. Verse 6.3 of this chapter is a slightly modified form of the Gita śloka II.71 in which this phrase occurs. Verse 6.3 mentions that a sthitaprajña karmayogin does not hanker after selfish gains—he, being nirmamo nirahaṁkāraḥ, works for Lokasaṁgraha, but maintains peace of mind under all circumstances.

By using Nirmamo Nirahaṁkāraḥ as a proxy for Lokasaṁgraha, it is stated in the next verse that every perfect person—irrespective of the type of yoga through which perfection is attained—works for Lokasaṁgraha. The next verse can therefore be called "Lokasaṁgraha through All Yogas Declaration".

सर्वयोगेभ्यो लोकसंग्रहघोषणा
SARVAYOGEBHYO LOKASAṀGRAHAGHOṢAṆĀ

६.४. निर्ममो निरहंकारो लोकसंग्रहसूचकः ।
न केवलं कर्मयोगे तथैव भक्तौ ज्ञाने च ॥
nirmamo nirahaṁkāro lokasaṁgrahasūcakaḥ
na kevalaṁ karmayoge tathaiva bhaktau jñāne ca

In the Gita, the use of the phrase "nirmamo nirahaṁkāraḥ" is indicative of being engaged in Lokasaṁgraha. Just as a sthitaprajña karmayogin is described as nirmamo nirahaṁkāraḥ, the same description has been given for a bhakta and a jñānin as well. This shows that, in the state of perfection, followers of all yogas—karmayoga, bhaktiyoga, jñānayoga—work for Lokasaṁgraha.

६.५. तदर्थं लक्षणं पश्य द्वादशाध्याये भक्तस्य ।
अष्टादशे ज्ञानिनोऽपि प्रवक्तं श्रीभगवता ॥
tadarthaṁ lakṣaṇaṁ paśya dvādaśādhyāye bhaktasya
aṣṭādaśe jñānino'pi pravaktaṁ śrībhagavatā

The truth of this statement is verified in this chapter by actually quoting the relevant ślokas of the Gita, for example, ślokas 53 and 54 of chapter eighteen which form part of the description of a perfect jñānin, and also ślokas 13, 14, 18, and 19 of chapter twelve which similarly form part of the description of a perfect bhakta.

६.६. अहंकारं बलं दर्पं कामं क्रोधं परिग्रहम् ।
विमुच्य निर्ममः शान्तो ब्रह्मभूयाय कल्पते ॥

ahaṁkāraṁ balaṁ darpaṁ kāmaṁ krodhaṁ parigraham
vimucya nirmamaḥ śānto brahmabhūyāya kalpate

This verse is the same as śloka 53 of chapter XVIII in the Gita. A perfect jñānin casts aside ahaṁkāra—egotism—and he is nirmama—free from the sense of mine-ness—also. Other characteristics of a perfect jñānin are: he is free from the use of force, arrogance, lust, anger, and personal possession. He is "śāntaḥ"—tranquil in mind, and he becomes worthy of becoming one with Brahman.

D.S. Sarma warns that the use of the word "śāntaḥ" as a part of the description of a jñānin (for example, in the above verse) should not be interpreted to mean as if the Gita supports "mere quietism" "divorced from service to society":

The Gita supplied a much needed corrective to the over-emphasis of jñāna and renunciation, which had led to mere quietism. It may be said that the whole Gita is a long and sustained protest against the dangers of quietism. . .[2] The unique feature of jñāna, as taught in the Gita, is that it is never divorced from service to society.[3] Unsympathetic critics of Hinduism have often ignored the Lokasaṁgraha message of the Gita and said that social service forms no integral part of our religion. They forget that the service to society is fundamental to the very concept of Hindu Dharma as taught by the Gita.[4]

What D.S. Sarma said as a scholar had already been boldly demonstrated in actual practice by Swami Vivekananda. Perhaps the best illustration of uniting Jñānayoga and Lokasaṁgraha is provided by Vivekananda's formulation of the concept of Practical Vedanta, and its continued implementation through the Ramakrishna Mission. 'Practical Vedanta', according to Vivekananda, meant an harmonization of theoretical knowledge—Vedanta—and practical action—Karmayoga:

Raise once more that mighty banner of Vedanta for on no other ground can you have that wonderful love until you see that the same Lord is present everywhere. The nation is sinking, the curse of unnumbered millions is on our heads—the unnumbered millions to whom we have talked of Vedanta and whom we have hated with all our strength, to whom we have talked theoretically that we are all the same and all are one with the same Lord, without even an ounce of practice . . . throw away everything, even your own salvation, and go and help others. Ay, you are talking bold words, but here is Practical Vedanta before you. The first part of this is that you should go to the sinking millions of India, and take them by hand, remembering the words of Lord Krishna. . .[5]

६.७. ब्रह्मभूतः प्रसन्नात्मा न शोचति न कांक्षति ।
समः सर्वेषु भूतेषु मद्भक्तिं लभते पराम् ॥
brahmabhūtaḥ prasannātmā na śocati na kāṁkṣati
samaḥ sarveṣu bhūteṣu madbhaktiṁ labhate parām

This verse is the same as śloka 54 of chapter XVIII in the Gita, and the description of a perfect jñānin is continued here. Having become one with Brahman, and being tranquil in spirit, he neither grieves nor desires. He is even-minded towards all people. He attains supreme devotion to Śrī Kṛṣṇa.

The fact that a perfect jñānin is engaged in Lokasaṁgraha is stated in these two verses by mentioning that he is nirmamo nirahaṁkāraḥ; and it is re-inforced by saying that he is even-minded towards all people—'sāmya' also denoting Lokasaṁgraha, as already explained in verses 5.9-13.

After having verified the link between Jñānayoga and Lokasaṁgraha, we next do the same thing for Bhaktiyoga, in verses 6.8-11.

६.८. अद्वेष्टा सर्वभूतानां मैत्रः करुण एव च ।
निर्ममो निरहंकारः समदुःखसुखः क्षमी ॥
adveṣṭā sarvabhūtānāṁ maitraḥ karuṇa eva ca
nirmamo nirahaṁkāraḥ samaduḥkhasukhaḥ kṣamī

This verse is the same as śloka 13 of chapter XII in the Gita, and with it begins the description of a perfect bhakta. He is engaged in Lokasaṁgraha because he is nirmamo nirahaṁkāraḥ. Other characteristics of his are: he has no ill will towards any being, he is friendly and compassionate, he is even-minded in pain and pleasure, and he is of a forgiving nature.

Mahatma Gandhi uses the characteristics of a Bhakta as described in chapter twelve of the Gita (quotations from which are included here) to set right some of the false notions that have become associated with bhakti in popular mind. Don't attach importance to external appearances, advised Gandhi; rather look for service activities as the real criteria of a Bhakta:

> In order that knowledge may not run riot, the author of the Gita has insisted on devotion accompanying it. . . This devotion is not mere lip worship, it is a wrestling with death. Hence the Gita's assessment of the devotee's qualities is similar to that of the sage's.
>
> Thus the devotion required by the Gita is no soft-hearted effusiveness. It certainly is not blind faith. The devotion of the Gita has the least to do with externals. A devotee may use, if he likes, rosaries, forehead marks, make offerings, but these things are no test of his devotion. . .
>
> The popular notion of bhakti is soft-heartedness, telling beads and the like, and disdaining to do even a loving service, lest the telling of beads etc. might be interrupted. This bhakti, therefore, leaves the rosary only for eating, drinking and the like, never for grinding corn or nursing patients. But the Gita says: 'No one has attained his goal without action. Even men like Janaka attained salvation through action. . .'[6]

Lokamanya Tilak also stresses the fact that the description of a Bhakta, as given in chapter twelve of the Gita, begins with a reference to the nature of his or her relationship with the society. If one ignores the interests of the world, says Tilak, one cannot hope to achieve unity with God:

> If a man seeks unity with the Deity, he must necessarily seek unity with the interests of the world also, and work for it. If he does not, then the unity is not perfect, because there is union between two elements out of the three (man and Deity), and the third (the world) is left out. I have thus solved the question for myself and I hold that serving the world, and thus serving His

will, is the surest way of salvation, and this way can be followed by remaining in the world and not going away from it.[7]

६.९. संतुष्टः सततं योगी यतात्मा दृढनिश्चयः ।
मय्यर्पितमनोबुद्धिर्यो मद्भक्तः स मे प्रियः ॥
saṁtuṣṭaḥ satataṁ yogī yatātmā dṛḍhaniścayaḥ
mayyarpitamanobuddiryo madbhaktaḥ sa me priyaḥ

This verse is the same as śloka 14 of chapter twelve in the Gita. A perfect bhakta is ever content, he exercises self-control, he is unshakable in determination, he can persevere because he has dedicated his mind and understanding to Śrī Kṛṣṇa and he is dear to Śrī Kṛṣṇa.

६.१०. समः शत्रौ च मित्रे च तथा मानापमानयोः ।
शीतोष्णसुखदुःखेषु समः संगविवर्जितः ॥
samaḥ śatrau ca mitre ca tathā mānāpamānayoḥ
śītoṣṇasukhaduḥkheṣu samaḥ saṁgavivarjitaḥ

This verse is the same as śloka 18 of chapter XII in the Gita. A perfect bhakta behaves alike towards friend and foe, neither honour nor dishonour can shake him from the right path, he is free from "dvandvas" or pairs of opposites like heat and cold, pleasure and pain, and so on, and he has no attachment to the fruits of his actions.

६.११. तुल्यनिन्दास्तुतिर्मौनी संतुष्टो येन केनचित् ।
अनिकेतः स्थिरमतिर्भक्तिमान्मे प्रियो नरः ॥
tulyanindāstutirmaunī saṁtuṣṭo yena kenacit
aniketaḥ sthiramatirbhaktimānme priyo naraḥ

This verse is the same as śloka 19 of chapter XII in the Gita. A perfect bhakta is not moved from the right path by criticism or praise, he is restrained in speech, he accepts things as they come and does not express dissatisfaction, he goes and lives wherever his services are needed because he is not tied down to any particular abode, he is a sthitaprajña—a man of steady wisdom—and he is dear to Śrī Kṛṣṇa.

The upshot of verses 6.8-11 is that a perfect Bhakta works for Lokasaṁgraha because he is 'nirmamo nirahaṁkāraḥ'; of course, this is re-inforced by mentioning other qualities of a Bhakta, and by saying that he is a sthitaprajña. Now the concluding verse of Part One.

६.१२. आत्मशान्तिस्तु योगस्य केवलं रूपमांशिकम् ।
पूर्णत्वं सर्वयोगानां प्राप्तव्यं लोकसंग्रहे ॥
ātmaśāntistu yogasya kevalaṁ rūpamāṁśikam
pūrṇatvaṁ sarvayogānāṁ prāptavyaṁ lokasaṁgrahe

Descriptions of those who have attained perfection are similar, irrespective of whether they are karmayogins or bhaktas or jñānins. They have peace of mind, they are tranquil in spirit, but this is only one side of the story. Their perfection and completeness lie in the fact that they are also engaged in Lokasaṁgraha—doing good to all people. Maintaining peace of mind in the midst of the struggles that they continuously wage for social justice, harmony, unity and welfare—particularly of the poor and the weak—this combination of Lokasaṁgraha and Śānti marks out the perfect Gita-followers.

Swami Vivekananda repeatedly referred to the significance of the above formulation, namely, a harmonious combination of Lokasaṁgraha and Śānti:

> He who sees in the midst of intense activity, intense calm, and in the midst of intense peace is intensely active, is wise indeed . . . This is the question: With every sense and every organ active, have you that tremendous peace so that nothing can disturb you? Standing on Market Street, waiting for the car with all the rush. . .going on around you, are you in meditation—calm and peaceful? In the cave, are you intensely active there with all quiet about you? If you are, you are a Yogi, otherwise not. . . The seers call him wise whose every attempt is free, without any desire for gain, without any selfishness. . . When your neighbour asks you, 'Come and help me', have you exactly the same idea when you are helping yourself?[8]

PART TWO

लोकहिते गीताप्रयोगकथाचयनम्

Lokahite Gītāprayogakathācayanam

GITA APPLICATIONS FOR SOCIAL CAUSES: A SELECTIVE NARRATION

CHAPTER SEVEN

रामभोहनरायेण स्त्रीवर्गरक्षार्थं गीताप्रयोगः
RĀMAMOHANARĀYEṆA STRĪVARGARAKṢĀRTHAM GĪTĀPRAYOGAḤ

RAMMOHUN ROY—USING THE GITA TO SAVE WOMEN'S LIVES

This is the opening chapter in Part Two which contains a selective narration of Gita applications made for social causes during the last two hundred years. These can be called "case studies". Five of them have been included in this book, namely, Raja Rammohun Roy, Swami Vivekananda, Lokamanya Bal Gangadhar Tilak, Sri Aurobindo, and Mahatma Gandhi. This chapter is devoted to Rammohun Roy, while the other case studies will follow in the succeeding chapters.

In order to understand and appreciate the significant contribution made by each leader of the social movement, essential background information needs to be provided. Also, it seems to be desirable to follow a fairly uniform pattern of presentation for each case study. Our plan is to start with a brief life-sketch of the leader under study, to be followed by a short statement of the social problem that he set out to tackle. Details of what he did will be given through the commentary on each verse. Finally, the role of the Gita in all this will be assessed. Advantages of such a presentation will become clear as we now proceed to follow this pattern for Raja Rammohun Roy (1772-1833).

A BRIEF LIFE-SKETCH

Rammohun Roy was born in 1772 when the British administration in Bengal was being consolidated. His father was a small Zamindar—land-owner—commanding respect of the village community as an orthodox Brahmin. His mother was a woman of great piety, descending from a family of priests.

Rammohun's parents wanted to give him good education. After learning Bengali and Persian in the village, Rammohun was sent to Patna for studying Arabic and to Banaras for studying Sanskrit. As a result of new ideas that arose from all these studies, seeds of discord with his orthodox father were sown because Rammohun had become a strong opponent of idol-worship.

Leaving his parental home, Rammohun travelled from place to place within India, and also went to Tibet to obtain first-hand knowledge of Buddhism. Rammohun's assertion of monotheistic doctrines gave offence to the Lama worshippers, and they even resolved to lay violent hands on him, but some kind-hearted Tibetan women saved him from imminent danger. From then on he became a strong supporter of women's causes.

Rammohun's willingness to get married in the usual orthodox style brought about a reconciliation between him and his father. This enabled Rammohun to widen the scope of his language studies, by including, at this stage, a study of English, Latin, Greek, and Hebrew.

Rammohun's knowledge of English and Persian enabled him to secure a job in the Revenue Department of the East India Company. He worked for the British administration till 1815. He was able to "retire" in 1815 because of the ancestral property that he got, and also because he wanted to reform the social and religious life of his country—an important aspect of which was his resolve to put an end to the evil custom of "suttee"—whereby a widow burnt herself to death along with the body of her dead husband.

After several years of preparatory work, Rammohun assumed, in 1818, the leadership of the movement to create public opinion against the suttee custom. He held "debates" with the orthodox suttee-advocates, and was able to convince them—at least philosophically—that to get a widow's consent for being burnt by creating a desire that this will take her to heaven, was a violation of the Niṣkāma Karma doctrine of the Gita.

The Governor-General, Lord William Bentinck, was encouraged by the change in public opinion—at least partially—and he invited Rammohun to discuss the suttee-question personally, in July 1829. On December 4, 1829, the suttee-custom was declared illegal by the Governor-General.

Orthodox Hindus filed an appeal to the King-in-Council, against the Governor-General's orders. Liberal Hindus asked Rammohun to go to England to present their point of view. Accordingly, he went to England and briefed the Solicitor General. He was present when the appeal was heard, and he felt that his life's mission was achieved when on July 11, 1832, the Privy Council confirmed the ban on "suttee'.

Rammohun was, however, unable to return to India because of his illness to which he succumbed, while still in England, in 1833.

We have concentrated our attention on suttee-abolition as the life's mission of Rammohun because this was closely linked with the Gita. However, we must briefly mention the second mission of his—the founding of Brahmo Samaj in 1828, for which the inspiration came exclusively from the Vedas and the Upanisads but not from the Gita.

Rammohun Roy is unanimously regarded as the pioneer of the social reform movement in modern India—the related term "reformism" being defined by Robert Bellah as " a movement that re-interprets a particular religious tradition to show not only that it is compatible with modernization but also that, when truly understood, the tradition vigorously demands at least important aspects of modernity".[1]

THE SOCIAL PROBLEM—SUTTEE—THAT HE SET OUT TO TACKLE

Although some instances of suttee occurred in different parts of India during the ancient and the middle ages, it was mainly during the seventeenth century that it became relatively more frequent, particularly in Bengal. The active role that the priestly class played in motivating, and even forcing, the widows to burn themselves has been documented by Tavernier and Bernier who travelled through India in that century. Without going into details, we mention only one point, contained in Tavernier's report, namely, that the priests were allowed to "rake for (the widow's ornaments) among the ashes when the party is burned".[2]

Another factor which contributed to suttee-occurrences in Bengal had three components: (i) a sudden increase of wealth in several of the joint Hindu families because of trading with the English merchants, (ii) the prevalence of the Dayabhaga Law of inheritance in Bengal, and (iii) the desire of property claimants—other than the widow—to obtain a greater share of the joint family property by eliminating the widow . The Dayabhaga Law and its relevance to suttee will be clarified in the commentary on verse 7.5.

So when Rammohun Roy took in hand the task of putting an end to the suttee-custom, what he had to face was a "conspiracy between the priests and the newly emerging richer sections of the Hindu society".[3]

With this background, we take up a verse-by-verse commentary.

७.१. योगिनः कर्म कुर्वन्ति सङ्गं त्यक्त्वात्मशुद्धये ।
तथैव स्वार्थरहिताः संलग्नाः जनताहिते ॥
yoginaḥ karma kurvanti saṁgaṁ tyaktvātmaśuddhaye
tathaiva svārtharahitāḥ saṁlagnāḥ janatāhite

The first line of this verse is the same as the second line of śloka V.11 of the Gita. Two of the guiding principles that underlie all the activities of the Gita followers are stated in this line, namely, first that they are not attached to the fruits of their actions, and secondly, that the process of self-purification goes on along with the activities. The third guiding principle is stated in the second line of verse 7.1, namely that, being free from the desire for selfish gains, these persons try their best to contribute to the good of the society.

७.२. लोकसंग्रहसंलग्नाः अनेके कर्मयोगिनः ।
यथा नारीरक्षणाय श्रीरायो राममोहनः ॥
lokasaṁgrahasaṁlagnāh aneke karmayoginaḥ
yathā nārīrakṣaṇāya śrīrāyo rāmamohanaḥ

There have been, and still are, many Karmayogins who follow the guiding principles stated in the preceding verse, and who thus carry on Lokasaṁgraha activities according to their own assessment of what the society needs and of how much they can possibly do. A good example of such a Karmayogin is provided by Raja Rammohun Roy who took up the cause of protecting women's lives, and more specifically, of preventing widows from being burnt—as suttees. As already mentioned during the presentation of the life-sketch, suttee was an evil custom according to which a widow was burnt to death along with the dead body of her husband. Rammohun himself had no authority to put an end to this evil custom. The only course of action open to him was to convince the people who were following this custom that this was not the right thing to do.

A notable feature of Rammohun Roy's attempt was that he adopted the technique of 'dialogue', or as he himself called it, 'a debate' between proponents of the two viewpoints—one opposing the 'suttee' custom, and the other supporting it.[4] Of the several arguments against the evil custom of the suttee, that Rammohun Roy tried to use in order to convince the orthodox sections of the Hindu society, the one which proved to be most effective was that the practice of alluring the widows by creating the desire for heaven was in violation of the Gita. This is taken up in the next verse, which can also be called "Widow-burning as a Gita-violation Declaration".

विधवादाहविषये गीताविरोधघोषणा
VIDHAVĀDĀHAVIṢAYE GĪTĀVIRODHAGHOṢAṆĀ

७.३. स्वर्गेच्छा गीताविरुद्धा प्राह श्रीराममोहनः ।
फलेच्छया कृतो दाहः कथं श्रीगीतासम्मतः ॥
svargecchā gītāviruddhā prāha śrīrāmamohanaḥ
phalecchayā kṛto dāhaḥ kathaṁ śrīgītāsammataḥ

The debate that took place between Rommohun Roy and the suttee-advocates in the year 1818 was intended to establish whether this custom had the sanction of the Hindu scriptures or not. The orthodox scholars argued that, although ancient scriptures make no mention of suttee, later smṛti-writers like Angiras say that the widow will thus go to heaven. The option involving re-marriage of widows was not a subject of debate—because of the prevalence of strong feelings against it at that time, although Roy did draw attention to the discriminatory element against women in this respect because the prevailing custom allowed re-marriage of men. This is how Roy put it :

> . . .the custom of marriage as to the respective sexes . . . (needs to be judged by contrast) . . . for one man may marry two or three or sometimes even ten wives, while a woman who marries but one husband, desires at his death to follow him, forsaking all

worldly enjoyments, or to remain leading the austere life of an ascetic.[5]

The options that the widow had, according to the orthodox opinion, were just two—either burn herself as 'suttee', or live the austere life of an ascetic. This is how the suttee-advocates argued:

> . . . They (i.e. the widows), according to the precepts of the śāstras, are not allowed to marry again after the demise of their husbands, and consequently despair at once of all worldly pleasure. Hence it is evident that death to these unfortunate widows is preferable to existence; for the great difficulty which a widow may experience by living a purely ascetic life, as prescribed by the śāstras, is obvious. . .[6]

The suttee-advocates made the burning option look more acceptable to the widow by giving the allurement—based on later smṛti-writers like Angiras—that a suttee goes to heaven. However, since the authoritativeness of the later smṛtis was obviously less in comparison to that of ancient scriptures, the debate soon reached a stage involving a comparison between a life of asceticism (without hankering after any reward) and a reward-promising suttee. Rommohun Roy reminded the suttee-advocates that the main theme of the Gita—"the essence of all śāstras"—is "the praise of works performed without desire for fruits".[7]

The orthodox scholars asserted that the performance of rites with a desire for fruits was approved of by the Vedas themselves. In reply, Roy explained that "the Vedic passages directing works for the sake of fruition are meant only for the most ignorant. Learned men should endeavour to withdraw all those ignorant persons from works performed with desire, but should never, for the sake of profit, attempt to drown them in the abyss of passion".[8] What Rommohun meant was that, within the Hindu tradition, the school of Uttara-Mīmāṁsā ultimately superceded that of Pūrva-Mīmāṁsā, that the spiritual content of the tradition was finally regarded as transcending the ritual content thereof—and that this was given a practical shape by the Niṣkāma Karma doctrine of the Gita.

Rammohun Roy's statement referred to above is summarized in verse 7.3. He declared: "Widow-burning is against the Gita, because the allurement in the form of a desire for heaven—phalecchā—that is given to widows is contrary to the Niṣkāma

Karma doctrine of the Gita. How can such widow-burning ever be approved by the Gita?"

७.४. कुरीतिभारेण त्रस्ता पुनर्विवाहवर्जिता ।
स्वर्गप्राप्तिप्रलोभेन विधवाग्नौ प्रज्वलिता ॥
kurītibhāreṇa trastā punarvivāhavarjitā
svargaprāptipralobhena vidhavāgnau prajvalitā

Rommohun Roy also argued that the promise of heavenly pleasures looked to the widow like a better alternative because she knew very well that superstitious beliefs and socially oppressive customs would make life extremely miserable for her if she did not agree to be burnt.

Support for this view of Roy has been provided by the following description of a traditional widow as recently given by Alaka Hejib and Katherine Young:

The appearance of a traditional widow suggested destitution. Her tonsured head or her flowing hair unadorned with flowers indicated her miserable status. . . Not only was she denied enjoyments, but every other opportunity for pleasure, such as participation in social gatherings, festivals, the partaking of rich food, indeed, entertainment or pleasure of any sort. . . Even when the family and society grieved ostensibly for her plight, they had more regret for her kārmic crime of "causing her husband's death". Thus widowhood of a woman entailed spiritual misfortune and implied the temporary absence of dharma in relation to the family. Not only she but also the family, the lineage and the community too had to share the blame for this adharma.[9]

७.५. कुलसम्पत्तिलोभस्तु वास्तविकः प्रयोजनः ।
धर्मरीतिः नाममात्रं श्रीराममोहनमते ॥
kulasampattilobhastu vāstavikaḥ prayojanaḥ
dharmarītiḥ nāmamātraṁ śrīrāmamohanamate

Rommohun Roy questioned whether the persons who supported widow-burning really believed in the heaven-rewarding argument or whether they were more interested in property-grabbing. Rammohun's conclusion on this issue has been summarized by B.B. Roy in the following words:

> The real cause of suttee was the worldly interest, but not the religious interest. The worldly interest is served under the cloak of religion. The law of inheritance prevailing in Bengal was Dayabhaga, whereas, in the Upper Provinces Mitākṣara was respected as the law of inheritance. According to the law of inheritance in Bengal (i.e. Dayabhaga) a widow was entitled to inherit the property of her deceased husband without regard to his condition in life, and therefore completely barred the claims of the father, mother, brothers, sisters and daughters of the deceased, who had all consequently a direct interest in the destruction of his widow. Whereas according to Mitākṣara the rights of surviving wives were more circumscribed, so the relatives of the husband were not much interested in her death. Actually the number of suttees in the Upper Provinces was comparatively very low.[10]

७.६. यां तु शिक्षा न प्रदत्ता दौर्बल्यभावनाश्रिता ।
दाहसमर्थकमते किं तया निष्कामकर्म ॥
yāṁ tu śikṣā na pradattā daurbalyabhāvanāśritā
dāhasamarthakamate kiṁ tayā niṣkāmakarma

The suttee-advocates realized—although they did not admit this—that Rammohun Roy had correctly understood the conspiracy between priests and the property-grabbing relatives of the widow. They also knew that giving allurements about heaven violated the Niṣkāma karma doctrine of the Gita. Therefore, said the suttee-advocates, since a successful adherence to Niṣkāma karma needed education and self-confidence—neither of which the widows had—the second best' alternative, i.e. suttee (or concremation) was being followed, because "to persuade them to forsake concremation in order to attempt the acquisition of knowledge is to destroy their hopes in both ways".[11] Furthermore, since Rammohun Roy was making a very effective use of the Gita in his arguments, the suttee-advocates themselves picked up a Gita-śloka (III.26) out of context and quoted it in support of their own actions.

७.७. गीताश्लोकं कथयन्तः किं त्वाश्रिताः भेदभावम् ।
संलग्नाः क्रूरकर्मणि कथमेतद्गीताज्ञानम् ॥
gītāślokaṁ kathayantaḥ kiṁ tvāśritāḥ bhedabhāvam
saṁlagnāḥ krūrakarmaṇi kathametadgītājñānam

Rammohun Roy pointed out that to keep women away from education and confidence-building opportunities, in the first place, and then to say that they are inferior and unfit for Niṣkāma Karma—both these showed discrimination—or bhedabhāva in Sanskrit. "How can you", asked Roy, "quote a Gita-śloka and pretend to be Gita-followers, because, according to the Gita, men and women are equally entitled to make spiritual progress?"[12] Roy's defence of the inherent capability of women, supported by examples from India's past history, deserves to be quoted below:

> The male part of the community, taking advantage of the women's corporal weakness, have denied to them, those excellent merits that they are entitled to by nature, and afterwards they are apt to say that women are naturally incapable of acquiring those merits. Is men's accusation against women consistent with justice? When did you ever afford them a fair opportunity of exhibiting their natural capacity? How then can you accuse them of want of understanding? As you keep women generally deprived of education and acquirements, you cannot in justice pronounce on their inferiority. Lilawati, Bhanumati and other women in the past were celebrated in their thorough knowledge of all the śāstras, and Yājñavalkya imparted divine knowledge of the most difficult nature to his wife Maitreyi who was able to follow and completely attain it. . .[13]

Rammohun Roy also explained why the Gita-quotation resorted to by the suttee-advocates was invalid. In the interest of clarity, we repeat that it was Gita śloka III.26 which was quoted by Roy's opponents, who tried to justify, as they put it, their support to women's desire for reward, on the plea that "even the Gita advises that ignorant persons who are devoted to works ought not to be dissuaded from performing them".[14] Roy's reply about the interpretation of this śloka went as follows:

> As to your quotation from the Gita, to show that persons devoted to works ought not to be dissuaded from the perfor-

mance of them, it may be observed that this text applies only to rites offered without desire of rewards, though applied by you to works performed for the sake of future enjoyment, in direct inconsistency with the authority of the Gita. The object of this, as well as of all the texts of the Gita, is to dissuade men from works performed with desire.[15]

Roy's reply, summarized in verse 7.7, besides being scholarly, also referred to the inconsistency, on the part of the suttee-advocates, between a pretended acceptance of the Gita and the actual performance of a cruel deed like the burning of living human beings. "What sort of knowledge of the Gita", asked Roy, "do you claim to have if, side by side with your quoting a Gita-śloka, you continue discrimination against women and even burn them alive?"

७.८. विधवानां देहदाहो मानवहत्या नान्यथा ।
एवं प्राह गीताज्ञाता श्रीरायो राममोहनः ॥
vidhavānāṁ dehadāho mānavahatyā nānyathā
evaṁ prāha gītājñātā śrīrāyo rāmamohanaḥ

After having invalidated all the arguments of the suttee-advocates, Rommohun Roy 'hit the nail on the head' and declared that the way suttee was usually performed—using physical force to prevent any escape from the flames—was nothing but a "woman murder":

Those who, in direct defiance of the authority of the śāstras, act the part of woman-murderers, in tying down the widow to the pile and subsequently applying the flame, burn her to death, can never expurgate themselves from the sin of woman-murder.[16]

Rammohun Roy was able to make such a strong accusation because he had personal knowledge—from as early as 1811—of the physical force applied to a widow to prevent her from escaping from the flames. In fact, the shock that he felt at that time led him to resolve "within himself"—in 1811—that to end this will be the mission of his life, as the following account shows:

At the death of his elder brother Jagamohun in 1811 the widow became a suttee. It is said that Rammohun had endeavoured to persuade her beforehand against this terrible step, but in vain. When, however, she felt the flames, she tried to get up and escape from the pile, but her orthodox relations and the priest forced her down with bamboo poles, and kept her there to die, while drums and brazen instruments were loudly sounded to drown her shrieks. Rammohun, unable to save her and filled with unspeakable indignation and pity, vowed within himself then and there that he would never rest until the atrocious custom was rooted out.[17]

७.९. कुत्र गताः गीताभक्ताः प्रश्नो राममोहनस्य ।
मानवहत्यां त्यजेयुः यान्दृष्ट्वा क्रूरकर्मिणः ॥
kutra gatāḥ gītābhaktāḥ praśno rāmamohanasya
mānavahatyāṁ tyajeyuḥ yāndṛṣṭvā krūrakarmiṇaḥ

Rammohun Roy believed that if the Niṣkāma Karma doctrine of the Gita could be truly grasped by at least some of the Hindus, then their very presence in the society—reinforced by their opposition to cruel deeds like the suttee—would provide a safeguard against social degeneration. This verse is therefore put in the form of an agony-filled query—almost like a prayerful wish—that must have agitated Rammohun Roy: "Where have gone the Gita-followers in whose presence it would be impossible for any one to commit cruel deeds like the burning of living human beings?"

७.१०. गीताज्ञानप्रयोगेन विधवादाहं संहर्तुम् ।
अभयशीलयत्नेन जनमतः संस्थापितः ॥
gītājñānaprayogena vidhavādāhaṁ saṁhartum
abhayaśīlayatnena janamataḥ saṁsthāpitaḥ

Rammohun Roy made a significant contribution to the social reform movement by providing the correct interpretation of the Niṣkāma Karma message of the Gita and by thus generating public opinion against the evil custom of widow-burning. He faced challenges and even threats to his life from the orthodox sections of the society, but he continued his efforts in the spirit of the Gita.

When orthodox Hindus decided to take the suttee question to England for a final decision by the Privy Council, liberal Hindus requested Rammohun Roy to go to England on their behalf and they even collected money to meet Roy's travel expenses. Roy gladly agreed to go but he said he would not take any money from the society because he was determined to fight for the just cause of the widows in the spirit of Karma-yoga. Rammohun also wanted to demonstrate his opposition to the social ban on sea-voyage which orthodox priests had imposed on the Hindus. He was aware of the risk to which he was thus exposing himself, because some of the orthodox Hindus even thought of assassinating him, as B.B. Roy (referring to the Asiatic Journal of August 1830) says:

> When the anti-abolitionists heard that Rammohun would go to England to counter their petition before the House of Lords, they decided to assassinate him. As a consequence, Francis Keith Martin came forward for his help and accompanied him, armed with a brass pistol and sword stick, when he came to town during those perilous days. Rammohun himself also kept a naval dagger in his pocket and a sword stick in his hand. His attendants were also well armed.[18]

७.११. स्त्रीवर्गहिते गीतायाः सामाजिकप्रकरणे ।
प्रथमः प्रयोगः इति रामरायस्य घोषितः ॥
strīvargahite gītāyāḥ sāmājikaprakaraṇe
prathamaḥ prayogaḥ iti rāmarāyasya ghoṣitaḥ

The way Rammohun Roy interpreted and used the Gita for a social cause, namely to save women's lives, has been recognized as the first major social application of the Gita in modern times of which written records are available.

Of course, the availability of written records did not, for a long time, imply the spread of knowledge based thereon. The fact that the important role played by the Gita, in connection with the suttee-abolition efforts of Rammohun Roy, was relatively unknown, even amongst scholars, prompted Arvind Sharma to publish a paper on this subject in 1983.[19] Eric Sharpe, writing in 1985, views Roy's use of the Gita as the "first entry" of this book "into the field of modern Indian politics"—the word "politics" probably intended to convey the general meaning of "social affairs".[20]

ROLE OF THE GITA

Only one aspect relating to the wider issue of the role of the Gita in Roy's work will be taken up here, and it can be presented in the form of a question: "Why did Roy take the help of the Gita for suttee-abolition, and what happened when he did not do so for Brahmo Samaj?" Obviously, there was no compulsion or imposition from any external authority. Hinduism being basically an unorganized religion, allowing for choices in many matters including preference for a scriptural text—Roy was free to use the Vedas, the Upaniṣads, the Gītā, the Rāmāyaṇa, the Mahābhārata, the Purāṇas and so on—either singly or in groups. Roy found the Gita the most helpful in proving that the suttee-custom was not the right dharma, because it violated the Niṣkāma Karma doctrine. Rammohun's advocacy of Karmayoga was reinforced—following the example of the Gita itself—by his appeal to Buddhiyoga. Furthermore, M.N. Jha interprets Roy's approach "as conforming to the ancient Indian doctrine of Lokasaṁgraha (people's welfare)".[21]

Niṣkāma Karma, Buddhiyoga, and Lokasaṁgraha—these lay behind the success achieved by Roy in suttee-abolition. Since these were not highlighted in Brahmo Samaj, it did not have the same practical, long-lasting impact on the society—although it did serve a useful purpose in the nineteenth century.

CHAPTER EIGHT

विवेकानन्देन संस्थापितं सेवाकार्यप्राधान्यम्
VIVEKĀNANDENA SAṀSTHĀPITAṀ SEVĀKĀRYAPRĀDHĀNYAM

VIVEKANANDA—ESTABLISHING PRIORITY TO SOCIAL SERVICE

The subject of the second case study is Swami Vivekananda (1863-1902). His life and work were closely connected with his spiritual Master, Śrī Ramakrishna (1836-1886). Before meeting his Master—and, in fact, before assuming monkhood names of which the final one was 'Swami Vivekananda'—he was called 'Naren'. The short life-sketch that we present of him is divided into four parts—before he met his Master, also his Master before meeting Naren, the two together, and finally, his carrying on the Master's work.

A BRIEF LIFE-SKETCH

(i) Naren Prior to Meeting Śrī Ramakrishna

Swami Vivekananda's pre-monkhood name was Narendra Nath Datta or Naren for short. His father, a solicitor in the Calcutta High Court, was known for his broad outlook on social and cultural matters. His mother too was highly educated, and about her influence, Vivekananda said later, "It is my mother who has been the constant inspiration of my life and work".[1]

In his boyhood, Naren exhibited talents in several fields—physical exercises, dancing, music, meditation—and at college, "he was distinguished for his brilliant intellect", as Romain Rolland writes.[2] A number of philosophic questions arose in Naren's mind, and he sought answers thereto, in turn, from rationalism and Brahmo Samaj, but remained unsatisfied.

(ii) Śrī Ramakrishna Prior to Meeting Naren

Śrī Ramakrishna, whose pre-sainthood name was Gadadhar, came from a poor Brahmin family. His father died when Gadadhar was seven years old, and the latter had to depend on whatever his elder brother Ramkumar could earn as a teacher. In 1855, Ramkumar became a priest in a new Kali temple at Dakshineshwar, near Calcutta. When Ramkumar died a year later, Gadadhar, the future Śrī Ramakrishna, began his astounding career of spiritual disciplines and attainments, as a temple priest and devotee of Mother Kali.

"Śrī Ramakrishna", writes Majumdar, "made his own life a laboratory for the synthesis of different systems of religion"—including Tantra, Vaiṣṇavism, Vedānta, Islam, Christianity.[3] "Tales of his sanctity", writes Embree, inspired "thousands (who) flocked to see him".[4] But equally inspiring was the spontaneity and depth of feeling with which Śrī Ramakrishna wanted to serve the poor. Shivananda narrates how Śrī Ramakrishna "went to a pariah's house, . . .cleaned it. . . and prayed: O Mother, make me the servant of the pariah."[5]

(iii) Naren and Śrī Ramakrishna Together

Naren's singing of a religious hymn at a friend's house in November 1880 drew the attention of Śrī Ramakrishna, who had the capacity to peep into the "depth of Naren's unsatisfied soul."[6] Śrī Ramakrishna asked Naren to come and see him at Dakshineshwar—starting in this way the process of obtaining Naren's participation in his mission. Initially, Naren resisted, but his attitude changed when he heard Śrī Ramakrishna say: "God can be realized. One can see Him and speak to Him as I speak to and see you. But who takes the trouble to do so?. . ."[7]

Naren got his B.A. degree but his father's sudden death in 1884 forced him to look for a job to maintain his widowed mother and younger brothers. On Śrī Ramakrishna's advice, Naren entered the Kali temple to seek the Mother's help, but, says Majumdar, "as soon as he stood before Kali, . . .he forgot the worldly affairs. . . and prayed for true knowledge and a spirit of devotion and renunciation. . ."[8]

The crisis in Naren's family passed off, and Śrī Ramakrishna gradually prepared Naren to be the head of the group of sincere devotees who would carry out the Master's Mission after he himself would be no more. Śrī Ramakrishna also taught Naren that the proper way of doing good to mankind was to view it as worship to God.

(iv) Vivekananda Carrying on Śrī Ramakrishna's Work

The work done by Swami Vivekananda during the sixteen-year period (1886-1902), after the passing away of the Master, to put into effect Śrī Ramakrishna's Mission, can be broadly divided into four significant stages, namely:

(i) Initial attempts in India from 1886 onward, culminating in the Kanyakumari resolve of 1892 "to organize sannyāsins for social service".[9]
(ii) First visit to the West, including speeches at the Parlia-ment of Religions, and subsequent work (1893-1896).
(iii) Founding of the Ramakrishna Mission (1897).
(iv) Strengthening of the organization and worldwide net-work of activities and relationships (1898-1902), till his departure from this world in 1902.

THE SOCIAL PROBLEMS THAT HE SET OUT TO TACKLE

Vivekananda's assessment of the social problems of India was realistic, rather than academic, because he wandered all over the country for years, with a staff and a begging bowl in his hand. The main problems that he thus identified were:

(i) Poverty, ignorance, disease and misery of the masses
(ii) Wide gulf between the rich and the poor, leading to lack of social unity and fellow-feeling
(iii) Tyranny over women, aggravated by child marriage, big gap in the ages of husbands and wives, ill-treatment of widows, etc.
(iv) Physical and moral weakness, perpetual sense of fear, and lack of self-confidence.

Besides identifying the above problems, Vivekananda traced them back to religious perversion and lack of proper education. Religious perversion, said Vivekananda, appeared in the ugly forms of exclusiveness, superstitions and touch-me-not-ism. Similarly, improper education meant that there was "no life-building, man-making, character-strengthening assimilation of ideas."[10]

With this background, we take up a verse-by-verse commentary.

८.१. गीताप्रयोगो द्वितीयः प्रमुखतो दरिद्रेभ्यः ।
कृतो विवेकानन्देन स्थापयित्वा नवमठम् ॥

gītāprayogo dvitīyaḥ pramukhato daridrebhyaḥ
kṛto vivekānandena sthāpayitvā navamaṭham

We presented in the preceding chapter a brief account of the first major social application of the Gita in modern times, namely, by Rammohun Roy. Now we take up the second such application, made by Swami Vivekananda, the focus this time being on serving the poor. In order that the social cause of serving the poor may receive continuing attention, Swami Vivekananda established a new Monastery—Maṭha—committed to the new ideal.

८.२. **रामकृष्णस्योपदेशो गीताशास्त्रादिसम्मतः ।**
आत्मनः श्रेयोऽर्थं सेवा लोकसंग्रहायापि च ॥
rāmakṛṣṇasyopadeśo gītāśāstrādisammataḥ
ātmanaḥ śreyo'rthaṁ sevā lokasaṁgrahāyāpi ca

Swami Vivekananda's Master, Śrī Ramakrishna gave the message of service, by his examples as well as by his teachings. He thus helped people understand how the Gita and the other scriptures had emphasized the importance of rendering selfless service—both for achieving personal salvation and for ensuring the good of humanity.

८.३. **श्रीमद्विवेकानन्देन संन्यासिनो नवादर्शः ।**
मोक्षार्थमात्मनस्तथा जगद्धिताय वर्णितः ॥
śrīmadvivekānandena saṁnyāsino navādarśaḥ
mokṣārthamātmanastathā jagaddhitāya varṇitaḥ

Swami Vivekananda told the monks of the new Monastery that he set up: "Instead of a narrow ideal of caring for one's own salvation only, I am giving you, on the basis of what I learnt from my Master, a new motto 'ātmano mokṣārthaṁ jagaddhitāya ca', that is, you have to work for two goals simultaneously, namely, your own mokṣa and the good of the world".[11]

This famous Sanskrit phrase—ātmano mokṣārthaṁ jagaddhitāya ca—was coined by Swami Vivekananda to summarize Practical Vedanta as a harmonious combination of Vedanta and Karma-yoga, which provided the appropriate socio-spiritual approach to India's problems.

८.४. द्वितीयादर्शविरोधः कृतः श्रीयोगानन्देन ।
किं तु सोऽपि विवेकेन सेवायोगे समाहितः ॥
dvitīyādarśavirodhaḥ kṛtaḥ śrījogānandena
kiṁ tu so'pi vivekena sevāyoge samāhitaḥ

The first goal—mokṣa—was easily understood by the monks of the new Monastery, but the second goal—good of the world—appeared to some of them to be unimportant, or even that it might take them away from the first goal. Swami Jogananda expressed his opposition to the second goal. However, Swami Vivekananda won him over, although it was obvious to those present there that he (Swami Vivekananda) had to pass through a violent storm.

Since this was a significant incident, it seems necessary to write in detail about it. When Swami Vivekananda explained his ideas at a representative meeting of the monks and lay devotees held at Calcutta on May 1, 1897, all the monks appeared to be satisfied with the new approach—worship of God through the service of the needy. However, a lingering doubt was still bothering some of them whether the real formulator of this concept was Vivekananda or Śrī Ramakrishna. They had heard Śrī Ramakrishna speak time and again against preaching, excessive study of the scriptures, and charitable activities, and exhort aspirants to intensify their love of God through prayer and meditation in solitude. Therefore they regarded Vivekananda's ideas as out of harmony with the Master's teachings. One of them said bluntly to Vivekananda, "You did not preach our Master in America; you only preached yourself". Vivekananda retorted with equal bluntness, "Let people understand me first; then they will understand Śrī Ramakrishna".[12]

But things came to a climax one day at Balaram's house in Calcutta, when Jogananda, a brother-disciple whom Śrī Ramakrishna had pointed out as belonging to his 'inner circle' of devotees, said that the Master had emphasized bhakti alone for spiritual seekers and that philanthropic activities, organizations, homes of service for the public good, and patriotic work were Vivekananda's own peculiar ideas, the result of his Western education and travel in Europe and America.

Swami Vivekananda first replied to it in good humour. But he suddenly flared up. "You think you have understood Śrī Ramakrishna better than myself. . . Your Bhakti is sentimental nonsense which makes one impotent. Hands off ! Who cares for your Ramakrishna ? Who cares for your Bhakti and Mukti ? Who cares what the scriptures say? I will go into a thousand hells cheerfully, if I can rouse my countrymen, immersed in Tamas, to stand on their own feet and be men inspired with the spirit of Karma-yoga. I am not a follower of Ramakrishna or anyone, I am a follower of him only who carries out my plans! I am not a follower of Ramakrishna or anyone, but him only who serves and helps others, without caring for his own Bhakti and Mukti."[13]

Swami Nikhilananda describes what happened next:

The Swami's voice was choked with emotion, his body shook, and his eyes flashed fire. Quickly he went to the next room. A few moments later, some of his brother-disciples entered the room and found him absorbed in meditation, tears flowing from his half-closed eyes. After nearly an hour the Swami got up, washed his face, and joined his spiritual brothers in the drawing-room. His features still showed traces of the violent storm through which he had just passed; but he had recovered his calmness. He said to them softly: "When a man attains bhakti, his heart and nerves become so soft and delicate that he cannot bear even the touch of a flower. . .I cannot think or talk of Śrī Ramakrishna long without being over-whelmed. So I am always trying to bind myself with iron chains of jñāna, for still my work for my motherland is unfinished and my message to the world not fully delivered. So as soon as I find that those feelings of bhakti are trying to come up and sweep me off my feet, I give a hard knock to them and make myself firm and adamant by bringing up austere jñāna. Oh, I have work to do ! I am a slave of Ramakrishna, who left his work to be done by me and will not give me rest till I have finished it."[14]

So profound and convincing was the impression created by this incident that no protest was afterwards made against Swami Vivekananda's plans and methods of work. The Karma-yoga-based socio-spiritual approach to India's problems formulated by Vivekananda was thus fully adopted by the Ramakrishna Mission. This is stated in the next verse.

८.५. श्रीमद्विवेकानन्दस्य लोकसंग्रहसंदेशः ।
सम्मानितो मतैक्येन रामकृष्णमिशनेन ॥
śrīmadvivekānandasya lokasaṁgrahasaṁdeśaḥ
sammānito mataikyena rāmakṛṣṇamiśanena

After the above incident, the plan of action as proposed by Swami Vivekananda for the Ramakrishna Mission, and in which the rendering of social service was given prominence, was unanimously adopted.

८.६. मिशनसदस्यैः सदा शिक्षास्वास्थ्यवर्धनाय ।
उपस्थितैः विषमेऽपि सेवोत्तमा सम्पादिता ॥
miśanasadasyaiḥ sadā śikṣāsvāsthyavardhanāya
upasthitaiḥ viṣame'pi sevottamā sampāditā

Under the most difficult circumstances, for example during the outbreak of plague, exemplary service was rendered by the members of the Ramakrishna Mission, whose work programme included the promotion of public health, education, etc.

The outbreak of plague in Calcutta during the summer of 1898, and again in 1899, proved to be difficult tests of the service-rendering capability of the Ramakrishna Mission. In May 1898, Swami Vivekananda himself started relief operations to help the afflicted. When a brother-monk asked him, "Swamiji, where will the funds come from?", he replied with a sudden fierceness of decision: "Why, we shall sell the newly-bought Maṭha grounds, if necessary ! We are sannyāsins; we must be ready to sleep under the trees and live on daily Bhikṣā (alms) as we did before. What! Should we care for Maṭha and possessions when by disposing of them we could relieve thousands suffering before our eyes !"[15] Fortunately, this extreme step was not necessary, for Vivekananda soon received promises of ample funds for his immediate work.

Again, when plague broke out in 1899, the Ramakrishna Mission undertook relief work under the leadership of Swami Sadananda, assisted by Sister Nivedita (the former Margaret Noble of UK) and others. About Sister Nivedita's exemplary service in the face of this serious challenge, the historian, Sir

Jadunath Sarkar writes as an eye witness:

When the sweepers had fled away, I chanced upon a white woman one day clearing the streets with broom and basket in hand. This was none other than Nivedita, whose courage and sense of civic duty spurred the local youths to take up the cleansing of the lanes and streets, following her example, and make their quarters free from the threat of the pestilence.[16]

Swami Sadananda himself similarly set an unprecedented example. If the stench of garbage accumulated in a narrow lane repelled even the practised sweepers, he would non-chalantly snatch the basket and spade from one of them and set about removing the decomposed heap till the sweepers too would step forward to help him. At the end, he would congratulate them and embrace them warmly, regardless of their social distance and dirty bodies. Or if there was an uncared-for patient, he would hug him and nurse him to recovery.

Swami Vivekananda believed that the appeal to the people to come forward and serve the needy can be strengthened by coining new words or phrases. An excellent example of this was his coining of the phrase "Daridra-Nārāyaṇa" to convey the message that "service to the poor is service to God". The next verse summarizing this idea of Swami Vivekananda can be called "Daridra-Nārāyaṇa Declaration".

दरिद्रनारायणघोषणा

DARIDRA-NĀRĀYAṆAGHOṢAṆĀ

८.७. न सेवा दैन्यभावेन नाहंकारात् मानेच्छया ।
हरिरूपदरिद्राय मत्वैवं ज्ञानप्रेरिता ॥
na sevā dainyabhāvena nāhaṁkārāt mānecchayā
harirūpadaridrāya matvaivaṁ jñānapreritā

An important characteristic of the service activity taken up by the Ramakrishna Mission was that it was founded on right knowledge—it viewed service of the poor as service of God—and therefore there was no arrogance, no feeling of superiority, and no desire for any selfish return in the form of honour, etc.

God to be served in the form of the poor was declared by Swami Vivekananda as "the only God that exists, the only God in whom I believe. . . my God the miserable, my God the poor of all races".[17]

८.८. दृष्ट्वा जीवं शिवरूपं तत्प्रतिं सेवासाहाय्यम् ।
मते विवेकानन्दस्य वेदान्तो व्यावहारिकः ॥
dṛṣṭvā jīvaṁ śivarūpaṁ tatpratiṁ sevāsāhāyyam
mate vivekānandasya vedānto vyāvahārikaḥ

Swami Vivekananda used the expression "Practical Vedanta" to convey his message, an important element of which was the rendering of selfless service to the needy, but with the knowledge that Jīva is Śiva.

To Śiva-worshippers, Swami Vivekananda said, "Jīva is Śiva", and he explained the implications of this famous teaching—which he himself had learnt from his Master, Śrī Ramakrishna—in the following words:

He who sees Śiva in the poor, in the weak and in the diseased, really worships Śiva; and if he sees Śiva only in the image, his worship is but preliminary. He who has served and helped one poor man, seeing Śiva in him, without thinking of his caste, or creed, or race, or anything, with him Śiva is more pleased than with the man who sees Him only in temples.[18]

८.९. वर्णितो वेदान्तज्ञानी समदृष्टिः सिद्धान्तेन ।
तस्मिंश्च कर्मयोगेन सेवाभावः पूर्णत्वाय ॥
varṇito vedāntajñānī samadṛṣṭiḥ siddhāntena
tasmiṁśca karmayogena sevābhāvaḥ pūrṇatvāya

To have an equal vision, to view everyone as the manifestation of the One—this has been a part of the ancient Vedanta philosophy. What Swami Vivekananda did was to combine this philosophy with Karmayoga, and thus to arrive at Practical Vedanta, in which the attainment of perfection and completeness is ensured by selfless service.

Drawing inspiration from the Upaniṣads and the Gita, Swami

Vivekananda made it clear that his plan of action (as he called it in January 1897) represented an harmonization of Vedanta and Karmayoga, or "Practical Vedanta", for short. He announced it at a largely attended gathering in Madras:

> My plan is to follow the ideas of the great ancient Masters. . . Circumstances have become a little different, and in consequence the lines of action have to be changed. . .
>
> The first work that demands our attention is that the most wonderful truths confined in our Upaniṣads must be brought out from the monasteries and scattered broadcast all over the land. . .
>
> One word more. This national ship. . .has been ferrying millions and millions of souls across the waters of life. . .If there are holes in this national ship, this society of ours, we are its children. Let us go and stop the holes. Say not one harsh word against this society. . . Our task is only to work, as the Gita says, without looking for results.[19]

८.१०. विश्वविख्यातसभायां गीताश्लोकान् समाश्रित्य ।
सर्वधर्मसमभावो विवेकेन संबोधितः ॥
viśvavikhyātasabhāyāṁ gītāślokān samāśritya
sarvadharmasamabhāvo vivekena sambodhitaḥ

Besides providing for a strong institutional support to social service activities, Swami Vivekananda devoted special attention to creating among people a feeling of equality and respect towards all religions. He spoke in favour of such equality and respect in large and distinguished gatherings like the World's Parliament of Religions, and he quoted Gita-ślokas that lent support to his ideas.

Three of the Gita-ślokas, in the form as quoted by Swami Vivekananda in his speeches at the Parliament of Religions, are: Whosoever comes to Me, through whatever form, I reach him; all men are struggling through paths which in the end lead to me. (IV.11). I am in every religion as the thread through a string of pearls. Wherever thou seest extraordinary holiness and extraordinary power raising and purifying humanity, know thou that I am there. (VII.7 and X.41).[20]

८.११. राजनीतिविषयेऽपि श्रीमद्विवेकानन्देन ।
परोक्षरूपेणोत्तमा जागृतिश्च समुत्पन्ना ॥
rājanītiviṣaye'pi śrīmadvivekānandena
parokṣarūpeṇottamā jāgṛtiśca samutpannā

A question is sometimes asked: "Knowing that political slavery was a great obstacle in the way of India's socio-spiritual regeneration, why was the Ramakrishna Mission set up as a non-political organization?" The answer in brief is that the time for a direct confrontation with the British had not arrived, and therefore Swami Vivekananda devoted his attention to programmes like creating an all-round awakening among the people which, in due course of time, helped the political cause also.

८.१२. आत्मविश्वासं धारय तदेव हरिविश्वासः ।
शब्दो विवेकानन्दस्य बभूव जागृतिमंत्रः ॥
ātmaviśvāsaṁ dhāraya tadeva hariviśvāsaḥ
śabdo vivekānandasya babhūva jāgṛtimantraḥ

As a part of the process of creating an all-round awakening among the people, Swami Vivekananda tried to generate amongst them self-confidence—faith in themselves—which he equated with faith in God. His exhortation and encouragement did have a significant impact—almost like a Mantra of Awakening.

८.१३. सेवारतवेदान्ताय सर्वधर्मसमन्वाय ।
नवादर्शप्रसाराय विवेकानन्दः पूजितः ॥
sevāratavedāntāya sarvadharmasamanvāya
navādarśaprasārāya vivekānandaḥ pūjitaḥ

Swami Vivekananda is honoured and remembered for the great contributions that he made, for example, he made social service as an integral part of Practical Vedanta, he tried his best to harmonize different religions, and he spread far and wide the ideals of fearlessness, self-confidence, etc. which helped bring about an all-round awakening among the people.

ROLE OF THE GITA

The task which Swami Vivekananda took in hand was much bigger than that attempted by Rammohun Roy, because instead of a specific issue (suttee-abolition as in the case of Roy), the goal of Vivekananda was to revolutionize the entire socio-spiritual outlook of the people. The Niṣkāma Karma doctrine of the Gita, centered on Lokasaṁgraha, enabled him to expand the "monastery-based Vedanta" into "practical Vedanta".[21] In fact, the new motto in Sanskrit that he proclaimed—ātmano mokṣārthaṁ jagaddhitāya ca—was inspired by the Gita śloka III.20 which contains within itself, both the individual goal—mokṣa—and the social goal—Lokasaṁgraha, the latter expressed by its equivalent "jagaddhita" in Vivekananda's motto.

To a country living in a perpetual sense of fear, Vivekananda reminded of the Gita śloka II.3 by which Śrī Kṛṣṇa gave the "Mantra of Awakening" at the very start of His statement—"Cast off this petty faintheartedness". God is standing before you, said Vivekananda, "as Daridra-Nārāyaṇa—the poor, the hunger-stricken, gazing with lustreless eyes, at the well-fed and the amply provided".[22]

To institutionalize the new socio-spiritual approach, in the face of opposition from his closest colleagues, needed immense strength and farsightedness. More than ninetyfive years have elapsed since the Ramakrishna Mission faced the initial challenges of rendering service to the needy under the most difficult circumstances. The fact that this institution not only maintained the spirit of dedication but also widened the coverage of service activities is a tribute to Swami Vivekananda and his followers.

The message of equal respect for all religions, which Swami Vivekananda gave to the Parliament of Religions, is equally—if not more—relevant today. R.C. Majumdar rightly sees in it "a vindication, a declaration to the world, of the wonderful doctrine preached in the Gita. . ."[23]

CHAPTER NINE

तिलकेन राजनैतिकसंघर्षायापि गीताप्रयोगः
TILAKENA RĀJANAITIKASAṀGHARṢĀYĀPI GĪTĀPRAYOGAḤ

TILAK—EXTENDING GITA-APPLICATIONS TO POLITICAL STRUGGLES TOO

Although Swami Vivekananda's efforts to arouse all-round awakening among the people contributed, in due course of time, to political awakening too, the Ramakrishna Mission was, by its charter, a non-political organization. The political and military control of the British administration in India was so tight that whatever political demands were to be made, they had to be expressed in a manner acceptable to the administration. The Indian National Congress was, in fact, started in 1885 as a political organization, with the support and approval of the British. The main function of this organization was to hold an annual meeting towards the close of the year, and to make some mild suggestions about giving to Indians a few more of senior administrative jobs. For transforming the Indian National Congress into a party carrying on mass struggles for self-rule, the credit goes primarily to Tilak (1856-1920), and his inclusion in this book is justified because he viewed it as an application of the Gita. Furthermore, Tilak's extending the Gita-applications so as to include political struggles was not an ordinary expansion of a quantitative nature; rather it was a significant qualitative extension—an addition, so to say, of a new dimension because it inevitably involved conflict with the police and ultimately with all the military might of the British empire.

With these introductory remarks, we now present a brief life-sketch, etc. of Tilak, as we did earlier of the other leaders.

A BRIEF LIFE-SKETCH

In an attempt to trace the likely causes of Tilak's revolutionary ideas in politics, a good deal of attention is often devoted to the fact that he was a Chitpavan Brahmin of Maharashtra whose ancestors—Peshwas—"assumed temporal as well as spiritual power over the people" in the eighteenth century.[1] Bal Gangadhar Tilak was born in 1856. His father was a school teacher and his mother practised religion in a form that involved frequent fasting.

Tilak lost his mother when he was only ten, and his father six years later. However, in spite of the untimely death of his parents, Tilak was able to complete his Bachelor's and Law degrees. Tilak started his career as a teacher, along with three other dedicated friends, in a private school in Poona "aiming to rejuvenate the land of their birth".[2]

Tilak, along with his colleagues, also ventured into journalism. The Marathi newspaper 'Kesari' soon became very popular, and the English newspaper 'Mahratta' also appealed to patriotic readers.

The next important activity with which Tilak was closely associated was the establishment of the Deccan Education Society in 1884, and the founding of the Fergusson College in 1885. However, Tilak's association with the Deccan Education Society came to a close in 1890, and there was, at the root of it, a conflict between him and Gokhale—a conflict that continued in Indian politics as between 'revolutionary' and 'reformist' approaches.

In 1893, Tilak tried to revive the religious enthusiasm of the Hindus by celebrating Gaṇapati festival as a public function. Two years later, he started organizing 'Shivaji festival' on an even bigger scale—a festival which was secular and through which he could also arouse the political consciousness of the people.

The Shivaji festival of 1897 proved to be a turning point in India's history. Tilak addressed the largely attended public meeting in Poona, portraying Shivaji not only as a great national hero but also as an adherent to the Karmayoga teachings of the Gita. He further said that since Shivaji murdered Afzul Khan for the good of the society, and not for selfish gain, his action was blameless, according to the Gita. A few days after this speech, a British Officer, Rand, was murdered by Damodar Chapekar, to take revenge—as Chapekar put it—for atrocities committed on the public. Although the police found no direct connection between Tilak's speech (in Marathi) and Chapekar's action, the non-Marathi-speaking jury found Tilak guilty of sedition and he was sentenced to eighteen months' imprisonment.

After the 1897-trial and imprisonment, Tilak became, on the one hand, a recognized enemy of the British, and on the other, "Lokamānya" (Revered by the people) in Indian public opinion.

During the anti-partition agitation in Bengal, which started in 1905, a bomb-throwing incident took place in 1908. Again Tilak was arrested—although no link could be established between him and the bomb-thrower—and he (Tilak) was sentenced to six years imprisonment and sent to Mandalay (Burma).

While Tilak was still in Mandalay, his wife died in Poona. But he knew that self-sacrifice was a part of the freedom struggle. Undaunted by calamities and hardships, Tilak wrote his most famous book "Gītārahasya"—a Gita-commentary in Marathi—while still in Mandalay jail.

The years 1916-18 saw Tilak as the "Uncrowned king of India".[3] His famous slogan "Swaraj is my birthright and I shall have it" was on the lips—and in the heart—of every freedom-fighter.[4] During 1919-20, the Gandhian era in Indian politics began, and the first All-India Non-cooperation movement under Gandhi's leadership started on 1st August 1920, just a few hours after Tilak breathed his last. As D.S. Sarma puts it: "Doubtless, it is Tilak's mantle that has fallen on Mahatma Gandhi. . ."[5]

THE PROBLEMS OF THE SOCIETY THAT HE SET OUT TO TACKLE

According to Tilak's assessment, the key to tackle the social problems of India lay in attaining political independence.

Therefore, in his view, the freedom struggle deserved a higher priority than efforts to reform the society. He also felt that disagreements between the reformers on the one hand, and orthodox elements in the society, on the other, could adversely affect the formation of a united front that was needed to fight against the British.

Tilak also believed that the re-awakening and freedom of India depends on the revival of her religion and the restoration of her ancient glory. In his opinion, ancient books—and particularly the Gita—contained concepts and ideas that could form a better foundation for all-round advancement of the country, as compared to half-baked ideas that reformers tried to put forward by copying the west. He recognized, at the same time, that traditional Gita-commentators too had, by emphasizing a non-activist message, done a great dis-service to the society.

Thus dissatisfied by reformers as well as by traditional scholars, Tilak set before himself the task of explaining that the real message of the Gita was karmayoga with a social content—Lokasaṁgraha—and that great leaders including Shivaji achieved success in the past because they had acted accordingly. To develop amongst the people a sense of pride in the country's past, thought Tilak, would help the freedom struggle.

K.M. Panikkar agrees that, in presenting a new interpretation of the Gita, Tilak rightly hoped to show the way to a socio-political revolution:

> (Tilak's interpretation of the Gita) fulfilled the urgent need to endow the Hindu people as a whole with a new ethic and a message for social action and to discover a dynamic doctrine which, while providing Hindus with modern social ideals, could enable them to transform their society.[6]

We now take up a verse-by-verse commentary.

९.१ राजनैतिके संघर्षे तीव्रप्रयोगो गीतायाः ।
कृतः प्रत्यक्षरूपेण लोकमान्यतिलकेन ॥
rājanaitike saṁgharṣe tīvraprayogo gītāyāḥ
kṛtaḥ pratyakṣarūpeṇa lokamānyatilakena

It was Lokamanya Tilak who applied the Gita, directly and actively, to the task of launching political struggles and also of carrying them on, in spite of acute difficulties and self-suffering including long-term imprisonment under harsh conditions.

९.२. गीतासारः कर्मयोगो लोकसंग्रहमूलकः ।
लोकसंग्रहप्राधान्यं श्रीतिलकेन घोषितम् ॥
gītāsāraḥ karmayogo lokasaṁgrahamūlakaḥ
lokasaṁgrahaprādhānyaṁ śrītilakena ghoṣitam

Prior to Tilak, the most famous Gita-commentaries were those of Śaṁkara and Ramanuja. According to Śaṁkara, the main teaching of the Gita was Jñānayoga, while according to Ramanuja the main teaching was Bhaktiyoga. It was Tilak who challenged both these famous commentators and declared that "Karmayoga is the main teaching of the Gita, and Lokasaṁgraha is the foundation of Karmayoga".[7] In this way, the credit for writing a full-length Gita-commentary, with emphasis on Lokasaṁgraha, goes to Tilak.

Swami Vivekananda had, prior to Tilak, started emphasizing the activistic message of the Gita but he did not write a full-length commentary thereon. V. Subramaniam agrees that the task initiated by Swami Vivekananda was taken to a "firing the imagination" stage by Tilak:

> By the turn of the (twentieth) century, a number of factors were combining to give the Gita the status of the bible of India's national struggle... This was the time when Tilak's new interpretation of the Gita, equating it with Karma-yoga was firing the imagination of the Indian intelligentia and of the nationalists in particular... And just recently, Vivekananda had increased that stress (on activism) with his lectures on Karma-Yoga, his highly activist conduct and his activist approach to all things religious and social.[8]

९.३ अर्जुनस्य कुरुक्षेत्रं वर्णितं महाभारते ।
अद्य मुक्तियुद्धभूमिः तत्क्षेत्रं तिलकमते ॥
arjunasya kurukṣetraṁ varṇitaṁ mahābhārate
adya muktiyuddhabhūmiḥ tatkṣetraṁ tilakamate

In order that the Gita might fire the imagination of people in his times, Tilak indicated what new meanings should be associated with the words used in the Gita. One such word was "Kurukṣetra"—the place where the battle between the Pāṇḍavas and Kauravas was fought. The original Gita speaks of Kurukṣetra as "Dharmakṣetra" or the sacred ground. Various commentators before Tilak had tried to explain why the term "Dharmakṣetra" was used in this context. Tilak adopted a new approach and boldly stated that the whole of India is the Dharmakṣetra for modern Indians. As Damodaran observes, "the attainment of freedom from the British rule was a religious mission for Tilak".[9] Faced with the oppression of the foreign rule, Tilak interpreted "dharma" as a relentless struggle against the British authorities and the forging of a national movement to restore the freedom and the glory of India. "Our life and our dharma will be in vain", said he, "in the absence of Swarāj—self-rule".[10]

१.४. हीनभावं परित्यज्य कुरुष्व मुक्तिसंग्रामम् ।
घोषणेयमुच्चारिता लोकमान्यतिलकेन ॥

hīnabhāvaṁ parityajya kuruṣva muktisaṁgrāmam
ghoṣaṇeyamuccāritā lokamānyatilakena

Tilak gave to the Gita a "revolutionary interpretation", as K.M. Panikkar called it. Give up all ideas of weakness, said Tilak to his countrymen; also, do not circumscribe your vision like a frog in a well, i.e. within the slavish boundary prescribed by "the Penal Code" of the British rulers. Fight for self-rule—Swarāj.

"The revolutionary interpretation of the Bhagavad-Gita", says Panikkar, "was primarily the work of Bal Gangadhar Tilak, the father of Indian Nationalism. . . The philosophy of the Hindus, so long considered to be contemplative and world-denying, was interpreted by Tilak as a dynamic doctrine for action for the welfare of the world. . . "[11]

Tilak told the people, in a modern Indian language—Marathi—that not only Arjuna benefited from the Gita, but also the Maratha Leader Shivaji in the seventeenth century. "Shivaj Maharaj", said Tilak, "strove to drive away (foreigners) from the land of his birth. . . He did nothing with a view to fill the small void of his own stomach (i.e. from interested motives). With benevolent intentions, he murdered Afzul Khan for the good of others. . . Do not circumscribe your vision like a frog in a well. Get out of the Penal Code, enter into the extremely high atmosphere of the Shrimat Bhagavat-Gita and then consider the action of great men".[12]

Tilak's speech, exhorting people to follow the path shown by the Gita as exemplified by Shivaji, resulted in his (i.e. Tilak's) trial and imprisonment, in July 1897. Tahmankar is of opinion that this proved to be a turning point in the history of India's fight for independence and democracy.[13] Non-availability of a vegetarian meal to Tilak, during imprisonment, would have put an untimely end to his life. However, luckily for Tilak and all Gita-lovers, Professor Max-Muller—impressed by Tilak's writings, organized a petition to the British Queen, leading to Tilak's release from imprisonment in 1898.

Tilak's call for action to achieve "rights", and his linking it with the Gita's message, gave a modern form to an ancient teaching. The next verse which summarizes this can be called a "Fighting for Rights Declaration".

अधिकाराय संघर्षघोषणा
ADHIKĀRĀYA SAṀGHARṢAGHOṢAṆĀ

९.५. कथितं नवरूपेण तेन श्रीकृष्णस्य वचः ।
क्षुद्रं हृदयदौर्बल्यं त्यक्त्वोत्तिष्ठाधिकाराय ॥
kathitaṁ navarūpeṇa tena śrīkṛṣṇasya vacaḥ
kṣudraṁ hṛdayadaurbalyaṁ tyaktvottiṣṭhādhikārāya

The second line of verse 9.5 is largely the same as in śloka II.3 of the Gita, except that the word "adhikāra"—meaning 'right'—has been incorporated therein to indicate how Tilak gave a modern interpretation to the Gita. Cast off petty faint-heartedness and get ready to fight for your rights—this was the type of the new language which Tilak used to interpret the Gita.

९.६. मुक्तियुद्धे लोकहिते प्राप्तुं लोकसमर्थनम् ।
स्वराज्यः प्राह तिलकः जन्मसिद्धोऽधिकारो मे ॥
muktiyuddhe lokahite prāptuṁ lokasamarthanam
svarājyaḥ prāha tilakaḥ janmasiddho'dhikāro me

Tilak's most famous statement was "Swaraj is my birthright and I will have it". This is quoted in verse 9.6. Only through such bold statements—accompanied with willingness to go to jail for having said so—was Tilak able to attract large scale support of the masses in the political struggle.

९.७. गीतानुयायिनोऽपि चेन्न त्यजेयुः पारतंत्र्यम् ।
कथं ते ज्ञानिनो भक्ताः अथवा कर्मयोगिनः ॥
gītānuyāyino'pi cenna tyajeyuḥ pāratantryam
kathaṁ te jñānino bhaktāḥ athavā karmayoginaḥ

Tilak asked his countrymen: "How can you say that you are Gita-followers if you do not exert to get rid of slavery? It does not matter whether you call yourself a Jñānin or a Bhakta or a Karmayogin; to follow the Gita means to fight for freedom."

The message underlying this verse is similar to the one conveyed by verses 7.7 and 7.9. Our idea is to show that, just as agony-filled queries arose in Rammohun Roy's mind at the sight of widow-burning, similar queries arose in Tilak's mind also when he saw that people claiming to be Gita-followers did nothing to get rid of slavery.

९.८. पारतंत्र्यं स्वातंत्र्यं वा केवलं आत्मनिर्णयः ।
त्यक्तपरतंत्रभावो यः सदा मुक्त एव सः ॥
pāratantryaṁ svātantryaṁ vā kevalaṁ ātmanirṇayaḥ
tyaktaparatantrabhāvo yaḥ sadā mukta eva saḥ

The closing words of verse 9.8 are the same as those of śloka V.28 of the Gita. According to the Jīvanumukta ideal of the Gita, liberation does not have to await the giving up of one's physical body; it can be experienced while one is still alive provided one becomes free from lust, fear and anger. Tilak visualized a parallel state of "political liberation" for which he told his countrymen: "If you want to be free, you can be free from tomorrow; all you need is firm determination to declare yourselves free, accompanied with willingness to suffer for having so declared. . ."

According to D.S. Sarma, Tilak was the first political leader to visualize the likely form of "non-cooperation with the foreign ruler", which would have been a step beyond the Congress policy of boycott as formulated at that time. Tilak spoke of such an idea on January 2, 1907:

> Your future rests entirely in your own hands. If you want to be free, you can be free. . . If you have not the power of active resistance, have you not the power of self-denial and self-abstinence in such a way as not to assist this foreign government to rule over you?. . . We shall not give them assistance to collect revenue and keep peace. . . When time comes we shall not pay taxes. Can you do that by your united efforts? If you can, you are free from tomorrow.[14]

९.९. एषा स्वातंत्र्यभावना न लभ्या बलहीनेन ।
सर्वान् हि प्राह तिलकः कुरुष्व मुक्तिसंग्रामम् ॥
eṣā svātantryabhāvanā na labhyā balahīnena
sarvān hi prāha tilakaḥ kuruṣva muktisaṁgrāmam

While telling the people "You can be free tomorrow through self-determination", Tilak of course knew that two pre-conditions are implicitly assumed. First, that those who declare themselves free must have inner strength and fearlessness. Secondly, that the declaration of freedom can be effective only if there is mass participation to an extent that it can be called 'participation by all the people'.

Tilak appealed to all his countrymen, small or big, to participate in the struggle for freedom, and also to contribute to one or other aspects of Lokasaṁgraha:

. . .Just as extremely small wheels are necessary along with large wheels in order that any machine should work properly, so also is it necessary that the authority of common-place persons should be exercised properly and fully in the same way as the authority of superior persons like Vyāsa and others, in order that the immense and ponderous activity or mechanism of the Cosmos should continue to work in a properly regulated manner. . .[15]

The above appeal of Tilak was based on the interconnectedness of the individual, the society and the cosmos. He put forth a similar plea to encourage 'participation by all' from the viewpoint of yoga-practitioners aiming to achieve 'perfection of buddhi':

. . .It is the highest ideal of everybody to make his mind like that of a Sthitaprajña. But it is stated already in the commencement of the Gita, that because this is the highest ideal, one need not wait for performing Action until that ideal has been reached. . .[16]

९.१०. जनकार्ये कारावासः तिलकेन प्रतिष्ठितः ।
अलिखत् सः कारावासे गीतारहस्यसद्ग्रन्थम् ॥
janakārye kārāvāsaḥ tilakena pratiṣṭhitaḥ
alikhat saḥ kārāvāse gītārahasyasadgrantham

It was through Tilak's own pioneering example that going to

jail as a freedom-fighter began to acquire a special status in people's thinking. For Tilak himself, a long stay in jail became instrumental towards his writing of his most famous book—a Gita commentary entitled "Gītārahasya".

Tilak was the first eminent political leader of India to be put behind the bars by the British administration in 1897. Because of a rapid deterioration of his health—due to which Max-Muller and others intervened—Tilak was released in 1898. However, a bomb throw by Khudiram Bose in the then Province of Bengal again led to Tilak's arrest in Bombay in 1908. Seven European jurors found Tilak guilty, while the two Parsis did not. Justice Davar asked Tilak if he had anything to say before sentence was passed. What Tilak stated in reply has since become a famous declaration of the belief in the ancient Hindu doctrine of Tapas or willingness to suffer for a just cause:

> What I wish to say is that in spite of the verdict of the jury I maintain that I am innocent. There are higher Powers that rule the destiny of things and it may be the will of Providence that the cause which I represent may prosper more by my suffering than by my remaining free.[17]

This time, Tilak was imprisoned in Mandalay jail in Burma for six years. Although this was a period of much suffering and pain to him (his wife died at Poona while he was far away), the imprisonment did provide, at the same time, "compulsory time off" from the busy life that Tilak had led in India. He made the best use of it for writing his most famous book "Gītā-Rahasya"—his Gita-commentary emphasizing Lokasaṁgraha-oriented Karma-Yoga as the main teaching of the Gita.

९.११. तस्य निष्कामकर्मणा गीतार्थप्रसारेण च ।
मुक्तिसंग्रामसंदेशः श्रुतः देशे गृहे गृहे ॥

tasya niṣkāmakarmaṇā gītārthaprasāreṇa ca
muktisaṁgrāmasandeśaḥ śrutaḥ deśe gṛhe gṛhe

It was through a widespread distribution of Tilak's Gita-commentary (original in Marathi), translated in various languages, and through Tilak's personal sacrifices and contacts with the people, that the message of the freedom struggle reached practically every household in the country.

९.१२. तिलको लोकसेवको गीताज्ञानप्रचारकः ।
लोकमान्यसम्मानेन सर्वहृदि संस्थापितः ॥
tilako lokasevako gītājñānapracārakaḥ
lokamānyasammānena sarvahṛdi saṁsthāpitaḥ

Tilak's image found a respectful place in the hearts of all the people—his image as a freedom-fighter, as a true well-wisher of the masses, as a great Gita scholar trying to share his knowledge with common people through the medium of languages currently in use. That is why people called him "Lokamānya", meaning "Revered by the people"

ROLE OF THE GITA

Tilak was the first Indian leader to initiate the political application of the Gita, to obtain mass support in the freedom struggle. In order to do this successfully, he gave an activistic interpretation of the Gita, reinforced with his willingness to undergo whatever suffering would be inflicted on him by the British rulers who did not want to grant Swaraj—self-rule to Indians. Of course, in this process, questions of social reform had to be postponed till, as Tilak put it, "we have the power to shape our own destiny".[18]

Tilak knew that the main difference between a "social" and a "political" application of Karmayoga was that the latter involved confrontation—saṁgharṣa—for which he justified the philosophy of 'measure for measure', in the following words:

> Under any circumstances, punishing evil-doers in the interest of general welfare, as was done by the Blessed Lord, is the first duty of saints from the point of view of Ethics. . . It is nowhere stated by our moral philosophers, that if protection against evil-doers cannot be obtained by saintliness, one should not give 'measure for measure', and protect oneself, but should allow oneself to become a victim of the evil-doings of villains. . .[19]

It was no wonder that Tilak, who gave to the freedom struggle a mass appeal based on the Gita, was considered by the British government "the greatest enemy of the empire". But even amongst Indians, the social-reform-oriented "Moderates"—including

Gokhale—called Tilak an "Extremist". All this made Tilak the most controversial figure in the socio-political history of modern India. But undoubtedly, to the people at large, he was "Lokamānya" meaning "Revered by the People".

In order to make the activistic interpretation of the Gita acceptable to the people in general, and to the scholars in particular, Tilak had to "challenge" the authors of the traditional Gita-commentaries—Śaṁkara and Rāmānuja—who had already attained so much fame. This was a very difficult task, even for Tilak whom Sukthankar calls "a spiritual and intellectual giant. . .who practised what he preached":

> . . .The Gita and its teachings would seem to have been the guiding beacon of his (Tilak's) life; and if one considers what he did for India, and compares it with what he has preached in the Gītārahasya, one will come to believe that he practised what he preached, (which few people do), and that his political activities were a concrete example of that Lokasaṁgraha which, according to him, was preached by the Gita to be the basis of Karmayoga.[20]

CHAPTER TEN

अरविन्दस्य लोकसंग्रहसंदेशः सर्वमुक्तिरूपेण
ARAVINDASYA LOKASAṀGRAHASANDEŚAḤ SARVAMUKTIRŪPEṆA

AUROBINDO—EXTENDING LOKASAṀGRAHA TO INCLUDE SALVATION FOR ALL

Śrī Aurobindo (1872-1950) made significant contributions to the Lokasaṁgraha message of the Gita, first as a Karmayogin, and later as a Pūrṇayogin. As a Karmayogin, Aurobindo was a close ally of Tilak, and they both used the Gita to strengthen the freedom struggle—through their own participation and imprisonment, and also by encouraging large numbers of people to do the same. As a Pūrṇayogin, Sri Aurobindo's interest in Lokasaṁgraha continued, but the emphasis shifted from secular to spiritual needs of the society. Without going into details of what the comprehensive philosophy of Pūrṇayoga meant for the society, we have picked up, as a specimen that seems to be particularly appealing, Śrī Aurobindo's vision of sarvamukti—meaning liberation for all.

With these introductory remarks, we now proceed with the standardized form of presentation, including a brief life-sketch, etc.

A BRIEF LIFE-SKETCH

A good deal of significance is often attached to Aurobindo's date of birth (15 August) as well as to the year (1872) in which he was born. When the date fixed for India's independence (15 August 1947) happened to be the same as Aurobindo's seventy-fifth birthday, he himself felt that "this coincidence" was not merely "a fortuitous accident, but as the sanction and seal of the Divine Force that guides my steps. . ."[1] Similarly—but perhaps less prominently—the year of Aurobindo's birth (1872) was significant not only as the centenary of Rammohun Roy's birth, but also because it was during that year that "the father of nationalism in Bengal"—Rajnarain Bose formulated the idea of basing Indian nationalism on the Hindu religion, which reached its climax about thirtyfive years later through Rajnarain's daughter's son Aurobindo.[2]

Aurobindo Ghose's father, an England-returned medical officer holding views diametrically opposed to Rajnarain Bose, was so strongly anglicized that he sent Aurobindo to England at the age of eight, hoping that he would come back as an ICS officer. During his thirteen-year stay in England, Aurobindo achieved high academic honours, but, as he himself put it, he "felt no call for the ICS. . .By certain manoeuvres he managed to get himself disqualified for riding. . ."[3]

Aurobindo returned to India in 1893, and spent the next twelve years at Baroda—mainly as Professor of English and French. But he utilized this time to lay the foundations for his future work by learning Sanskrit and several of the modern Indian Languages and, above all, by assimilating the spirit of Indian civilization and Hindu religion.

The partition of Bengal in 1905 marked the beginning of what can be called the "Karmayogin phase" of Aurobindo's life. Like Tilak, Aurobindo attained fame not only as a great political leader but also as a journalist—the papers with which Aurobindo was associated being "Bande Mātaram" and "The Karmayogin". And it was the same act of bomb-throwing by Khudiram Bose in April 1908 which resulted in Tilak's trial in Bombay and Aurobindo's trial in Calcutta.

Aurobindo's yearlong stay in the Alipur jail as an under-trial prisoner proved to be the most momentous period in his life. In jail he read the Gita, and as he himself said, "I was able to do the Sādhanā of the Gita. . . It was Śrī Kṛṣṇa whom I saw (everywhere). . . In the court, it was not the Magistrate whom I saw. . .it was Śrī Kṛṣṇa. . . He said, 'I am guiding, therefore fear not. . .' "[4]

Aurobindo was acquitted—and Karan Singh notices in this historic event "an ironic twist of destiny" by virtue of which the Judge trying the case was one Mr. Beachcroft who was at Cambridge with Aurobindo and had stood second to him in Greek.[5] Aurobindo emerged from the jail with the firm conviction that he was merely an instrument—nimittamātram in the terminology of the Gita śloka XI.33—in the hands of the Divine.

Aurobindo put on the title page of his paper "The Karmayogin" a picture of Śrī Kṛṣṇa teaching Arjuna at Kurukṣetra. In the July 31, 1909 edition of this paper, he wrote, almost prophetically, that India will become free—through a spiritual revolution—but that the country "must wait for the man who is to come" and who will be like the Sthitaprajña of the Gita.[6]

In 1910, Aurobindo "received a command from above", withdrew from politics and went to Pondicherry.[7] Through a life of intense Sādhanā spread over forty years—aiming to achieve "progress of humanity"—Aurobindo not only wrote books on the Gita, Human Unity, Pūrṇa Yòga, etc. but as D.S. Sarma says, the highlight of his Mission was "his actual practice of Pūrṇa Yoga".[8] He received immense support from Mira Richard who came from France "to join in the spiritual work needed for the world", and who co-ordinated all the activities of the Aurobindo Ashrama as "The Mother".

Śrī Aurobindo "withdrew from the physical body" on 5 December 1950. However, The Mother continued implementing Aurobindo's ideas. Śrī Aurobindo International University Centre was started in 1951, and "Auroville—The Cradle of a New World" was founded in 1968.

THE PROBLEMS OF THE SOCIETY THAT HE SET OUT TO TACKLE

Even before Aurobindo returned from England at the age of 21, he had made up his mind to do something to help his country rise again, politically as well as spiritually. But he also knew that mere wishful thinking would be of no avail; his own capability to help the society needed to be built up through a carefully thought out programme of study, observation, and practical discipline—Sādhanā, as it is called in Indian philosophy.

The preparatory phase of Aurobindo's life in India lasted twelve years, from 1893 till 1905—the closing year of this phase being determined, as it were, by circumstances beyond Aurobindo's control. The political uprising in Bengal, in protest against the British plan to partition the province, was for Aurobindo "a call for action". During the next five years, he devoted all his attention to political activities, but he viewed the freedom struggle from a larger angle, as "God's work". Aurobindo characterized social reform, educational reform, industrial expansion, and all attempts towards the moral improvement of the race "without aiming first and foremost at political freedom", as "the very height of ignorance and futility".[9]

With the intensification of his Sādhanā—spiritual discipline—Śrī Aurobindo really felt that he was merely an instrument of the Divine, and so he acted in response to "commands from above", not for the sake of India alone but in the interest of the whole of humanity. The Pondicherry phase, covering the last forty years of his life, began with apparent abruptness in 1910, in response to such "a command from above", as we already mentioned. However, in spite of an ever-increasing spiritualization of the angle from which he viewed the problems of the society, there was a basic continuity of purpose, namely "the progress of humanity".

Kishor Gandhi, the author of "Social Philosophy of Śrī Aurobindo and The New Age" also stresses the continuity element underlying the enlargement of the scope of Śrī Aurobindo's work:

> . . . (Śrī Aurobindo's) retirement to Pondicherry in 1910 did not signify the cessation of the work that he had been carrying on till then but a continuation of it with a deeper and wider vision and a greater effective power than before; only it was carried on from a different station and with different means not visible to the normal outward sight. . . This enlargement of the scope of his work.. .became commensurate with the whole world-Movement. . .[10]

We now take up a verse-by-verse commentary.

१०.१. श्रीअरविन्दघोषेण पाश्चात्यशिक्षाप्राप्तेऽपि ।
कृतस्तु मुक्तिसंग्रामः त्यक्त्वा शासकीयपदम् ॥
śrīaravindaghoṣeṇa pāścātyaśikṣāprāpte'pi
kṛtastu muktisaṁgrāmaḥ tyaktvā śāsakīyapadam

Aurobindo Ghose was sent to England by his father to receive western education and to qualify for the Indian Civil Service. However, he was moved by patriotic considerations, and rather than work for the British administration, he adopted a path which, in due course of time, led to his active participation in the struggle for the country's liberation from a foreign rule.

१०.२. वन्दे मातरमित्युक्त्वा कार्याः क्रान्तिप्रसारार्थं ।
अरविन्देन वेगेन मुक्तियुद्धाय सम्पन्नाः ॥
vande mātaramityuktvā kāryāḥ krāntiprasārārthaṁ
aravindena vegena muktiyuddhāya sampannāḥ

The patriotic slogan "Bande Mātaram"—meaning "Hail Mother"—was on Aurobindo's lips, and he devoted himself vigorously to spread revolutionary ideas so that the freedom struggle could become a mass movement.

१०.३. श्रीगीतोक्तसाधनया प्राप्ता हरिध्यानस्थितिः ।
तदारविन्दः कृष्णेन कारागृहे सम्बोधितः ॥
śrīgītoktasādhanayā prāptā haridhyānasthitiḥ
tadāravindaḥ kṛṣṇena kārāgṛhe sambodhitaḥ

Aurobindo's devotion to the Gita and to Śrī Kṛṣṇa became prominent during his stay in the jail as a freedom-fighter. There he studied the Gita thoroughly, did the 'sādhanā'—spiritual practices—in accordance with the Gita, became absorbed in spiritual thoughts, and felt as if he was seeing Śrī Kṛṣṇa all around him.

Aurobindo's famous "Uttarpara speech", delivered immediately after his acquittal in 1909, clearly described how Śrī Kṛṣṇa talked to him in the jail:

> Then He placed the Gita in my hands. His strength entered into me. . . It was Śrī Kṛṣṇa whom I saw (everywhere). . . In the court, it was not the Magistrate whom I saw. . . it was Śrī Kṛṣṇa who sat there. . . He smiled and said, 'I am guiding, therefore fear not. . . Remember that it is I who am doing this, not you nor any other. . .[11]

१०.४. सर्वधर्मान् परित्यज्य मामेकं शरणं व्रज ।
अहं त्वा सर्वपापेभ्यो मोक्षयिष्यामि मा शुचः ॥
sarvadharmān parityajya māmekaṁ śaraṇaṁ vraja
ahaṁ tvā sarvapāpebhyo mokṣayiṣyāmi mā śucaḥ

This verse is the same as śloka XVIII.66 of the Gita, and it is quoted here to describe how Śrī Aurobindo surrendered himself whole-heartedly to Śrī Kṛṣṇa. From then on he felt as if the entire direction of his life was being determined by Śrī Kṛṣṇa Himself.

१०.५. प्राप्तं श्रीअरविन्देन समर्पणत्वं सम्पूर्णम् ।
न केवलं स्वमोक्षाय लोकसंग्रहार्थे सदा ॥
prāptaṁ śrīaravindena samarpaṇatvaṁ sampūrṇam
na kevalaṁ svamokṣāya lokasaṁgrahārthe sadā

Śrī Aurobindo achieved a state of complete surrender to Śrī Kṛṣṇa, but he did not view it narrowly as a way merely to his personal liberation; rather he always felt that the almighty Power was transforming everything to achieve universal good—Lokasaṁgraha.

Śrī Aurobindo has written extensively about 'samarpaṇam of sarvadharmān' or 'surrender without reservations', but the main idea to be stressed in our present context is that this leads to "universal good", as the following short extract from "Essays on the Gita " shows:

. . .An Almighty Power will take up our virtue and sin, our right and wrong, our strength and our weakness, cast away their tangled figures, sarvadharmān parityajya, and transform all into its transcendent purity and universal good and infallible force. . .[12]

१०.६. तृतीयाध्याये गीतायां लोकसंग्रहसप्तकम् ।
एते हि विशिष्टाः श्लोकाः श्रीघोषारविन्दमते ॥
tṛtīyādhyāye gītāyāṁ lokasaṁgrahasaptakam
ete hi viśiṣṭāḥ ślokāḥ śrīghoṣāravindamate

Regarding the seven Lokasaṁgraha ślokas (III.20-26) of the Gita, Śrī Aurobindo wrote: "There are few more important passages in the Gita than these seven striking couplets".[13]

१०.७. वर्णितं नवरूपेण श्रीअरविन्दयोगिना ।
पुरुषप्रकृतिज्ञानं लोकयात्राप्रकाशकम् ॥
varṇitaṁ navarūpeṇa śrīaravindayoginā
puruṣaprakṛtijñānaṁ lokayātrāprakāśakam

A special feature of Śrī Aurobindo's "Essays on the Gita" is how he gave a new interpretation to the Gita-concepts of Purushottama and Parā Prakriti, and linked therewith irrevocably, action performed for purposes of Lokasaṁgraha.

Śrī Aurobindo views the Purushottama as "greater than the Akshara", and as "no aloof and unrelated Indefinable", and he summarizes the Gita's message as a call from Śrī Kṛṣṇa to Arjuna in the following words:

> . . .I demand of you. . .action complete and divine. . ., done for God in you and others and for the good of the world. This action I propose to you, first no doubt as a means of perfection in the supreme Spiritual Nature—Parā Prakriti—but as a part too of that perfection . .[14]

१०.८. कर्मयोगिन्-पत्रिकायां संदेशो देशवासिभ्यः ।
दत्तः श्रीअरविन्देन मुक्तियुद्धो महामखः ॥
karmayogin-patrikāyāṁ saṁdeśo deśavāsibhyaḥ
dattaḥ śrīaravindena muktiyuddho mahāmakhaḥ

Through the weekly paper, the Karmayogin, of which Aurobindo was the editor, he tried to inspire the readers to contribute what they could to the cause of freedom of the country, in the spirit of the Gita. Aurobindo interpreted the term "Yajña" from the political angle and declared: "In today's context, the freedom struggle is the great Yajña".[15]

Aurobindo wanted his countrymen to be ready to sacrifice their all—even lives—in the struggle for freedom:

> Liberty is the fruit we seek from the sacrifice, and the Motherland, the Goddess to whom we offer it; into the seven leaping tongues of the fire of the yajña we must offer all that we are and all that we have. . . Freedom was never won from the gods by a grudging giver.[16]

१०.९. एतस्यां पत्रिकायां हि गीतायाः कृष्णस्य चित्रम् ।
अग्रपृष्ठे संस्थापितं अवतारप्रतीकेन ॥
etasyāṁ patrikāyāṁ hi gītāyāḥ kṛṣṇasya citram
agrapṛṣthe saṁsthāpitaṁ avatārapratīkena

Religious symbols had inspired large numbers of people, particularly in Bengal, to take part in the anti-partition uprising. To the symbols which had already assumed importance prior to Aurobindo's editing of the weekly paper, the Karmayogin, Aurobindo himself made a significant addition in the form of the "Kurukṣetra Battlefield." He presented this symbol—Śrī Kṛṣṇa, the Avatāra, giving the Gita-teaching to Arjuna at Kurukṣetra—on the title-page of the Karmayogin Journal.

Ursula King attaches great importance to Aurobindo's contribution in popularizing the Kurukṣetra picture as a religious symbol carrying a political message:

> This motif (a picture of Krishna at Kurukṣetra) decorates the title page of Aurobindo's weekly review 'Karmayogin', published at the height of his political activity in Calcutta between 1909-10. . . Religious and political nationalism are closely intertwined in this review which preaches a new Karmayoga through the very effective vehicle of the ideal Karmayogin symbol.[17]

१०.१०. न केवलं कर्मयोगे लोकसंग्रहसंदेशः ।
घोषितः पूर्णयोगेऽपि श्रीअरविन्दघोषेण ॥

na kevalaṁ karmayoge lokasaṁgrahasaṁdeśaḥ
ghoṣitaḥ pūrṇayoge'pi śrīaravindaghoṣeṇa

Śrī Aurobindo gave the Lokasaṁgraha message not only when he was a Karmayogin; he also gave it—albeit in a modified form—in the context of Pūrṇayoga. The type of modification that he made is explained in the next verse.

१०.११. आदौ तु लोकसंग्रहो लोकयात्रासम्पन्नाय ।
पूर्णयोगप्राप्ते तस्मिन् अध्यात्मतत्त्वप्राधान्यम् ॥

ādau tu lokasaṁgraho lokayātrāsampannāya
pūrṇayogaprāpte tasmin adhyātmatattvaprādhānyam

As a Karmayogin, Lokasaṁgraha activities are mainly secular, aimed at helping people in their life's journey in the practical world—Lokayātrā. However, in the context of Pūrṇayoga, the emphasis is shifted from the secular to the spiritual.

V. Madhusudan Reddy views Pūrṇayoga as a spiritualized transformation of Lokasaṁgraha:

The liberated individual being, united with the Divine in self and spirit, becomes in his natural being a self-perfecting instrument for the perfect outflowering of the Divine in humanity. . . This we see in a seed-form in the Gita's vision of the Lokasaṁgraha dharma.[18]

The next verse can be called the "Liberation for all" declaration.

सर्वमुक्तिघोषणा
SARVAMUKTIGHOṢAṆĀ

१०.१२. मुक्तिः वैयक्तिकामात्रा सर्वमुक्तिध्येयाद्विना ।
स्वार्थाश्रिता ह्यपर्याप्ता श्रीघोषारविन्दमते ॥
muktiḥ vaiyaktikāmātrā sarvamuktidhyeyādvinā
svārthāśritā hyaparyāptā śrīghoṣāravindamate

According to the Pūrṇayoga philosophy of Śrī Aurobindo, the only worthwhile goal is "Liberation for all". If anyone aims at achieving merely personal liberation, it should be characterized as narrow, selfish and inadequate.

Śrī Aurobindo used the term "Integral Yoga" or "Pūrṇa Yoga" to denote the technique by which one can ascend to the Supramental plane and then descend back to the material plane with a view to helping others achieve a similar Spiritual Evolution as quickly as possible. Two of the most striking features of this Yoga, according to Basant Kumar Lal's analysis are:

(i) the specific inclusion of both ascent and descent, and
(ii) aiming at 'sarvamukti' or the collective liberation of the mankind.[19]

Regarding Śrī Aurobindo's goal of collective human liberation, Karan Singh remarks that although this view has affinity with the Bodhisattva doctrine of Mahayana Buddhism and the traditional Hindu doctrine of Jivanmuktas or Siddhas, "it has seldom been so clearly put forward as the spiritual goal as in the theory of Śrī Aurobindo".[20] Calling this a "unique feature" of Aurobindo's yoga, Karan Singh adds that it is "stunning in its daring ambition and immensity":

Aurobindo is emphatic that his Yoga is not merely directed towards individual salvation but is for humanity as a whole. . . Having ascended the Yogi must again come down so that he can help the mass of humanity. . . Thus conceived, his (yoga) is stunning in its daring ambition and immensity.[21]

A question is often asked: "As a Karmayogin, Aurobindo was fighting for India's independence. When he withdrew from politics, and started the Sādhanā—spiritual practices—which ultimately made him a Pūrṇayogin, what did he think would happen to India's freedom struggle?" The next two verses summarize the answer to this question.

१०.१३. अरविन्ददृष्टिः दिव्या प्रस्तुता स्वर्णलेखेन ।
देशो मुक्तो भविष्यति कालेन स्थितप्रज्ञेन ॥
aravindadṛṣṭiḥ divyā prastutā svarṇalekhena
deśo mukto bhaviṣyati kālena sthitaprajñena

Nearly seven months prior to his withdrawal from politics—that is, almost prophetically endowed with a vision of the future—Aurobindo wrote in the weekly paper 'The Karmayogin' that a man comparable to the Sthitaprajña of the Gita will come and India will become free by moral force.

T.V. Parvate, who wrote Tilak's biography in 1958, is of opinion that Aurobindo had envisaged the desirability, if not the feasibility, of winning India's independence through an unarmed revolution. In one of his speeches, Aurobindo had said, "On their fidelity to Swadeshi, to boycott, to passive resistance, rested the hope of a peaceful and spiritual revolution. On that it depended whether India would give the example unprecedented in history of a revolution worked only by moral force and peaceful pressure."[22] However, Aurobindo realized that neither he nor any of the other leaders who were in India at that time seemed capable of leading such a 'spiritual revolution'. Almost prophetically he wrote in the Karmayogin on 31 July 1909 that the country 'must wait for the man who is to come':

The party is there, not less pervading and powerful than before but in want of a policy and a leader. The first it may find, the second, only God can give. The men who have led hitherto, have been strong men of high gifts and commanding genius, great enough to be protagonists of any other movement; but even they were not sufficient to satisfy one which is the chief current of a worldwide revolution. Therefore, the Nationalist Party, custodians of the future, must wait for the man who is to come, calm in the midst of calamity, hopeful under defeat, sure of eventual emergence of triumph and always mindful of the responsibility which they owe not only to India, but to the world.[23]

१०.१४. वक्तव्यमेतत् पूर्णत्वं प्राप्तं खलु कालान्तरे ।
आगमदजयो गाँधी स्थितप्रज्ञः सत्याग्रही ॥

vaktavyametat pūrṇatvaṁ prāptaṁ khalu kālāntare
āgamadajayo gāṁdhī sthitaprajñaḥ satyāgrahī

The prophetic statement that Śrī Aurobindo made in 1909—foreseeing how India will become free through the efforts of a Sthitaprajña— did indeed turn out to be true, because Mahatma Gandhi launched the Satyagraha-based non-violent struggle from the year 1919-20 onward and he equated the ideal Satyagrahi with the Sthitaprajña of the Gita.

Details as to how the ideal Satyagrahi was equated by Mahatma Gandhi with the Sthitaprajña of the Gita are given in chapter eleven.

When India became free on Aurobindo's seventy-fifth birthday, he sent a worldwide message, and spoke of his dreams:

The first of these dreams was a revolutionary movement. . . Another dream was for the resurgence and liberation of the people of Asia. . . The third dream was a world-union. . . Another dream, the spiritual gift of India to the world has already begun. . . The final dream was a step in evolution which would raise man to a higher and larger consciousness. . . The difficulties in the way are more formidable than in any other field of endeavour, but difficulties were made to be overcome.[24]

The next verse, being the closing verse of this chapter, attempts to summarize how Śrī Aurobindo is held in high esteem for his great contributions to the progress of humanity.

१०.१५. समर्पणबुद्धिप्रदो लोकसंग्रहप्रेरकः ।
अरविन्दः पूर्णो योगी द्रष्टारूपेण पूजितः ।
samarpaṇabuddhiprado lokasaṁgrahaprerakaḥ
arvindaḥ pūrṇo yogī draṣṭārūpeṇa pūjitaḥ

Śrī Aurobindo, the Pūrṇayogin, taught us how we can dedicate ourselves whole-heartedly to the Divine Will and work continuously for the progress of humanity. He indeed had a prophetic vision about the liberation of all—sarvamukti, and we all bow to him with deep respect for the message that he gave through his life.

ROLE OF THE GITA

The Gita gave to Śrī Aurobindo a clear "vision" as to how one can make a complete "surrender (to God) without reservations", and then act in the world for "universal good. . .as an instrument of God"—or nimittamātram as it is called in the Gita. Initially he followed the Karmayoga teachings of the Gita, but later he supplemented what he learnt from the Gita, with the results of his own Sādhanā, to formulate his theory of Spiritual Evolution, in which the concept of the Supermind has a crucial role. He also developed a new technique, called Integral Yoga, or Pūrṇa Yoga, by means of which the Yogi rises to the Supra-mental plane and then descends back to the material plane to help others achieve a similar Spiritual Evolution as quickly as possible.

Since the Sannyāsa-oriented interpretation of the Gita was still attracting many people in the days when Śrī Aurobindo wrote his "Essays on the Gita", he emphasized Śrī Kṛṣṇa's teaching on the non-avoidability of action. "The Divine Teacher", wrote Aurobindo, "gives His own example. . . and says, 'I have no work that I need to do. . . but I still abide verily in the paths of action—varta eva ca karmaṇi (III.22). . .' The Sanskrit word "eva" implies, I abide in it and do not leave it as the Sannyāsin thinks himself bound to abandon work' ".[25] Panikkar says that "this new interpretation—conveyed by Aurobindo in his own unique style—won immediate recognition as a masterly exposition of the permanent truths of the Gita in the context of modern life and in the language of modern thought".[26]

Even the Pūrṇa Yoga or Integral Yoga of Śrī Aurobindo has

important social implications because he had specifically stated the main objectives of his "quest for truth" to include "the application of our ideas to the problems of man's social and collective life".[27] Integral Yoga, according to Lal, includes Sarvamukti or the collective liberation of the mankind. In Madhusudan Reddy's opinion, Integral Yoga seeks to fulfil the Lokasaṁgraha ideal of the Gita in a modified form:

> The liberated individual being, united with the Divine in self and spirit, becomes in his natural being a self-perfecting instrument for the perfect outflowering of the Divine in humanity. This we see in a seed-form in the Gita's vision of the Lokasaṁgraha dharma.[28]

D.S. Sarma attributes Śrī Aurobindo's greatness more to 'his actual practice of Pūrṇa Yoga' than to his writings:

> The importance of the mission of Śrī Aurobindo lies not so much in his restatement of the integral spiritual ideal taught in the Ṛgveda, the early Upaniṣads and the Gita, and his clearing the air of imperfect ideals like quietism, illusionism and asceticism, as in his actual practice of Pūrṇa Yoga.[29]

CHAPTER ELEVEN

गाँधिना अहिंसाप्रतिपादनं लोकसंग्रहार्थे

GĀNDHINĀ AHIṀSĀPRATIPĀDANAṀ LOKASAṀGRAHĀRTHE

GANDHI—ESTABLISHING AHIṀSĀ AS ESSENTIAL TO LOKASAṀGRAHA

The fifth and the last case study in this book relates to Mahatma Gandhi (1869-1948). The unique contribution that he made was to establish, by thought, word and deed, that Ahiṁsā—non-violence—was the only means through which Loka-saṁgraha—the good of the society—could be achieved. Ahiṁsā is now being viewed by steadily increasing numbers of people as the Yugadharma—the path most appropriate to the needs and circumstances of the modern age. It is a memorable part of world history how the method of 'group non-violence'—as distinguished from individual non-violence—was applied as an experiment by Gandhi in South Africa from 1906 onwards, and how it led to India's independence in 1947. For Gita-scholars, an interesting aspect of this memorable history was that Mahatma Gandhi derived the Ahiṁsā doctrine from the Gita, although those who gave priority to śabda—words—over intuition, experimentation and realization did not quite agree with such derivation. In our opinion, finding new meanings in the Gita for promoting Lokasaṁgraha is a worthy cause, because the good of the society has priority over literal word meanings.

With these introductory words, we now proceed to present a brief life-sketch, etc. of Mahatma Gandhi.

A BRIEF LIFE-SKETCH

Mohandas Karamchand Gandhi was born at Porbandar (Gujarat) on October 2, 1869. His father was Prime Minister of a small princely state. About his mother—who had a long-lasting influence on his life—Gandhi remembered her daily prayers, saintliness and fasting.

Two plays which Gandhi witnessed during his boyhood left an indelible impression on his mind. One was about the filial love of Śravana. The other was about the devotion to truth of Harish Chandra—how he went through so many ordeals but did not waver.

Among other influences of a religious nature, which started in Gandhi's early life, "toleration for all branches of Hinduism and sister religions" is attributed to his father's close and friendly ties with Shiva worshippers as well as Jain monks.[1] Chanting God's name—or Rāmanāma—was taught to Gandhi by his nurse, Rambha.

At the age of eighteen Gandhi went to England to study law, but only after he had taken three solemn oaths—to obtain clearance from his mother for going abroad—that he would not touch wine, woman and meat during his stay in England. There was "peer pressure", says Gandhi, "but who dare harm whom God protects?"[2]

Gandhi's first reading of the Gita took place in England, through the translation by Edwin Arnold, entitled "The Song Celestial". The second chapter in particular—containing the Sthitaprajña-verses (II.54-72)—made a long-lasting impression on his mind.

Gandhi returned to India with a Law degree in 1891. He tried to set up legal practice in Bombay, but found it hard to make both ends meet. Then he tried his luck at Rajkot, but he had a very unpleasant experience with the British Political Agent. Luckily for him, a job offer came from an Indian firm doing business in South Africa. Accordingly, Gandhi went to South Africa in 1893.

The twenty-one years (1893-1914) that Gandhi spent in South Africa are the most important from the viewpoint of the development of his personality—how he decided to spend all his time for social causes, how religious influences—and particularly the Gita—moulded his philosophy of life, and how he developed a new technique of non-violent social action—Satyāgraha.

"Satyāgraha was born", says D.S. Sarma, "on September 11, 1906".[3] The Indian community in South Africa wanted to prevent a discriminatory Ordinance from becoming law, and on the advice of Gandhi, three thousand persons declared their "solemn determination not to submit to the Ordinance, if it became law, and to suffer all penalties attaching to such non-submission".[4] This "experiment" in non-violent social action continued for eight years, bravely facing governmental repression, resulting in the imprisonment of Gandhi, his wife, and many more. Finally, in 1914, all the demands of the Satyagrahis were acceded to. The head of the South African Government, General Smuts himself wrote about Gandhi:

> However often we may differ from him, we are conscious all the time of his sincerity, his unselfishness, and above all of his fundamental and universal humanity. He always acts as a great human, with deep sympathy for men of all classes and all races and especially for the under-dog.[5]

Back in India in the beginning of 1915, Gandhi tested—successfully—the applicability of the Satyagraha technique, in relation to five local problems affecting farmers, mill-workers, railway passengers, etc. during the years 1915-18.

During 1919-20, the leadership of the Indian freedom movement passed on from Tilak to Gandhi. Both viewed it as a practical application of the Karmayoga of the Gita. However, Gandhi's insistence on truth and non-violence as the basis of all social and political activities was considered unrealistic by Tilak. The first All-India non-cooperation movement under Gandhi's leadership started on August 1, 1920—just a few hours after Tilak passed away from this world.

The confrontation with the British went on, but parallel to the 'agitational' element, Gandhi attached equal importance to the 'internal growth' element to which he gave the meaningful name: Constructive Programme, and which included:

(i) Hindu-Muslim or communal unity
(ii) Removal of untouchability
(iii) Khadi and other village industries
(iv) Uplift of women
(v) Basic education, adult education, education in hygiene
(vi) National language, supplementing one's own language
(vii) Working for economic equality.[6]

Gandhi's long imprisonment on many occasions enabled him to write his own commentary (in Gujarati) on the Gita, a special feature of which is his "claim of an endeavour to enforce the meaning (of the Gita) in my own conduct for an unbroken period of forty years".[7]

India's freedom was won on 15 August, 1947 but at the cost of the country's partition resulting in Hindu-Muslim disturbances. About Gandhi's efforts to restore peace and harmony, Louis Fischer says: The fact that Gandhi's fast restored Calcutta to its senses and peace, the fact that his presence reduced the mass killing in Delhi to occasional outbursts,. . .the fact that hardened bandits laid their arms at his feet. . .—all this remains to inspire. . .[8]

Within six months of India's independence, Gandhi faced the assassin's bullet, on 30 January 1948, with the words 'He Rāma'. Ramesh Betai summarizes Gandhi's feelings in those days:

> It is remarkable that absolute devotion to God, total surrender to His will, directing all one's activities and one's very self towards becoming an instrument in the hands of God—these were the most remarkable features of Gandhiji's utterings in these last days. And he had read just this in the Gita.[9]

THE PROBLEMS OF THE SOCIETY THAT HE SET OUT TO TACKLE

Initially, that is in 1906, the issue for which Gandhi launched the Satyāgraha campaign was related to discriminatory legislation against the people of Indian origin in South Africa. The occasion assumed historical significance because the Indian community, under Gandhi's leadership, publicly declared that they will not resort to violence in their campaign. This meant, in effect, that large numbers of people were willing to suffer penalties which, they knew, the Government of South Africa would impose on them for breaking a law of the State, howsoever unjust the law might appear to be to the Indian community.

After ups and downs that were experienced by the Satyagrahis during their eight year long non-violent struggle, Gandhi's experiment in South Africa proved to be successful. Encouraged by this, and on his return to India in early 1915, five small scale tests of the applicability of the new technique under Indian conditions were made by Gandhi, on local issues affecting farmers, mill-workers, railway passengers, etc.

In 1919, the question arose whether the fight for India's independence can be waged through the non-violent Satyagraha technique. In Tilak's opinion this was not feasible, but a majority of delegates of the Indian National Congress were prepared to follow Gandhi. Ironically, both Tilak and Gandhi quoted the Gita in support of their respective points of view. With Tilak's failing health, the Gandhian era in India's freedom struggle began.

But Gandhi did not confine his attention to fighting against the British alone. Since the fight was to be non-violent, a good deal of work needed to be done to train the people in the new technique, and steps had to be taken to maintain the unity and morale of the people. Thus came into prominence the Gandhian Constructive Programme—a comprehensive plan of action which included communal unity, removal of untouchability, Khadi and other village industries, uplift of women, a new type of education, etc.

For Gandhi, the freedom struggle as well as the constructive programme was a part of what he called "experiments" centered on putting the Gita ideals into practice. There was no limit as to what type of problem could be tackled, the only restriction was that the approach and the method had to be non-violent. Also, the ultimate beneficiary was no longer India but the whole of humanity. As Mahatma Gandhi himself put it, "For me the road to salvation lies through incessant toil in the service of my country and humanity. I want to identify myself with everything that lives. I want to live at peace with both friend and foe. So my patriotism is for me a stage on my journey to the land of eternal freedom and peace".[10]

We now take up the verses one-by-one.

११.१. सामाजिकं वैषम्यं च संहर्तुं राजनैतिकम् ।
अहिंसाप्रयोगः कृतो गीतापालकगाँधिना ॥

sāmājikaṁ vaiṣamyaṁ ca saṁhartuṁ rājanaitikam
ahiṁsāprayogaḥ kṛto gītāpālakagāṁdhinā

It was through Mahatma Gandhi, who believed in putting Gita-teachings into practice, that non-violent methods were applied to tackle crisis situations, both on the social and political fronts.

Of the four other leaders, whose case studies are included in this book, two, namely Rammohun Roy and Swami Vivekananda, concentrated their attention on socio-religious but non-political problems, while the other two, namely Lokamanya Tilak and Sri Aurobindo—the latter during the Karmayogin phase—gave priority to political freedom, suggesting postponement of attention to social problems. During the Gandhian phase, both social and political problems were tackled simultaneously.

११.२. यद्यपि वर्णिता गीता युद्धभूमौ कुरुक्षेत्रे ।
तथापि तस्यामहिंसा श्रीमोहनदासमते ॥
yadyapi varṇitā gītā yuddhabhūmau kurukṣetre
tathāpi tasyāmahiṁsā śrīmohanadāsamate

Although the Gita-teaching was given by Śrī Kṛṣṇa to Arjuna on the battlefield of Kurukṣetra, yet, says Gandhi, the real message of the Gita is non-violence, and not violence.

In order not to keep thinking all the time about the background provided by the Mahābhārata war at Kurukṣetra, Gandhi takes the view that the Mahābhārata and the Gita are largely allegorical. He regards Duryodhana and his party as the baser impulses in man, and Arjuna and his party as the higher impulses. The persons described in the Mahābhārata, says Gandhi, may be historical, but the author has used them merely to drive home the religious theme, namely, that Truth outweighs everything else on earth. Gandhi continues:

> The author of the Mahabharata has not established the necessity of physical warfare; on the contrary he has proved its futility. He has made the victors shed tears of sorrow and repentance, and has left nothing but a legacy of miseries. In this great work the Gita is the crown.[11]

११.३. सामाजिक्यामहिंसायां वस्तुतो लोकसंग्रहः ।
तस्मिंश्चैव परं श्रेयो यः पश्यति स पश्यति ॥
sāmājikyāmahiṁsāyāṁ vastuto lokasaṁgrahaḥ
tasmiṁścaiva paraṁ śreyo yaḥ paśyati sa paśyati

Mahatma Gandhi extended the scope of application of non-violent methods from the individual level to the group level. He declared that real Lokasaṁgraha—the good of the society—could be achieved only through a mass scale application of non-violence. Furthermore, said Gandhi, the road to Śreyas—Mokṣa or salvation—goes through Lokasaṁgraha. One who has such a vision has the right vision, in the opinion of Mahatma Gandhi.

The last half-line of this verse, namely "yaḥ paśyati sa paśyati", is a favourite Gita expression, having been used three times therein—in ślokas V.5, XIII.27 and XIII.29.

The next verse can be called "Ahiṁsā-for-Lokasaṁgraha Declaration".

अहिंसावृत्त्या लोकसंग्रहघोषणा

AHIṀSĀVṚTTYĀ LOKASAṀGRAHAGHOṢAṆĀ

११.४. धर्मं चर लोकसंग्रहमूलम् ।
त्यज लोकसंहारं यथाशक्यम् ॥
द्विमंत्राभ्यां प्रेरितो गाँधीमतः ।
हिंसावृत्त्या कुतो लोकसंग्रहः ॥

dharmaṁ cara lokasaṁgrahamūlam
tyaja lokasaṁhāraṁ yathāśakyam
dvimantrābhyāṁ prerito gāṁdhīmataḥ
hiṁsāvṛttyā kuto lokasaṁgrahaḥ

According to Mahatma Gandhi, Ahiṁsā is essential for Lokasaṁgraha. How can one hope to bring about the good of the society, asks Gandhi, if one is guided by violence? This can also be expressed in the form of two underlying mantras—guiding principles. First, that we should put into practice only that dharma which is rooted in Lokasaṁgraha. Secondly, that we should avoid doing, as far as possible injury or violence to others—Lokasaṁhāra.

११.५. अहिंसया मुक्तिप्राप्तिः सम्पन्ना गाँधिनेतृत्वे ।
अपूर्वा विश्वेतिहासे यद्यप्यपूर्णत्वदोषः ॥

ahiṁsayā muktiprāptiḥ sampannā gāṁdhinetṛtve
apūrvā viśvetihāse yadyapyapūrṇatvadoṣaḥ

The achievement of India's independence through non-violent struggles conducted under the leadership of Mahatma Gandhi was a unique event in the world's history—whatever might have been its imperfections. This has been so acclaimed by all.

११.६. सत्याग्रही कः प्रश्नस्य स्पष्टोत्तरो गाँधीमते ।
सत्याग्रही स्थितप्रज्ञो यथा वर्णितो गीतायाम् ॥

satyāgrahī kaḥ praśnasya spaṣṭottaro gāṁdhimate
satyāgrahī sthitaprajño yathā varṇito gītāyām

Mahatma Gandhi coined the word "Satyāgraha" to denote the non-violent method of carrying on the struggles for social justice and human rights including political independence. He explained in a variety of ways as to what Satyagraha is. Here we want to draw attention to one of the replies that he gave in response to the question: ".Who is a Satyagrahi—the ideal person who can conduct the Satyagraha campaign?" Mahatma Gandhi answered that the Sthitaprajña of the Gita is an ideal Satyagrahi.

In the commentary on verses 10.13-14, we referred to Śrī Aurobindo's statement, made in 1909, that a person resembling the Sthitaprajña of the Gita will come and fight without arms to achieve India's freedom. The Gandhian era began nearly ten years after that, and the ideal Satyagrahi—leading the freedom struggle—was equated by Mahatma Gandhi with the Sthitaprajña of the Gita.[12] For example, the following qualifications and "Rules for the Satyagrahi", which were laid down by Gandhi, resemble the Gita-description of Sthitaprajña:

(i) A Satyagrahi will harbour no anger—nor any hatred in his heart against the opponent. . .
(ii) He will suffer the anger of the opponent.
(iii) In so doing he will put up with assaults from the opponent, never retaliate; but he will not submit, out of fear of punishment or the like, to any order given in anger.
(iv) A Satyagrahi will never insult his opponent.
(v.) The issue for which Satyagraha is launched should be a true and substantial one. . .
(vi) In the end he must be ready to lay down his life. . .[13]

११.७. न केवलं मुक्तिशत्रुः द्रष्टव्यो जनदोषोऽपि ।
आन्तरिकः दोषः एव दारुणो रिपुरात्मनः ॥
na kevalaṁ muktiśatruḥ draṣṭavyo janadoṣo'pi
āntarikaḥ doṣaḥ eva dāruṇo ripurātmanaḥ

In order to carry on the non-violent Satyagraha struggle against the might of the British Empire, what sort of preparation on the part of the people was envisaged by Mahatma Gandhi? In contrast to an army of soldiers—who have to get ready their arms and ammunition to hit the enemy—the non-violent activists have to cleanse themselves of inner weaknesses like fear, hatred, attachment to selfish interests, etc. To a Satyagrahi, the risk of violence entering into the struggle depends not only upon the opponent's use of force but also on the lack of adequate training in the technique of non-violence. Gandhi carried on his "mass education" through writings, speeches, personal advice, and continuous field level training of volunteers by local leaders. The Sthitaprajña ślokas of the Gita (II.54-72) were recited everyday at Gandhi's prayer meeting.

११.८. अस्पृश्यवर्गान् संपश्य भावेनात्मौपम्येन हि ।
वस्तुतो हरिजनास्ते संदेशः श्रीमोहनस्य ॥
aspṛśyavargān saṁpaśya bhāvenātmaupamyena hi
vastuto harijanāste saṁdeśaḥ śrīmohanasya

An important issue of inner cleansing, to which Mahatma Gandhi paid special attention, was related to the raising of the low social status of the so-called "untouchables". Don't ill-treat them, said Gandhi, because by keeping the streets clean and by performing low-paid public health jobs, they are rendering great service to the society. Feel as if they are just like you—this was Gandhi's appeal on behalf of the untouchables—and he gave them a new name "Harijan" meaning "God's own people".

Since orthodox elements believing in the evil custom of untouchability asked for scriptural support for his message of social equality, Mahatma Gandhi (in his response during the 1930s) quoted the Gita. Two of the Gita-ślokas used by Gandhi in this context are reproduced as verses 11.9 and 11.10. The situation was similar to the demand made by suttee-advocates more than a century earlier, in response to which Rammohun Roy had also used the Gita to justify fair treatment towards women, based on the principle of equality.

११.९. विद्याविनयसम्पन्ने ब्राह्मणे गवि हस्तिनि ।
शुनि चैव श्वपाके च पण्डिताः समदर्शिनः ॥
vidyāvinayasampanne brāhmaṇe gavi hastini
śuni caiva śvapāke ca paṇḍitāḥ samadarśinaḥ

This verse is the same as the Gita śloka V.18. S. Radhakrishnan's translation of this śloka and a part of his comments thereon are reproduced below:

Sages see with an equal eye, a learned and humble Brahmin, a cow, an elephant or even a dog or an outcaste. "Seeing with an equal eye" means we look at things from the standpoint of the Ultimate Reality present in all. . . This view makes us look upon our fellow beings with kindliness and compassion. The wise see the one God in all beings and develop the quality of equalmindedness which is characteristic of the Divine.[14]

११.१०. आत्मौपम्येन सर्वत्र समं पश्यति योऽर्जुन ।
सुखं वा यदि वा दुःखं स योगी परमो मतः ॥

ātmaupamyena sarvatra samaṁ paśyati yo'rjuna
sukhaṁ vā yadi vā duḥkhaṁ sa yogī paramo mataḥ

This verse is the same as the Gita śloka VI.32. Again, Radhakrishnan's translation and a part of his comments are reproduced below:

He, O Arjuna, who sees with equality everything, in the image of his own self, whether in pleasure or in pain, he is considered a perfect yogi. Even as he desires good to himself, he desires good to all. . . He harms no creature as, in the words of Śaṁkara, he sees that whatever is pleasant to himself is pleasant to all creatures, and that whatever is painful to himself is painful to all beings.[15]

Ramesh Betai summarizes the success achieved by Mahatma Gandhi on the untouchability front, through the authoritative support of the Gita:

The Gita told him that all men are equal, all men deserve the supreme blessings of God, the Gita bars no one from divine attainment that he calls self-realization. This spirit that he derived from the Gita made him a life-time servant of and upholder of the rights of the untouchables in particular and the down-trodden of the society in general. He rightly opined that untouchability is a blot on Hindu society and religion and he prided in calling himself a Bhangi (i.e. scavenger). Eradication of untouchability is one of the greatest works of Gandhiji and for this he derived justification from the Gita.[16]

११.११. मुक्तियुद्धे च नारीभिः दत्तः पूर्णः सहयोगः ।
तथैव रचनात्मके सर्वाङ्गिके कार्यक्रमे ॥

muktiyuddhe ca nārībhiḥ dattaḥ pūrṇaḥ sahayogaḥ
tathaiva racanātmake sarvāṁgike kāryakrame

There were two parts of Mahatma Gandhi's plan of action. First, Satyagraha movements were launched, involving non-violent non-cooperation or civil disobedience. Secondly, there was a comprehensive constructive programme. Both the parts of Gandhi's plan were so organized as to enable women to make significant contributions, and they did so with great efficiency and devotion.

'Uplift of women' constitutes, like the removal of untouchability, an important plank in Gandhi's constructive programme. The fact that the Gita makes no distinction between man and woman strengthened Gandhi's belief in the need to provide equal opportunities to women. He always wanted India's womanhood to rise, to realise its due status, work and duty in society. He wanted women to have due education. He wanted them to become real partners in the lives of their husbands and family; he wanted women to play a leading role in the Satyagraha movements and in the reconstruction of the country. So many of his activities were guided by these ideas.

११.१२. सर्वधर्मसमभावः सम्बोधितः पूर्वमपि ।
प्रदत्तं मुक्तिसंग्रामे विशिष्टं स्थानं गाँधिना ॥

sarvadharmasamabhāvaḥ sambodhitaḥ pūrvamapi
pradattaṁ muktisaṁgrāme viśiṣṭaṁ sthānaṁ gāṁdhinā

"Equal respect for all religions" was an important teaching of Śrī Ramakrishna, based on his personal experiences. Swami Vivekananda spread this message far and wide. This became a critical issue during the freedom struggle, because of the need to present a united front. High priority was attached to "Hindu-Muslim or communal unity" in the constructive programme of Mahatma Gandhi.

Inter-religious harmony, in general, and Hindu-Muslim unity, in particular, turned out to be the cause for which Gandhi fasted several times, and because of which ultimately he faced the assassin's bullet. In his prayer meetings, verses from various scriptures—including the Gita and Koran—were recited. Louis Fischer attaches great significance to 'the fact that Hindus would listen to Koran verses and that Moslems would not object to hearing holy words of Islam from the mouth of a Hindu'.[17] Gandhi's argument was that, even after the partition of the country, Muslims in the 'secular state of India' should feel safe and equal to all other citizens. He helped restore communal harmony in Calcutta by undertaking a fast in September 1947 till the city's leaders pledged to keep peace. In January 1948, just a couple of weeks before his assassination, Gandhi's fast in Delhi helped restore inter-communal goodwill. A few days later, that is on 20 January 1948, when Gandhi survived a bomb explosion, Lady Mountbatten came to congratulate him. Betai records Gandhi's reply—given in 'perfect equanimity of spirit and perfect fearlessness':

> On this occasion, I have shown no bravery. If somebody fired at me point-blank and I faced bullet with a smile, repeating the name of Rama in my heart, I should indeed be deserving of congratulations.[18]

And indeed, it is well-known that this is exactly what happened ten days later, when, on 30 January 1948, Nathuram Godse assassinated Gandhi by his bullet.

११.१३. न पूर्णतया सफलः प्रयत्नो राजनैतिकः ।
किं तु गाँधीमार्ग एव कालान्तरे हितकरः ॥
na pūrṇatayā saphalaḥ prayatno rājanaitikaḥ
kiṁ tu gāṁdhīmārga eva kālāntare hitakaraḥ

It can be said that, because of the partition of India and communal disturbances that occurred at that time, the success achieved by Mahatma Gandhi on the political front was significant but incomplete. However, it became clear that the long-term interests of humanity can be best served by following the Gandhian way of non-violence.

११.१४. आधाराः रायविवेकतिलकाः ।
अरविन्दो नवदिशासूचकः ॥
अहिंसया लोकहितं सदैव ।
युगधर्मदीपो गाँधी-प्रयोगः ॥
ādhārāḥ rāyavivekatilakāḥ
aravindo navadiśāsūcakaḥ
ahiṁsayā lokahitaṁ sadaiva
yugadharmadīpo gāṁdhī-prayogaḥ

The process of discovering and disseminating the social message of the Gita, and of updating it to suit the changing conditions of the society, is necessarily long and arduous. The five leaders, whose contribution has been described in this and the preceding case studies, played significant roles in this process. For example, we can say that Rammohun Roy, Swami Vivekananda and Lokamanya Tilak laid a solid foundation for tackling social, religious and political problems with the help of the Gita. Śrī Aurobindo carried this process further and declared, almost prophetically, that even seemingly impossible tasks, like bringing about a revolution only by moral force and peaceful pressure, can be done by the Sthitaprajña of the Gita. This was one of the new directions of Gita applications—or navadiśā in Sanskrit—foreseen by Śrī Aurobindo. Mahatma Gandhi identified Ahiṁsā—non-violence—as the essential tool of the Sthitaprajña, without which Lokasaṁgraha—the good of the society—was impossible. The inspiration to recognize Ahiṁsā as the Yugadharma—the guiding principle for the modern age—thus came from Gandhi's experiments—or Prayoga as he calls them in his autobiography—but only after great contributions were made by other leaders to arrive at that stage. A corollary of this is that the process of updating the social message of the Gita must continue.

ROLE OF THE GITA

Gandhi's main contribution in regard to the application of the Gita to social and political causes was that he developed, in 1906, the Satyāgraha-technique based on Ahiṁsā. But how could Gandhi, a coolie barrister as he was then called, feel that, in 1906, he had the spiritual courage as well as moral and material support of the Indian community so as to recommend to them the breaking of a law, howsoever unjust it might be? D. S. Sarma attributes this to the taking of "significant steps" by Gandhi during the years 1903-6—the first step being an "intense study of the Gita":

> The first step was his intense study of the Bhagavad-Gita which from 1903 became his infallible guide in conduct. . .He wanted to put into practice the Gita teaching—that one should be in the world, but not of it. He wanted to practice aparigraha (not having any possessions) and samabhāva (treating all as equals). . . (He decided) that all his future savings, if any, would be utilized for the benefit of the community.[19]

When Gandhi was in South Africa, there were, besides the Gita, two other strong influences on his philosophy of life, namely Ruskin and Tolstoy. Ruskin's "Unto This Last" impressed Gandhi so much that he translated it into Gujarati under the title "Sarvodaya". To Tolstoy, Gandhi gave credit for enunciating convincingly the "Bread Labour Law". However, after Gandhi returned to India and made a deeper study of the Gita, he found that the ideas underlying "Sarvodaya" and "Bread Labour" were included in the comprehensive Gita-ideals of 'Sarvabhūtahitam', 'Svadharma', and 'Yajña'.

A similar statement can be made about Gandhi's tracing the expression 'civil disobedience' to Thoreau. Although Gandhi used the same expression, he explained how the Indian experiment was wider in terms of application as well as stricter in regard to the emphasis on non-violence.[20]

In regard to the political application of the Gita, Tilak had already started significant activities from 1897 onward. Panikkar has explained how the Lokasaṁgraha ideal stressed by Tilak was supplemented by the Ahiṁsā doctrine of Gandhi, and further, how the unique combination of Ahiṁsā and Lokasaṁgraha resulted in an exemplification of the image of a Sthitaprajña in the personality of Gandhi:

> To Gandhiji, it was not sufficient that the ideal should be Lokasaṁgraha. . . It was even more important that the means should be ethically right. . . If activism was what Tilak emphasized, it is the Sthitaprajña doctrine that Gandhiji taught by his commentary on the Gita. . .and through the practical interpretation he gave to it through his own life.[21]

PART THREE

रेखाङ्कनं नवरूपाणां लोकसंग्रहस्य

Rekhāṁkanaṁ Navarūpāṇāṁ Lokasaṁgrahasya

OUTLINE OF NEW FORMS OF LOKASAṀGRAHA

CHAPTER TWELVE

अहिंसया भेदभावमुक्तये नवयुक्तिप्रयोगा:

AHIṀSAYĀ BHEDABHĀVAMUKTAYE NAVAYUKTIPRAYOGĀḤ

EVOLVING NEW BUT NON-VIOLENT WAYS OF ENDING DISCRIMINATION

This chapter begins the process of updating the Lokasaṁgraha message of the Gita, and relating it more closely to issues like discrimination which come in the way of achieving social harmony in the present-day world. For this purpose, we propose that new but non-violent ways—or 'yukti' in Sanskrit—of tackling social problems need to be evolved, through experimentation—or 'prayoga'—under different situations. Also, a selective use of some new words to express these new ways of promoting social causes may be as important as the giving of new meanings to old words.

We start by recalling the nature of social relationships that are envisaged under the Vedantic ideal, and then examine as to why this ideal has not been achieved and with what results. Since our attention is mainly focussed on voluntary, non-governmental action, we propose that the observance of non-violence may be accepted as a constraint subject to which the struggles for human rights and social justice should be carried out.

We feel it is very important that the Lokasaṁgraha ideal should not be presented like an outdated, impracticable utopia, because that would be against the very spirit of the Gita. In this context, it may not be out of place to recall Nehru's observation that the high degree of perfection implied by some of the ancient Indian ideals could not possibly have much influence on practice.[1] While this remark might be generally true of some of the lofty ideals of ancient Hinduism and early Buddhism, it can be stated that the approach of the Gita—and even more so of the modern interpreters thereof—encourages everyone's participation in the battle of life—and, therefore, also in Lokasaṁgraha

Having thus clarified that the suggestions made in this book have to be subjected to the criterion of practicability, we now take up the verses of this chapter one-by-one.

१२.१. अधुना घोरे वैषम्ये लोकसंग्रहभावना ।
सुज्ञातव्या पालितव्या प्राप्तुं भेदभावमुक्तिम् ॥
adhunā ghore vaiṣamye lokasaṁgrahabhāvanā
sujñātavyā pālitavyā prāptuṁ bhedabhāvamuktim

The starting point for trying to put into practice the Lokasaṁgraha ideal is to recognize that we are in the midst of a serious social crisis—or vaiṣamya. No doubt there are other crises as well—psychological, spiritual, religious, economic, environmental, political—but for the time being we want to refer mainly to the social crisis. In order to pull our society out of the crisis, and to achieve the all-round upliftment of all members of the society without any discrimination, we should understand clearly what the Lokasaṁgraha approach is, and in what new forms it can be expressed, and then should try to implement it as far as we can.

The Sanskrit word for crisis—vaiṣamya— is intended to recall Śrī Kṛṣṇa's opening statement in the Gita śloka II.2, when He reminds Arjuna that he (Arjuna) was engulfed in a crisis—viṣame samupasthitam. Whatever might have been Arjuna's crisis, we feel that discriminatory attitudes, based on religion, race, sex, language, caste or class, etc. constitute the main social crisis—in the form of disharmony and disunity—in today's world.

१२.२. पारस्परिकं सौहार्द्यं वेदान्तेन समर्थितम् ।
किं तु तस्य व्यवहारे पालनं खलु वाञ्छितम् ॥
pārasparikaṁ sauhārdyaṁ vedāntena samarthitam
kiṁ tu tasya vyavahāre pālanaṁ khalu vāñchitam

Social relationships need to be given the highest priority. Vedanta, the ancient Indian philosophy, provides the surest foundation for mutually supportive and friendly relationships, but we have to take care that the high philosophic ideas of the oneness of all life and the inherent divine potential of every human being do get reflected in our behaviour.

Swami Vivekananda used the expression "Practical Vedanta" to emphasize the Karmayoga-inspired, service-oriented application of Vedanta:

The nation is sinking, the curse of unnumbered millions is on our heads—the unnumbered millions to whom we have talked of Vedanta and whom we have hated with all our strength, to whom we have talked theoretically that we are all the same and all are one with the same Lord, without even an ounce of practice. . .[2]

१२.३. यदा यदा सामाजिकं एकत्वं न्यायसङ्गतम् ।
तदा तदा समुन्नतिं प्राप्ता हि देशवासिनः ॥
yadā yadā sāmājikaṁ ekatvaṁ nyāyasaṁgatam
tadā tadā samunnatiṁ prāptā hi deśavāsinaḥ

The people of India also need to learn lessions from their old history. Whenever the Indian society provided for just, stable and friendly inter-relationships between its different sections, those were also the periods when the country as a whole achieved prosperity and greatness in the various fields of activity. As against this—and this is important from the viewpoint of learning lessions—whenever there was disunity and disharmony in the society, the country fell a prey to foreign military invasions and suffered losses on all fronts.

१२.४. तदर्थं विषमां स्थितिं धर्मजातिलिङ्गभेदम् ।
कर्तुं दूरं हि यत्नेयुः किं त्वहिंसायोगेनैव ॥
tadarthaṁ viṣamāṃ sthitiṃ dharmajātiliṁgabhedam
kartuṁ dūraṁ hi yatneyuḥ kiṁ tvahiṁsāyogenaiva

Therefore, it is important that Gita-followers should help put into motion ideas and suggestions on the basis of which people may make serious efforts, individually as well as collectively—but based only on non-violence—to remove the causes which have brought about the crisis in social relationships. Even small scale, local efforts can be very helpful, because these can lead to the formulation and practice of measures—and our emphasis is on voluntary measures—to minimize exploitation and discrimination based on sex, caste, creed, etc. and also to narrow the gap between the have's and the have not's. In order to make the message of non-violence easier to understand and appreciate, for modern societies, effective use of some new words like "Ahiṁsā-yoga" on the part of scholars as well as activists will obviously be advantageous—care being taken to emphasize the practicability of whatever new ideas are put forward.

A trend towards adopting policies and programmes based on non-violence is visible in several parts of the world, and significant contributions in this direction have been, and are being, made in difficult and challenging situations, and some of them have been given recognition through Peace prizes and other similar gestures. Advantage should be taken of this new awareness of possibilities of solving age-old conflicts by conducting , as it were, newer and newer experiments—or prayoga in Sanskrit—in the use of non-violent techniques.

A non-violent technique—not necessarily new in name but having the potential of new applications—may be one involving in-depth dialogue or debate of the type used by Rammohun Roy as early as in 1818. Those who were supporting the evil custom of 'suttee' or widow-burning—on one plea or the other—were told by orthodox priests that some of the religious books were in favour of this custom. But Rammohun Roy was confident of proving that this practice was in violation of authoritative scriptures like the Gita. So he entered into a 'debate' with the 'suttee-advocates', details about which have been given in chapter seven. The relevant point in the present context is that Roy utilized the technique of 'debate', and achieved success in trying to create public opinion against the evil custom of suttee, which was obviously based on discriminatory attitudes against women in general, and widows in particular.

The dialogue-technique need not involve just two sides, because discussions could simultaneously be held between several viewpoints, as took place at the Parliament of Religions addressed by Swami Vivekananda in 1893. Without going into details, it is relevant to note that speeches made at this Parliament did contribute to the creation of a feeling of equal respect towards all the religions of the world.

The next verse views the role of "Ahiṁsā-yoga" as a protective—and at the same time creative—device against dangers from two sides or rather two approaches—one being a tame acceptance of the status quo in which weaker sections of the society suffer, and the other being associated with fundamentalism and terrorism. This can therefore be called "Double Danger Declaration".

उभयगर्तघोषणा
UBHAYAGARTAGHOṢAṆĀ

१२.५. एकतः शोषणस्थितिः अन्यतो ह्यातङ्कदंशा ।
उभयविभ्रंशशङ्कां संहर्तुमहिंसायोगः ॥
ekataḥ śoṣaṇasthitiḥ anyato hyātaṁkadaśā
ubhayavibhraṁśaśaṁkāṁ saṁhartumhiṁsāyogaḥ

Any one interested in tackling social problems in the present-day world needs to surmount the risk, as it were, of "pitfalls on both sides"—and we hope this "double danger" is picturesquely conveyed by the Sanskrit word "garta", preceded by "ubhaya". The first risk arises from a continuation of the status quo because the existing situation involving discrimination and exploitation of the weaker sections of the society is unsatisfactory, and it might explode at any time. The second risk arises from fundamentalists and terrorists, who, pretending to help the poor and the weak, spread violence and terror in the society but are unable to do real good to any one—not even to themselves. Under these circumstances, the role of "Ahiṁsā-yoga" is to steer clear of both these types of risks, that is, neither accept the status quo nor terrorism, but find a non-violent solution—a sort of "middle path"— to tackle the acute social problems.

Sissela Bok and Devaki Jain characterize the Ahiṁsā-yoga approach as "methodology-based" rather than "issue-based", and they envisage its application in small "territories" to begin with, to be gradually extended to wider issues and territories:

> We are most interested in the Gandhian alternative. Gandhi, far from denying the presence of violence in the world, meant to carve out spaces, territories in human interaction, where violence would nevertheless not be used. . . Once these territories have thus been carved out, they can be enlarged, extended, and become models for others. . .

A women's united platform need not be completely issue-based, but could well be methodology-based (for example, based on the way of non-violence).[3]

The phrase "ubhayagarta" used in verse 12.5 draws its inspiration from "ubhayavibhraṣṭaḥ", which occurs in śloka VI.38 of the Gita, and which means 'fallen from both or losing on both the fronts'. We feel that the dilemma facing social activists in the present-day world calls for new experimentation—or 'prayoga'—so that non-violent techniques can help save the situation. This is taken up in the next verse.

१२.६. अहिंसापरिपक्वार्थं नवप्रयोगाः कर्तव्याः ।
आश्रित्य स्वावलम्बनं स्थित्वा मध्यममार्गे च ॥

ahiṁsāparipakvārthaṁ navaprayogāḥ kartavyāḥ
āśritya svāvalambanaṁ sthitvā madhyamamārge ca

The need of the hour is to gain confidence in the application of non-violent methods under the very difficult conditions that exist in the society today. Such methods can help the needy, but the latter too must fully participate in the proper application of the methods—signifying their resolve to stand on their own feet, or 'svāvalambanam' in Sanskrit. More and more applications of non-violent methods—almost like so many experiments—need to be tried out for this purpose. Only through such experiments can public opinion turn in favour of non-violent methods—which have generally taken the form of adopting a sort of a 'middle path', both individually and collectively.

The use of the word 'prayoga'—or experiments—has been inspired by the title of Mahatma Gandhi's autobiography. In fact, experimentation with non-violence provides the key to his life, as he himself expressed in the following words:

> It gives me ineffable joy to make experiments proving that Love is the supreme and only Law of Life. . . Had violence, i.e. hate, ruled us, we should have become extinct long ago. . . I have been experimenting with non-violence, . . .and I see more and more signs of progressive Ahiṁsā and diminishing Hiṁsā. . .[4]

Among those who successfully followed the Gandhian method for getting discriminatory laws removed, for example in America, the name of Dr. Martin Luther King could be mentioned, particularly because his techniques have been recorded in detail, and can be consulted by those who want to apply a similar technique elsewhere.[5]

In case anyone thinks that the suggestions made here are too ambitious, it may be useful to recall Gandhi's assurance that even seemingly impossible things could become possible through non-violence:

In this age of wonders, no one will say that a thing or an idea is worthless because it is new. To say it is impossible because it is difficult, is again not in consonance with the spirit of the age. Things undreamt of are daily being seen, the impossible is ever becoming possible. We are constantly being astonished these days at the amazing discoveries in the field of violence. But I maintain that far more undreamt of and seemingly impossible discoveries will be made in the field of non-violence.[6]

Ultimately, a comprehensive approach to tackle the social problems needs to be developed, but this calls for slow but steady effort—or "Ahiṁsaka Yatna-yoga". Every member of the society should appreciate the need for making some effort—howsoever small—to adopt and spread mutually supportive ideas, namely that the aim is not merely one's own benefit but also the benefit of all. In other words, a sense of social responsibility needs to be cultivated in each individual. An obvious pre-requisite for this—according to Gita-followers—is to make people aware of what Radhakrishnan calls the cause-and-effect relationship between individual improvement and social betterment. "The way to social betterment", says Radhakrishnan, "is through improvement in the individual nature".[7]

One way of utilizing this linkage is to associate a double meaning with the term "middle path"—one at the social level and the other at the individual level.

At the social level, we spoke above of the need to avoid dangers associated with status quo, on the one hand, and terrorism, on the other, and to adopt a non-violent approach—or a sort of a middle way. A pre-requisite for this, at the individual level, is to appreciate the usefulness of avoiding extremes, or in other words, of trying to adopt, as far as possible, a balanced, middle path. The Gita does not look favourably on ways of living that are associated with extremes and excesses—be they in regard to desires, consumption, pleasures, and acquisition of things merely for personal possession, because from the wider point of view, they tend to create social tensions and conflicts. Two Gita-ślokas advocating the 'middle path' outlook will be presented below (as verses 12.8-9), but before that we want to complete the implications of Radhakrishnan's observation referred to above.

To have a sense of social responsibility is a basic element in the improvement in the individual nature which, according to Radhakrishnan's interpretation of the Gita, is essential for social betterment. This has been stressed in the above verses. Another basic element needed to bring about improvement in the individual nature is the cultivation of the spirit of self-help so as to discourage the habit of depending on the Government or on voluntary social service groups whose role is erroneously viewed to be spoon-feeding. This has been referred to as 'svāvalambanam' in verse 12.6, but, because of its great significance, the original Gita śloka on this subject is itself reproduced as the next verse.

१२.७. उद्धरेदात्मनात्मानं नात्मानमवसादयेत् ।
आत्मैव ह्यात्मनो बन्धुरात्मैव रिपुरात्मनः ॥
uddharedātmanātmānaṁ nātmānamavasādayet
ātmaiva hyātmano bandhurātmaiva ripurātmanaḥ

This verse is the same as śloka VI.5 of the Gita, and which has been explained by Swami Vivekananda in the following manner, as containing "the greatest lession" of self-help:

> It is a tremendous error to feel helpless. Do not seek help from anyone. We are our own help. If we cannot help ourselves, there is none to help us. The Gita says, "Thou thyself art thy only friend, thou thyself thy only enemy. There is no other enemy but this self of mine, no other friend but myself". This is the last and greatest lession. . .[8]

The main idea behind Mahatma Gandhi's constructive programme also was that the poor villagers, instead of feeling helpless and asking for charity, should stand on their own feet, as much as possible.

Next we present two Gita-ślokas about the 'middle path'.

१२.८. नात्यश्नतस्तु योगोऽस्ति न चैकान्तमनश्नतः ।
न चातिस्वप्नशीलस्य जाग्रतो नैव चार्जुन ॥
nātyaśnatastu yogo'sti na caikāntamanaśnataḥ
na cātisvapnaśīlasya jāgrato naiva cārjuna

This verse is the same as śloka VI.16 of the Gita, in which the importance of following the middle path—of avoiding extremes—is enunciated as being necessary to achieve success in the yoga of life. S. Radhakrishnan's translation of this śloka, and comments thereon, are as follows:

"Verily, yoga is not for him who eats too much or abstains too much from eating. It is not for him, O Arjuna, who sleeps too much or keeps awake too much. (Gita śloka VI.16). We must be free from animal cravings. We must avoid excess in all things. Compare with this the middle path of the Buddhists, the golden mean of Aristotle."[9]

१२.९. युक्ताहारविहारस्य युक्तचेष्टस्य कर्मसु ।
युक्तस्वप्नावबोधस्य योगो भवति दुःखहा ॥
yuktāhāravihārasya yuktaceṣṭasya karmasu
yuktasvapnāvabodhasya yogo bhavati duḥkhahā

This verse is the same as śloka VI.17 of the Gita. In continuation of the preceding verse, the middle path is further explained here by saying that, along with moderation in eating and sleeping, a fair amount of recreation is also necessary. Moreover, says Śrī Kṛṣṇa, the effort that you put into the performance of your duty should be balanced, disciplined, and appropriate to your circumstances. Only in this way can sorrows of life be destroyed and happiness achieved.

The teaching about balance and moderation is considered so important in the Gita that it is repeated in the closing chapters also. For example, in ślokas XVI. 7-17, demoniac beings are characterized as having insatiable desires, for the gratification of which they employ unjust means, unmindful of the damage and destruction that they cause to the society and the world. Śloka XVIII.25 warns against assuming responsibilities which are beyond one's capacity—pauruṣam. Similarly, śloka XVII.21 does not approve of whatever is given unwillingly, grudgingly, or whenever the giver feels hurt while giving. A strong warning is given is ślokas XVII.5-6 against going to extremes while performing tapas—austerity.

१२.१०. आचरन् मध्यममार्गं स्वधर्मं सेवाप्रेरितम् ।
नवरूपगीताशिक्षां स्वयं कुर्याच्च कारयेत् ॥

ācaran madhyamamārgaṁ svadharmaṁ sevāpreritam
navarūpagītāśikṣāṁ svayaṁ kuryācca kārayet

Three points of the Gita-teaching are brought together in this verse for purposes of stressing their importance in the modern society. First, that the middle path explained in the preceding verses—and interpreted so as to take care of specific situations—should be followed. Secondly, that the svadharma concept of the Gita, before being adopted to delimit the scope of one's duty, should be interpreted in such a constructive way that it does include some element of Lokasaṁgraha—the good of the society. Thirdly, while performing svadharma and following the middle path, encouragement should be given to other members of the society also to do the same—not from a sense of superiority or interference in other people's affairs, but as well-wishers and partners interested in the good of all.

The third point in the preceding paragraph, aimed at bringing about a unity of purpose and cooperative effort in the society for just causes, is closely linked with the Gita śloka III.26 in which Śri Kṛṣṇa asks the wise men not to be content by their own actions, but also to encourage others to act as well. The word 'joṣayet' (meaning to encourage or induce) occurring in this śloka (i.e. Gita III.26) encouraged Śrī Aurobindo to envisage 'universal action' for Lokasaṁgraha:

> To act for Lokasaṁgraha, impersonally, for the keeping and leading of the peoples on the path to the divine goal, is a rule which rises necessarily from the oneness of the soul with the Divine, the universal Being, since that is the whole sense and drift of the universal action . . .[10]

१२.११. विशाले यंत्रसमूहे गतिशीलाः सर्वे यंत्राः ।
लघुदीर्घभेदाद्विना यत्नो वाञ्छितः सर्वेषाम् ॥
viśāle yantrasamūhe gatiśīlāḥ sarve yantrāḥ
laghudīrghabhedādvinā yatno vāñchitaḥ sarveṣām

This verse tries to express, in brief, Tilak's idea that Lokasaṁgraha activities can best achieve their purpose only when there is maximum possible participation therein. A complicated machine will function properly only when all its parts—large or small—carry out their respective functions in a co-ordinated manner. Similarly, all the members of the human society—irrespective of whether they occupy a high position or a low position—need to put in their respective best for commonly agreed social causes. Tilak's own explanation, which forms the basis of this verse, is reproduced below:

Just as extremely small wheels are necessary along with large wheels in order that any machine should work properly, so also is it necessary that the authority of common-place persons should be exercised properly and fully in the same way as the authority of superior persons like Vyāsa and others, in order that the immense and ponderous activity or mechanism of the Cosmos should continue to work in a properly regulated manner. . .[11]

Verses of this chapter stress the importance of taking a realistic view of how the society functions, and recognize that, in spite of all exhortations and efforts to impart education in social values, some problems of exploitation, discrimination, denial of justice and of human rights, are likely to continue in the foreseeable future. Social activists are therefore advised not to resort to violent methods while trying to help the weaker sections of the society. Not only that, they have to create public opinion against the use of violent methods, that is, against the approach of fundamentalists and terrorists. In other words, Gita-followers have to try so that non-violence gets accepted—in due course of time—as the yugadharma of the new age. In spite of all the difficulties, a case-by-case effort to restrict social activism to non-violent methods is worth trying for, and Gita-followers should be prepared for long-lasting struggles in the cause of Lokasaṁgraha. Iyer has quoted Spratt's analysis (written in 1939) of how Gandhi's first 'experiment' with non-violence in South Africa (conducted during 1906-14) saw ups and downs, but only to confirm the efficacy of the new method:

> It was conducted against very heavy odds by poor and ignorant people—the majority indeed were illiterate—but there was hardly an instance of breach of the principles. It dragged on in all for eight years: the longest fight Gandhi has ever conducted. People became disheartened. At one time he could count upon only sixteen followers, but in the end the "law of growth" prevailed. Almost the whole community again entered the fight, and satisfactory terms were obtained. He was left with an apparently immovable faith in the capacity of ordinary poor people to undergo these trials and to observe the principles; and a no less indestructible faith in the efficacy of the method.[12]

CHAPTER THIRTEEN

यज्ञो नवरूपेण
YAJÑO NAVARŪPEṆA

MODIFYING YAJÑA AND GIVING IT NEW FORMS

This chapter explains that an important factor underlying the widespread acceptability of the Gita was that, while retaining some of the old symbols and particularly their names, it modified their meaning and content by introducing therein new concepts like that of the abandonment of selfish desires. The most impressive example of this approach of the Gita is provided by what the Vedas called the Yajña, and in respect of which the Gita—still retaining the same name, Yajña—made revolutionary changes to suit the changing socio-economic conditions of the people. An equally significant fact to be noted in this connection is that the modern Gita-followers, drawing inspiration from the revolutionary approach of the Gita, carried it still further and gave to the term "Yajña" more and more meanings so as to be able to tackle social, economic, political, and even environmental problems of the modern age. This chapter intends to draw attention to this fascinating aspect of India's socio-cultural history by indicating briefly how the Gita redefined the concept of Yajña, and also some of the newer types of socially relevant meanings that have been given to Yajña during modern times.

In order that the full significance of the Yajña-related phase of India's history can be properly appreciated, a short account is given below of what the Vedas had envisaged and what new ideas were introduced therein by the Gita as well as by some of the modern Gita-followers.

Yajña is a Vedic term and it denoted a particular type of ceremonial act, or "sacrificial ritual"—to use Tilak's interpretation—utilized for worshipping the Sun, Fire, Indra, Varuṇa, Rudra, and other Vedic Deities.[1] Offerings that were made into the sacrificial fire included sesamum, rice, and other specified materials. According to Mahatma Gandhi, "it is possible that, in the age prior to that of the Gita, offerings of animals as sacrifice was permissible."[2] Vedic Mantras uttered at the time of making sacrifice included the words "idaṁ devatāya. . . idaṁ na mama", that is, "this is for the deity. . . not for me". Yajñas were performed not only for personal benefit but also for the benefit of the community. The Brāhmaṇa-portion of the Vedas contains detailed descriptions of the ways in which different Yajñas have to be performed. Since the different Brāhmaṇas sometimes contained contradictory directions, Jaimini harmonized them through his "Mimāṁsā-Sūtras" or the "Pūrva-Mimāṁsā". The Yajña-doctrine is therefore also known as the Mīmāṁsā-doctrine.

Although Upaniṣads are also part of the Vedas, they are later in point of time than the Brāhmaṇas. During the Upaniṣadic period, the emphasis shifted from the sacrificial ritual, that is, Yajña or Karma, to the Knowledge of Brahman, that is, Jñāna. The Upaniṣads declared that Yajñas can only take one to heaven—which is temporary—whereas permanent bliss or release from the cycle of birth and death can be attained through Jñāna. Yajña as a sacrificial ritual was pushed to the background also because of the growth of the doctrine of non-sacrifice, that is, Ahiṁsā.

The Gita partly carried further the Upaniṣadic approach but it also introduced therein the important doctrine of Niṣkāma Karma, that is, putting into action all effort but not hankering after worldly or heavenly desires, that is , the doctrine of non-attachment to selfish gains. The Gita explained that Karma need not be confined to ritualistic sacrifices performed with the desire to obtain non-permanent benefits; rather, Karma, viewed as the basis of all life and uplifted as a way of obtaining permanent release, can become a Yoga, in no way inferior to Jñāna. Yajña had a place in such Karma-Yoga, but only if its (that is, Yajña's) meaning and content were modified.

The Gita associated new meanings with Yajña, not abruptly but in stages, explicitly on some occasions and implicitly on others. For example, the subject of Yajña is first introduced in the Gita śloka III.9 along with a reference to the Mīmāṁsā doctrine of the importance of Yajña, and then its (that is, Gita's) own doctrine of acting without attachment is added thereto. The idea of sharing "food" with "others" is then mentioned in the Gita śloka III.13, as a corollary of Yajña, condemning thereby the mentality of those who prepare food "only for themselves". Then, in ślokas III.14-16, the Gita presents " a wheel of Yajña or socially oriented karma", to establish the principle of interdependence of the individual, the society and the cosmos. As Upadhyaya summarizes the message of these Yajña-related ślokas:

> The wheel of the world, according to the Gita, goes on by means of sacrifice or renunciation, and one who does not discharge his selfless service to the world lives only in vain. [3]

Other modifications in the meaning of Yajña, made by the Gita or its modern interpreters, will be referred to in the course of the commentary on the verses of this chapter.

१३.१. यज्ञदानतपः कर्म ज्ञेयं नवीनरूपेण ।
अनुसृत्य गीताभावं प्राप्तुं सर्वभूतहितम् ।
yajñadānatapaḥ karma jñeyaṁ navīnarūpeṇa
anusṛtya gītābhāvaṁ prāptuṁ sarvabhūtahitam

It is helpful to adopt the Gita-approach, namely, to retain the names of traditional concepts—like Yajña, Dānam, Tapas—but to associate new meanings with them, in a manner that can best achieve the good of all beings.

The expression 'sarvabhūtahitam', meaning 'the good of all beings', is intended to recall Gita ślokas V. 25 and XII. 4 where the phrase 'sarvabhūtahite ratāḥ' occurs.

१३.२. देवानां प्रसंगादुक्तो भावो यज्ञस्य गीतायाम् ।
देवान् भावयतानेन ते देवा भावयन्तु वः ॥
devānāṁ prasaṁgādukto bhāvo yajñasya gītāyām
devān bhāvayatānena te devā bhāvayantu vaḥ

The idea that mutual help and cooperation are the guiding principles of Yajña, is conveyed in śloka III.11 of the Gita. Of course, this is stated in the context of the inter-relationship between human beings and gods—because this was the original framework envisaged for the Vedic Yajña. The advice to the human beings was "By Yajña, you should foster the gods, and in return let the gods foster you".

१३.३. देवतुल्यभावेनैव ज्ञेयो जनसहयोगः ।
परस्परं भावयन्तः श्रेयः परमवाप्स्यथ ॥
devatulyabhāvenaiva jñeyo janasahayogaḥ
parasparaṁ bhāvayantaḥ śreyaḥ paramavāpsyatha

The preceding verse quoted the first line of śloka III.11 of the Gita, and the second line thereof is quoted in the present verse. The message of mutual cooperation for good causes is explicitly given here: "By fostering one another you shall attain to the supreme good". But to understand that this message is for the human society, a simple modification needs to be made in the meaning of the word "devas"—the traditional meaning of which was "gods", but of which the new meaning should be taken to be "the whole creation of God", as suggested by Mahatma Gandhi in his commentary on śloka III.11.

Further extracts from Mahatma Gandhi's commentary on śloka III.11 are given below:

Yajña is a word full of beauty and power. Hence with the growth of knowledge and experience and with the change of time, its meaning is likely to grow and change. Yajña literally means worship; hence sacrifice; hence any sacrificial act or any act of service. And in this sense every age may and should have its own particular yajña. For mankind lives by yajña, sacrifice. . .

Yajña means an act directed to the welfare of others, done without receiving or desiring a return for it, whether of a temporal or a spiritual nature. 'Act' must be taken in its widest sense, and includes thought and word, and 'others' embraces not only humanity but all life. Therefore, it will not be a yajña to sacrifice lower animals even with a view to the service of humanity. . .[4]

१३.४. अधुना नवरूपेण यज्ञेन सर्ववर्णानाम् ।
सर्वलोकहितकार्ये निःस्वार्थो हि सहयोगः ॥
adhunā navarūpeṇa yajñena sarvavarṇānām
sarvalokahitakārye niḥsvārtho hi sahayogaḥ

Following the lead given by the Gita, which has been carried further by Lokasaṁgraha-activists, newer and newer meanings should be associated with the word "Yajña" so that it may include unselfish, mutual cooperation in actions aimed at benefiting all the members of the human society, without any discrimination—based on race or other considerations.

Tilak found in the long history of Hinduism, ample justification for periodically giving newer and newer interpretations to Vedic and other traditional terms (including Yajña):

> When the sacrifice of wealth. . . fell into disuse, and the devices of attaining perfection came more and more into vogue, the meaning of the word 'yajña' was widened. . . The principle at the root of this is the tendency to indicate subsequent religious methods by the same technical terms as had come to be formerly accepted in the religion.[5]

As a follow-up of the above, Tilak argues that it is better to offer animal tendencies like desire, anger, egotism, etc. which are in everyone's body, by way of sacrifice into the fire of mental control, than to offer commodities or animals into sacrificial fire.[6] Swami Chinmayananda also highlighted the cooperative spirit—which he called the true Yajña-spirit—in which socially useful work should be done to remove "all causes for the sorrows in social life. . .":

> The Yajña-spirit is the spirit of self-dedicated activities. . . The Creator created the world along with the spirit of service and the capacity for sacrifice. . . This law of Sevā (service) is faithfully followed by every sentient and insentient member of the cosmos instinctively. Man alone is given the freedom to act as he likes and to the extent he disobeys this universal law of service—Yajña—to that extent he comes to suffer, because he, with his arrogant and egoistic actions, brings discord in the harmony of the existence around him.[7]

The next verse, suggesting the inclusion of environmental protection among the defining criteria for Yajña in modern times, can be called "Environment-friendly Yajña Declaration".

वातावरणानुकूलो यज्ञघोषणा
VĀTĀVARAṆĀNUKŪLO YAJÑAGHOṢAṆĀ

१३.५. लोकसंग्रहप्रेरितं कृतं निःस्वार्थभावेन ।
नवीनरूपं यज्ञस्य वायुरक्षणकारकम् ॥

lokasaṁgrahapreritaṁ kṛtaṁ niḥsvārthabhāvena
navīnarūpaṁ yajñasya vāyurakṣaṇakārakam

Two of the elements that have characterized the new forms of Yajña have been, first, that the activities were inspired by Lokasaṁgraha—the good of the whole society—and secondly, that the participants in these activities did not want to derive any selfish gains therefrom. One more element, which has been occasionally mentioned so far but which needs to be given prominence in this connection, is that the activities should be such as may contribute to environmental protection also. This last point can also be stated in a preventive way, namely that activities doing harm to the earth's environment—air, water, etc.—should be discouraged, the idea being that environmental considerations should also guide the determination of activities that can be included in Yajña.

An environment-friendly interpretation of Lokasaṁgraha has been put forward by J.G. Arapura because he wants to highlight the protective aspect of this Gita-message, in the face of newer and newer types of threats. For example, says Arapura, there are threats to life itself due to environmental pollution caused by toxic substances, deforestation, and improper handling of wastes of all types. Scientific discoveries (including nuclear energy) are being misused to such an extent that human civilization, which took thousands of years to build, might be subjected to sudden, mass destruction. Additional hazards to environment and health, according to Arapura, are also due to uncontrolled increase in the population in those areas which already suffer from inadequacy of resources, malnutrition, poverty, and natural disasters. Arapura believes that the Gita-concept of Lokasaṁgraha needs to be spelt out in such a way as to enable an ethical input (howsoever small) in the formulation of an inter-disciplinary effort for environmental protection and human welfare.[8]

१३.६. सूत्रयंत्रसुचालनं यज्ञो हि मुक्तिसंग्रामे ।
भूदानं च वितरणं यज्ञः श्रीविनोबामते ॥
sūtrayantrasucālanaṁ yajño hi muktisaṁgrāme
bhūdānaṁ ca vitaraṇaṁ yajñaḥ śrīvinobāmate

New forms of Yajña that have attracted country-wide attention during the modern history of India are worth recalling, for example, during the non-violent freedom struggle led by Mahatma Gandhi, the spinning wheel become a symbol of Yajña, and subsequently, when Vinoba Bhave tried to devise a non-violent method to help the poor, landless people, the land-gift movement and the land-distribution activities associated therewith were presented as Yajña, inviting participation of all.

Mahatma Gandhi was very emphatic that the Gita ślokas III.9-16 which speak of the origin of Yajña and of the importance of continuing in motion the wheel of yajña, should be interpreted in such a way as to solve the most pressing problems of today's society. He raised the question: What is meant by saying that mankind was created along with Yajña?, and he also suggested an answer: Just as we cannot escape the cycle of birth, old age and death, so also bodily labour is our lot in life from which there is no escape. In a country like India, extremely backward that it was, he saw not only laziness and a dislike for physical labour and lack of care to do one's own small jobs on one's own, he also saw that a sense of hatred for physical labour even for one's own needs existed in the society, and so he wanted that dignity of labour should be established. He also saw that for removing the grave sin of untouchability, the sense of dignity of labour and self-dependence as also keenness for service should be emphasized. He therefore took the view that labouring enough for one's food has been classed in the Gita as a yajña. He suggested similarly that the wheel of yajña in śloka III.16 should in today's conditions mean the spinning wheel. "For me", said Gandhi, "nation-wide spinning is a yajña. It is the symbol of unity of Indian humanity, of its economic freedom and equality and, therefore, ultimately, in the poetic expression of Jawaharlal Nehru, 'the livery of India's freedom' ".[9]

Vinoba Bhave carried further the Gandhian approach and argued that chapter seventeen of the Gita, in which Yajña, Dānam and Tapas are viewed as "triple duty", should be interpreted with reference to three levels of creation, namely, nature, society, and body. According to this interpretation, Yajña represents the effort made to replenish nature's loss, Dānam is the help given through body, mind, material resources and other means to discharge the debt to society, and Tapas is self-discipline needed for removing the deficiencies and distortions in the body caused by normal wear and tear.[10]

But even within the 'triple duty' framework—denoted by yajña-dānam-tapas as a trio—Vinoba views Yajña as the most comprehensive term. Selfless participation by all, with the feeling that we are merely discharging our debt to 'the order of creation'—this, according to Vinoba, is Yajña in the comprehensive sense, which includes Dānam and Tapas also:

> So far we have regarded yajña, dānam and tapas as if they were three different things, but to tell the truth, there is no difference between them. For the three orders of nature, society and the body are not absolutely distinct. Society is not outside creation; nor for that matter is the body. These three together make up the beautiful order of nature. The creative effort we make, the dānam we give, and the tapas we perform—all these can be called yajña in the comprehensive sense. . .
>
> Whatever we do in a yajña should not be done for our own sake but with the feeling that it is one's duty to make up for the loss that one has caused. This is not altruism. We are, from the beginning, debtors. We are born into the world with a load of debt on our heads. Whatever we do to discharge this debt is yajña or service, not altruism. . .We have to do yajña to replenish loss, to purify things and to create new things.[11]

Since Vinoba developed these ideas further in the context of his Bhoodāna (land-gift) movement, details thereof will be given in chapter fourteen which is devoted to Dānam and Tapas.

१३.७. एवं सुवर्णिते यज्ञे नास्ति काष्ठप्रज्वलनम् ।
यज्ञाय काष्ठज्वलनमनुचितं गाँधीमते ॥

evaṁ suvarṇite yajñe nāsti kāṣṭhaprajvalanam
yajñāya kāṣṭhajvalanamanucitaṁ gāṁdhīmate

In the traditional form of Yajña, the sacrificial fire—which meant burning of wood—was considered as essential. However, this was not the case with the newer forms of Yajña referred to in the preceding verse. In fact, Mahatma Gandhi suggested that, in the present circumstances of the country, burning of wood should not be considered as essential for Yajña.[12]

१३.८. आदौ काले वनानां तु बाहुल्यं दृष्टं भारते ।
तदा काष्ठप्रज्वलनं न हि यज्ञे वर्तमाने ॥
ādau kāle vanānāṁ tu bāhulyaṁ dṛṣṭaṁ bhārate
tadā kāṣṭhaprajvalanaṁ na hi yajñe vartamāne

Mahatma Gandhi's argument was that, in Vedic times, there were large forest areas in the country, and since the clearing of these forests was a socially useful task, burning of wood became a symbol of Yajña. However, present-day conditions being entirely different—wood is now a scarce commodity—the traditional form of Yajña should be modified.[13]

In śloka IV.24, the Gita itself has envisaged that agni—that is, fire—as well as other ingredients that together make a traditional Yajña could be interpreted symbolically. Śrī Aurobindo emphasized the symbolic meaning of Yajña and said that making sacrifices in the struggle for freedom, without selfish motives, constituted Yajña:

> Liberty is the fruit we seek from the sacrifice, and the Motherland, the Goddess to whom we offer it; into the seven leaping tongues of the fire of the yajña we must offer all that we are and all that we have. . .[14] The fire of sacrifice, agni, is no material flame. . . it is the fire of self-knowledge. . . For the man who has this knowledge and lives and acts in it, there can be no binding works, no personal and egoistically appropriated action. . .[15]

१३.९. नवीना भाषा यज्ञस्य गीताज्ञानानुकूलैव ।
सृष्टिचक्रप्रवर्तनं जपश्च यज्ञौ गीतायाम् ॥
navīnā bhāṣā yajñasya gītājñānānukūlaiva
sṛṣṭicakrapravartanaṁ japaśca yajñau gītāyām

In trying to give newer and newer meanings to Yajña, to contribute to the good of the society, modern Lokasaṁgraha-activists have only followed the Gita-approach, because the Gita itself has mentioned the following as examples of Yajña:

(i) japa, that is, repetition of God's name (śloka X.25)
(ii) keep moving the wheel of the world (ślokas III.14-16).

The Bhakti movement followed the advice of the Gita and stressed the importance of japa. Mahatma Gandhi also found it very useful.

Regarding the wheel-related verses III.14-16 of the Gita, Upadhyaya's interpretation emphasizing 'selfless service to the world' has already been referred to. Radhakrishnan sees in these verses a message of interdependence:

> In these verses the Vedic conception of sacrifice as an interchange between gods and men is set in the larger context of the interdependence of beings in the cosmos. . . Sacrifice is the law of life. The individual and the cosmos depend on each other. There is a constant interchange between human life and world life. He who works for himself lives in vain.[16]

Yajña as a symbolic way of relating human beings with other elements in the cosmos can be expressed, according to Manusmṛti (2.27 and others), through five principal yajñas prescribed for householders:

- (i) Brahma-yajña or a study of Vedas
- (ii) Deva-yajña or prayer to deities
- (iii) Pitri-yajña or offerings dedicated to ancestors
- (iv) Manuṣya-yajña or hospitality to human beings
- (v) Bhūta-yajña or offering of food to other creatures.

The last two of the five yajñas, if interpreted in practical rather than ritualistic terms, can help strengthen linkages between yajña and Lokasaṁgraha. To achieve this, says Tilak, it is necessary that, while doing something for others, the words "idaṁ na mama" should come not merely from the lips but from the heart:

> The most important element in a Yajña is the giving up of the idea of mineness (mamatva) with reference to the object thrown into the sacrificial fire, by uttering the words "idaṁ na mama" (i.e. this is not mine) at the time of throwing. . . In short, one may say that doing a particular karma, in which there is no selfish purpose, with a pure frame of mind, is a yajña in itself.[17]

CHAPTER FOURTEEN

तपोदानं नवरूपेण
TAPODĀNAṀ NAVARŪPEṆA

MODIFYING DĀNAM AND TAPAS AND GIVING THEM NEW FORMS

Just as chapter thirteen examined how the traditional concept of Yajña was modified, first by the Gita and subsequently, in modern times, by Lokasaṁgraha-activists, similarly the present chapter looks into two other traditional concepts, namely, Dānam and Tapas, which denote charity and austerity, respectively. In fact, the three concepts—Yajña, Dānam, Tapas—are often spoken of as a trio, in the Upaniṣads as well as in the Gita. For example, Bṛhadāraṇyaka Upaniṣad (4.4.22) mentions these three together as a means to know Brahman, which has been characterized as "lokānāṁ asambhedaḥ", that is, "one who protects the worlds from falling apart". In Vinoba Bhave's opinion, this is similar to Lokasaṁgraha of the Gita.[1] A translation of the relevant passage from the Bṛhadāraṇyaka Upaniṣad follows :

> That infinite Brahman is the lord of all, the ruler of beings, the protector of beings. It is like a bridge which protects the worlds from falling apart. It is the Brahman whom the Brahmins wish to know by the study of the Vedas, and also by means of yajña, dānam, and tapas, performed without attachment. (Bṛhadāraṇyaka Upaniṣad 4.4.22)

In the Gita also, in chapter eighteen, while presenting a summary of the whole teaching, Śrī Kṛṣṇa has prominently picked up Yajña, Dānaṃ, Tapas as three virtuous action programmes in which everyone should participate, without attachment or desire for the fruits thereof. This important statement of Śrī Kṛṣṇa occurs in ślokas XVIII.5-6, and it is declared to be "His firm and final view", as the following translation of these two ślokas shows:

> Acts of yajña, dānam, and tapas are not to be relinquished but should be performed; for these are purifiers of the wise. But even

these acts ought to be performed, without attachment or desire for fruits. This, O Arjuna, is my firm and final view. (Gita XVIII.5-6)

In chapter nine of the Gita also, and particularly in śloka IX.27, in which Śrī Kṛṣṇa asks Arjuna to dedicate all acts to Him, three of the acts specifically mentioned for dedication are: yajña, dānam, tapas.

Besides the above references where all three acts—Yajña, Dānam, Tapas—are spoken of as a trio, there are of course others where the importance of Yajña, or of Tapas, is separately emphasized. For example, the second part of the Gita śloka IV.31 says: "This world is not for him who offers no yajña, how then any other world, O Arjuna?" Similarly, the first part of the Gita śloka XVIII.67 says: "Never speak the Gita to one who does not do tapas (among other things)."

After having shown in the previous chapter how the new forms of Yajña have contributed, and can still contribute, to Lokasaṁgraha, a similar look into Dānam and Tapas is now presented.

१४.१. नवीना भाषा यज्ञस्य यथोक्ता लोकरक्षार्थम् ।
तथैवाधुना वाञ्छिता तपसो दानस्यापि च ॥
navīnā bhāṣā yajñasya yathoktā lokarakṣārtham
tathaivādhunā vāñchitā tapaso dānasyāpi ca

Just as new definitions of Yajña have been made to support movements aimed at protecting and helping all members of the human society, similarly it is desirable to associate new ideas with Dānam and Tapas as well.

१४.२. नवीना भाषा दानस्य धनाहंकारवर्जिता ।
संविभागस्वरूपा हि वर्णिता श्रीशंकरेण ॥
navīnā bhāṣā dānasya dhanāhaṁkāravarjitā
saṁvibhāgasvarūpā hi varṇitā śrīśaṁkareṇa

While attempting to give new definitions to Dānam, it is highly encouraging to find that Śaṁkara, whose Gita-commentary is the earliest available one, defined Dānam as saṁvibhāgaḥ or equal division or sharing. Such a revolutionary approach can make Dānam acceptable as a social policy, even to those who prefer fundamental changes in distribution of resources rather than superficial acts of giving (which might encourage begging). Also, Śaṁkara's definition implies that the possession of wealth as well as the act of sharing it with others should be free from a sense of egotism, or ahaṁkāra.

१४.३. तद्दानं विनोबामते ज्ञेयं ऋणप्रकरणे ।
देयं हि संविभागार्थमात्मौपम्येन भावेन ॥
taddānaṁ vinobāmate jñeyaṁ ṛṇaprakaraṇe
deyaṁ hi saṁvibhāgārthamātmaupamyena bhāvena

In modern times, it was Vinoba Bhave who, starting from Śaṁkara's definition of Dānam as equal distribution or sharing, put into motion a non-violent revolutionary movement to obtain land for the poor, landless people. Vinoba made it clear that the person donating a part of his or her land voluntarily should be guided by the Vedantic philosophy that the same ātman resides in all beings. Furthermore, said Vinoba, the act of giving should be viewed as a means of discharging one's "debt to society".[2]

Since the Bhoodān (land-gift) movement of Vinoba marks an important application of the Gita to tackle a socio-economic problem, some details thereof may be mentioned here. Vinoba started this movement in the early fifties as a counter-point to the Communist activities in the Telangana area of Andhra Pradesh in India. The situation there acquired the characteristics of a class struggle when the tenants, under communist leadership, seized land from the landlords. Violent clashes took place between the peasants who tried to retain the land, and the police whose function according to the law of the country was to help return the land (by using force if necessary) to the landlords. Vinoba told the people that seizing land against the consent of the landlords as well as retaking land by force would only embitter relations between the peasants and the landlords and would cause widespread suffering. He also felt that there were many loopholes in the scheme of land reforms and redistribution attempted through legislative measures of the government. According to Vinoba, all three activities—forcible seizure, police protection, and compulsory re-distribution—involved the use of violence. Citing the Gita and other scriptures, Vinoba made the plea that all land belongs to God and those who hold it in trusteeship should voluntarily part with one-sixth of what they have, to be re-distributed among the landless.

Although Vinoba uses a traditional word 'dānam' (meaning charity, gift), his interpretation (drawing support from Śaṁkara) gives it a modern flavour. Vinoba says that when he accepts land on behalf of the poor, he is not accepting it as charity from the rich. Rather he is offering a peaceful alternative to the rich to save themselves from a violent revolution.

Vinoba presents a four-way categorization of an individual's economic relationship with the society—Dānam being one of them—namely:

(i) Theft
(ii) Begging
(iii) Earning one's livelihood (Śarīrayātrā)
(iv) Dānam.

First, Vinoba defines theft (in the light of the Gita ślokas III.11-12) as a situation in which an individual takes from the society goods and services but gives nothing in return. The second category is begging (Gita śloka II.5) when an individual takes more from the society than what he or she gives in return. The third category (śarīrayātrā occurring in Gita śloka III.8) represents a state of equality of what one takes and what one gives. Fourthly, dānam (occurring in Gita chapter XVII and others) refers to a situation in which one is apparently giving more to society than what one is (currently) receiving in return, but Vinoba says, this should be viewed as discharging old debts:

> Dānam, the rite of giving was instituted in order to discharge our debt to society. I have received from society boundless service, therefore I in my turn should serve society. 'Doing good' is serving someone from whom we have received no service, but in this case we have already received everything from society.[3]

Vinoba appealed for voluntary sharing, not only of land—which is the main productive resource in rural India—but also of other useful resources. For example, he extended his concept of dānam to include śrama-dān (voluntary labour for projects of public utility), buddhi-dān (dedicating one's intellectual capability, partly or wholly), sampatti-dān (sharing of one's wealth), etc. In Arapura's opinion, the real significance of Vinoba's movement based on Dānam lies not so much in measurable economic gains but rather in its attempt to build a spiritual and moral basis to the social life:

> The real aim of this movement is to put humanity through a spiritual discipline calculated to humanize it and to cure the basic ills that mar the spiritual image of man in the context of social existence.[4]

१४.४. ऋणभावाद्दत्तं दानं कृतज्ञताप्रकाशकम् ।
नोचिता तत्प्रसंगे हि मानेच्छाहंकारस्तथा ।।

ṛṇabhāvāddattaṁ dānaṁ kṛtajñatāprakāśakam
nocitā tatprasaṁge hi mānecchāhaṁkārastathā

When something is given with the feeling that thereby one is discharging old debts, then the giver is not likely to expect, in return, honour from other members of the society; rather, the giver should be grateful that he or she was given an opportunity to do something for others. Such an approach on the part of the giver can also save him or her from any sense of egotism.

The advice that the giver should "be grateful to the man you help" formed an important element in Swami Vivekananda's formulation of the Karmayoga technique of avoiding pain of vain expectation:

> We think that we have helped some man and expect him to thank us, and because he does not, unhappiness comes to us. Why should we expect anything in return for what we do? Be grateful to the man you help, think of him as God. Is it not a privilege to be allowed to worship God by helping our fellow men? If we were really unattached, we should escape all this pain of vain expectation, and could cheerfully do good work in the world.[5]

A significant element in the Gita's formulation of Dānam, which deserves to be stressed under modern conditions also, is to make sure that the recipient of our help is a worthy person—or 'pātra' in Sanskrit—or in other words, that we help only worthy causes. A corollary of this, which is useful as a policy statement, is that we refuse to help unjust causes. The next verse highlighting this can be called "Withdrawal of Help from the Unjust Declaration".

त्यक्तनीतये असहकारघोषणा
TYAKTANĪTAYE ASAHAKĀRAGHOṢAṆĀ

१४.५. दानं साहाय्यप्रदानं देयं केवलं पात्रेभ्यः ।
त्यक्तनीतये तद्रूपं संज्ञितमसहकारम् ॥
dānaṁ sāhāyyapradānaṁ deyaṁ kevalaṁ pātrebhyaḥ
tyaktanītaye tadrūpaṁ saṁjñitamasahakāram

The fact that the Gita advises Dānam to be given only to one who is a worthy recipient, can be so interpreted as to yield the doctrine of "non-cooperation with the unjust". The argument can run like this. First, offering one's assistance and cooperation is also a type of Dānam. Secondly, ślokas XVII.20 and 22 of the Gita clearly prescribe that Dānam should be given only to one who deserves—and never to one who is unworthy. Thirdly, one who has gone astray from the path of justice and righteousness is an unworthy person. Fourthly, it follows from the preceding statements that the Gita gives us the important doctrine of withdrawing cooperation from the unjust.

The restriction about giving dānam only to a 'pātra' introduces a value judgment which is of great social significance. The Ṛg Veda hymn X.117 had advised that 'the wealthier man should give unto the needy'. By declaring that some types of dānam—even to the needy—could be undesirable, the Gita made dānam a potential tool of Lokasaṁgraha.

It is well-known that the technique of non-violent non-cooperation was a part of the Gandhian Satyagraha. What is noticeable in the present context is, that the verse 14.5 links it with the Gita concept of a 'pātra'. The Gandhian idea was that the masses should withdraw cooperation from a government that, in the non-cooperators' view, was extremely unjust, oppressive or corrupt. The purpose of non-cooperation was to put so much pressure upon the government that the act of governance itself might become impossible. As Mahatma Gandhi put it:

> I believe, and everybody must grant, that no government can exist for a single moment without the cooperation of the people, willing or forced, and if people suddenly withdraw their cooperation in every detail, the government will come to a standstill. . . Cooperation with a just government is a duty; non-cooperation with an unjust government is equally a duty.[6]

Having examined how the new forms of Dānam as well as the doctrine of non-cooperation derived therefrom can help social causes, we now consider how the traditional concept of tapas has similarly been modified. To begin with, we must note that the importance of tapas as a basic virtue was stressed in the Vedas, and even more so in the Upaniṣads—not necessarily as a part of the trio 'yajña-dānam-tapas". For example, Muṇḍaka Upaniṣad (III.1.5) lists four basic virtues, namely, satya, tapas, jnāna, brahmacarya. As before in the case of dānam, the Gita declared that not all varieties of tapas can be considered useful. Verses 14.6-10 attempt to summarize the Gita's ideas relating to tapas.

१४.६. पुनश्च तपस्वरूपं श्रीकृष्णादेशं संपश्यन् ।
सात्त्विकमेव मन्तव्यं न घोरं न वा तामसम् ॥

punaśca tapasvarūpaṁ śrīkṛṣṇādeśaṁ saṁpaśyan
sāttvikameva mantavyaṁ na ghoraṁ na vā tāmasam

In ślokas XVII.14-16 of the Gita, tapas of three types (of body, speech, mind) is described, and then in ślokas XVII.17-19, there is a description of sāttvika, rajas and tamas varieties of tapas (applicable to all three types of tapas). One more variety of tapas which is akin to tāmasika tapas, and is called in the Gita as "ghora tapas", is described in ślokas XVII. 5-6. Within this broad framework, the main point to be noted in the present context is that Śrī Kṛṣṇa advises us to go in for sāttvika tapas only. With a view to reinforcing this advice, Śrī Kṛṣṇa also says: Avoid tāmasika tapas and ghora tapas.

It will be useful to understand what specific actions—of body, speech, mind—are referred to by the above-mentioned advice of Śrī Kṛṣṇa, and particularly those which have a bearing on the good of the society. This is done next, in verses 14.7-10.

१४.७. अशास्त्रविहितं घोरं तप्यन्ते ये तपो जनाः ।
दम्भाहंकारसंयुक्ताः कामरागबलान्विताः ॥
aśāstravihitaṁ ghoraṁ tapyante ye tapo janāḥ
dambhāhaṁkārasaṁyuktāḥ kāmarāgabalānvitāḥ

Having mentioned in verse 14.6 that Śrī Kṛṣṇa wants us to avoid "ghora tapas" and "tāmasika tapas", details as to what constitutes these two varieties of tapas are given in verses 14.7-9. In fact, verses 14.7-8 are the same as ślokas XVII.5-6 of the Gita. Śrī Kṛṣṇa says in the present verse that "ghora tapas", that is, violent austerities are not approved of by the scriptures. Those who perform violent austerities are vain and conceited, and they are impelled by the force of lust and passion.

१४.८. कर्षयन्तः शरीरस्थं भूतग्राममचेतसः ।
मां चैवान्तःशरीरस्थं तान्विद्ध्यासुरनिश्चयान् ॥
karṣayantaḥ śarīrasthaṁ bhūtagrāmamacetasaḥ
māṁ caivāntaḥśarīrasthaṁ tānviddhyāsuraniścayān

This verse is the same as śloka XVII.6 of the Gita in which Śrī Kṛṣṇa's advice against "ghora tapas" is continued. Śrī Kṛṣṇa says that those who perform violent austerities are unwise; they oppress the group of elements in their body and Me also dwelling in the body. O Arjuna, know these people to be demoniac in their resolve.

१४.९. पुनश्च भगवान् प्राह यत्तपः पीडाकारकम् ।
परस्योत्सादनार्थं वा तत्तामसमुदाहृतम् ॥
punaśca bhagavān prāha yattapaḥ pīḍākārakam
parasyotsādanārthaṁ vā tattāmasamudāhṛtam

Just as Śrī Kṛṣṇa advises Arjuna to avoid "ghora tapas", similarly He warned him against falling a prey to tāmasika tapas. Two of the most harmful features of tāmasika tapas, as specified in śloka XVII.19 of the Gita, are highlighted here, namely, first that tāmasika tapas involves self-torture, and secondly that its object is to cause injury to others.

Commenting on tāmasika tapas, Swami Chidbhavananda says that "occasionally, such performers of austerities stumble upon some psychic power which they utilize for hurting, wrecking or destroying others".[7]

१४.१०. सात्त्विके तपसि किं तु कष्टसहनं लोकार्थे ।
तस्मिन् सत्यमहिंसा च वाक्यं प्रियहितं तथा ॥

sāttvike tapasi kiṁ tu kaṣṭasahanaṁ lokārthe
tasmin satyamahiṁsā ca vākyaṁ priyahitaṁ tathā

After having described, in verses 14.7-9, the harmful features of "ghora tapas" and tāmasika tapas, the benevolent features of sāttvika tapas are brought together in the present verse. A clear distinction is made here between violent self-torture indulged in for causing harm to others (as done in ghora tapas and tāmasika tapas), and non-violent self-suffering voluntarily accepted to arouse public sympathy for just social causes (as envisaged in sāttvika tapas). This feature of sāttvika tapas is based on Mahatma Gandhi's interpretation of Gita-ślokas XVII.14-17. Furthermore, ahiṁsā or non-violence is mentioned in these ślokas as one of the elements of bodily tapas. Similarly, tapas of speech includes—besides other virtues—the utterance of words which give no offence but are truthful, pleasant and beneficial.

Mahatma Gandhi showed how new applications of tapas could be made for social causes. For example, he used tapas to prepare the Satyagrahis to undergo self-suffering, particularly in connection with the Civil Disobedience movement. According to Iyer's analysis, this represented a 'more difficult' type of Satyagraha, because 'only a few' could be expected to practise tapas for the good of the society:

> Non-cooperation was conceived in a much wider context as an instrument of social action. . . Civil disobedience is more difficult than non-cooperation because it presupposes the habit of willing obedience of laws without fear of their sanctions. . .
>
> Gandhi's emphasis was on Ahiṁsā in non-cooperation and on Tapas in civil disobedience, although both concepts contained elements of self-suffering and non-violence. Non-cooperation made fewer spiritual demands on its users. . . Civil Disobedience called for a spirit of tapas or self-suffering, which in practice only

a few were capable of exemplifying. . .[8]

Śrī Aurobindo viewed sāttvika tapas or tapasyā as "that which is done with a highest enlightened faith, as a duty deeply accepted or for some ethical or spiritual or other higher reason and with no desire for any external or narrowly personal fruit in the action".[9] He stressed his belief therein when he told Romain Rolland why he withdrew from 'mediocre politics' and how, in his opinion, a life of 'tapasyā' could contribute to the 'progress of humanity': India possesses in its past, a little rusty and out of use, the key to the progress of humanity. It is to this side that I am now turning my energies, rather than towards mediocre politics. Hence the reason for my withdrawal. I believe in the necessity for tapasyā (a life of meditation and concentration) in silence for education and self-knowledge and for the unloosing of spiritual energies. Our ancestors used these means under different forms; for they are the best for becoming an efficient worker in the great hours of the world.[10]

Śrī Aurobindo used his tapasyā to develop a new technique, called Integral Yoga, or Pūrṇa Yoga, by means of which the Yogi rises to the Supra-mental plane and then descends back to the material plane to help others achieve a similar Spiritual Evolution as quickly as possible. The point that needs to be stressed now is that the way Aurobindo looks at tapasyā has important social implications, because he had specifically stated the main objectives of his "quest for the truth" to include "the application of our ideas to the problems of man's social and collective life".[11]

१४.११. एवं सुपरिभाषितं यज्ञदानतपः कर्म ।
निःश्रेयसकरं तथा लोकसंग्रहपूरकम् ॥

evaṁ suparibhāṣitaṁ yajñadānatapaḥ karma
niḥśreyasakaraṁ tathā lokasaṁgrahapūrakam

It should be clear from chapters thirteen and fourteen that newer and newer forms of Yajña, Dānam, and Tapas have been devised in such a way that they can help Lokasaṁgraha activities, and all this being in conformity with the Gita technique of Niṣkāma Karma, the persons who participate therein can also be assured of their salvation—although they should not entertain any desire for selfish gains.

CHAPTER FIFTEEN

पुरुषार्थाः लोकसंग्रहसमन्विताः
PURUṢĀRTHĀḤ LOKASAṀGRAHASAMANVITĀḤ

PURUṢĀRTHAS HARMONIZED WITH LOKASAṀGRAHA

According to the Hindu tradition, any study of the philosophy of life would remain incomplete unless due attention is given therein to the four Puruṣārthas or goals of life or values. Swami Ranganathanada translates the word 'Puruṣārtha' as 'sought after by the human being', and says that "all human urges, aspirations, and purposes are covered by the four comprehensive puruṣārthas. . . "[1] There is no unanimity about the order in which the puruṣārthas should be mentioned—some put 'artha' in the beginning, some others put 'kāma', while some begin with 'dharma'. For our present purposes, we take the order 'artha-kāma-dharma-mokṣa', meaning 'wealth-pleasure-moral value-salvation'.

Following the Kaṭhopaniṣad, the goals of life can also be classified into two broad categories, namely, preyas (pleasant) and śreyas (good). Scholars like Mishra have suggested that a correspondence between preyas and śreyas, on the one hand, and the four puruṣārthas, on the other, can be established as follows:

(i) Preyas includes artha and kāma, and
(ii) Śreyas includes dharma and mokṣa, but can denote either one of them also in different contexts.[2]

Hiriyanna has studied the four puruṣārthas as a system of values.[3] Following his approach, and that of Mishra referred to above, we indicate in this chapter (among other things) how the Gita modified the Kaṭhopaniṣad view about 'preyas'. Although we have spoken about it in Part One, chapter five, but we feel it is important to look into this aspect of the value system as a special topic as we do here. In this process, our emphasis gradually shifts to the suggestion, put forward in verse 15.7, that the moral value 'dharma' should be interpreted so widely as to include 'social values' also. In a way, this only means going to the root 'dhṛ' from which the word 'dharma' comes, and the well-known phrase 'dhāraṇād dharmaḥ' is used by Śrī Kṛṣṇa in the Karṇaparva of the Mahabharata when he says:

> The word 'dharma' comes from the root 'dhṛ' which means 'to hold or uphold'; so all human beings are held together by dharma. That by which the holding together of all human beings takes place is dharma.[4]

The inclusion of social values in the moral value 'dharma' is thus fully justified. In fact, Hiriyanna implies the same thing when he says that 'other-regarding virtues' are as much a part of dharma as 'self-regarding virtues' are:

> There are several lists of virtues whose cultivation is signified by 'dharma'. For example, Yājñavalkya reckons them as nine—ahiṁsā, satya, honesty, cleanliness, sense-control, dānam, self-discipline, compassion, and forbearance. Some of them like ahiṁsā, dānam, and compassion have a reference to the good of others, while some others like satya, cleanliness, and self-discipline serve to develop one's own character and will. It should not, however, be thought that this division into self-regarding and other-regarding virtues is a hard and fast one; for, as an individual has no life of his own independent of society, the former has a bearing on the latter, as surely as the latter has on the former.[5]

In spite of the obvious inclusion of social values (other-regarding virtues) in 'dharma', there is still a risk that those who interpret 'dharma' narrowly might forget the social unity and welfare aspect of 'dharma'. No such risk can be associated with the word 'Lokasaṁgraha', because social values are automatically included therein. In fact, the most obvious meanings of the compound word 'Lokasaṁgraha'—taking into account the dictionary meanings of 'Loka' and 'Saṁgraha', as done by Tilak—include 'binding human beings together, and protecting (human beings as well as the world), and also maintaining and regulating them through mutual cooperation'.[6]

With these introductory remarks, which will help appreciate the arguments of this chapter, we now take up the verses one-by-one.

१५.१. पुरुषार्थाः हि चत्वारः प्रेयस्तेषामर्थः कामः ।
तथा धर्मश्च मोक्षश्च श्रेयः प्रसंगात् वर्णितौ ।।
puruṣārthāḥ hi catvāraḥ preyasteṣāmarthaḥ kāmaḥ
tathā dharmaśca mokṣaśca śreyaḥ prasaṁgāt varṇitau

It is well-known that the Hindu tradition speaks of four Puruṣārthas, namely, artha, kāma, dharma, mokṣa. The first two Puruṣārthas taken together—artha meaning wealth, and kāma meaning pleasure—can also be called preyas, meaning 'the pleasant'. Similarly, the third and the fourth Puruṣārthas taken together—dharma meaning moral value, and mokṣa meaning salvation—can be called śreyas, meaning 'the good'. However, depending on the context, śreyas can denote dharma alone, or mokṣa alone, or dharma and mokṣa together.

The correspondence between the four Puruṣārthas, on the one hand, and the two broad goals—preyas and śreyas—on the other, has been studied by several scholars. Here we have largely utilized the study by Mishra.[7]

१५.२. प्रेयः कठोपनिषदि न वाञ्छितं हि धीमता ।
स्वीकृतिः किं तु गीतायाः धर्माविरुद्धरूपेण ।।
preyaḥ kaṭhopaniṣadi na vāñchitaṁ hi dhīmatā
svīkṛtiḥ kiṁ tu gītāyāḥ dharmāviruddharūpeṇa

The two goals—śreyas and preyas—are highlighted in the dialogue between Yama and Nachiketa in the Kaṭhopaniṣad. Śreyas, meaning good, is presented there as the choice of the wise, while Preyas, meaning pleasant, is presented as the choice of the unwise. However, the Gita modified this view. Although it did not use the term 'preyas', it recognized the importance of its components—artha and kāma—provided that they are in conformity with dharma.

The phrase 'dharmāviruddhaḥ' used in this verse has been taken from the Gita śloka VII.11.

१५.३. न्यायेनार्जितोऽर्थस्तथा दुरुपयोगवर्जितः ।
दत्तः त्रस्तवर्गहिते प्राप्तव्यः संजयमते ।।
nyāyenārijito'rthastathā durupayogavarjitaḥ

dattaḥ trastavargahite prāptavyaḥ saṁjayamate

The Gita's approach to the question of wealth and prosperity can be summarized by saying that, subject to three conditions, the effort to earn money is fully justified. The first condition is that the wealth is earned by just means. Secondly, there is no misuse of wealth, for example, no consumption of drugs and other harmful things, no anti-social display of wealth, no arrogance, no hoarding of wealth nor attachment thereto, and no donation to unjust causes. Thirdly, after utilizing a reasonable portion of wealth for personal and family needs, the rest is spent for just social causes, and particularly to help the poor, oppressed people.

The above conditions are based on statements that occur in the Gita in chapters sixteen, seventeen, eighteen, seven and eleven. For example, Śrī Kṛṣṇa tells Arjuna in śloka XI.33: enjoy a prosperous kingdom but consider yourself to be an instrument of the Divine, that is, free from egotism as if you are the doer. Acquisition of wealth by unjust means is characterized as demoniac in śloka XVI.12. Śrī Kṛṣṇa's warning against donating wealth to unjust causes is contained in śloka XVII.22, a reference to which has been made in chapter fourteen also.

The Gita's positive attitude towards 'artha' has been interpreted by Lokasaṁgrha-activists as well as scholars as an encouragement to a productivity-oriented approach to the socio-economic problems of the modern society. Śrī Ramakrishna told his disciple Naren (the future Vivekananda) that "religion is not for empty bellies".[8] As a follow-up of that, productive activities for bringing about rural uplift were included in the work-programme of the Ramakrishna Mission.[9] Indira Rothermund also suggests possibilities for arousing poor villagers to give up their passivity and to engage themselves in productive effort :

> The Indian farmers could be persuaded to put in greater effort to improve their lot by pointing out to them, for example, that Lord Krishna in the Gita had emphasized this type of activity.[10]

The 'constructive programme' of Mahatma Gandhi attached much importance to utilizing the productive capability of villagers, in Khadi and other village industries. Gandhi wanted that everyone should support these activities by purchasing their products, even if, in strictly economic terms, they were more expensive than imported or mill-made items. Symbolically, Khadi became the backbone of the independence struggle, and as M.M. Verma puts it, "it produced common bonds of fraternity".[11]

The advice about the conditions that make wealth acceptable, although scattered in different ślokas of the Gita, is summarized in the last śloka thereof, where Sanjaya concludes his narration. Because of its usefulness as a summary, śloka XVIII.78 is quoted next.

१५.४. यत्र योगेश्वरः कृष्णो यत्र पार्थो धनुर्धरः ।
तत्र श्रीर्विजयो भूतिर्ध्रुवा नीतिर्मतिर्मम ॥
yatra yogeśvaraḥ kṛṣṇo yatra pārtho dhanurdharaḥ
tatra śrīrvijayo bhūtirdhruvā nītirmatirmama

Wherever there is Śrī Kṛṣṇa, the Lord of Yoga to give the Gita-teaching for the guidance of mankind, and there are people like Arjuna, the archer, to implement whole-heartedly and with full energy the Gita-teaching, then wonderful results like the following are sure to be achieved, namely, good fortune, victory, welfare, and a stable moral order.

Radhakrishanan has explained that this summarization includes the double purpose of human life, personal perfection and social efficiency:

The tremendous facts of life divine are: yoga, the realization of God through worship and entire submission to His will, and dhanuḥ or active participation in the furtherance of the cosmic plan. Spiritual vision and social service should go together. The double purpose of human life, personal perfection and social efficiency, is indicated here.[12]

१५.५. तथैव कामो निष्पापो नीतिन्यायसमर्थितः ।
शरीरयात्रापूरकः लोकयात्राहितेऽपि च ॥
tathaiva kāmo niṣpāpo nītinyāyasamarthitaḥ
śarīrayātrāpūrakaḥ lokayātrāhite'pi ca

Having stated the conditions which make Artha—wealth—acceptable, a similar look into Kāma—pleasure—is now presented. According to the Gita, Kāma can play a useful role in the world, and particularly as an essential part of every householder's duty to achieve an appropriate population balance, provided that it (Kāma) is regulated by Dharma and is in conformity with ethical, moral and legal standards. In fact, such Kāma constitutes a part of what are called now-a-days 'basic needs', and which, in the Gita śloka III.8, is denoted by 'Śarīrayātrā'. We want to draw attention not only to 'Śarīrayātrā'—which is essentially individual-based—but also to its counterpart at the social level, namely 'Lokayātrā' or the basic needs of the whole society.

Kāma meaning pleasure represents psychological value. Hiriyanna interprets Gita's approach to Kāma as drawing a line between Kāma as a value and Kāma as a disvalue, because, says Hiriyanna, "Not everything desired is necessarily desirable".[13] That variety of Kāma—but not any other—is a true value which is in accord with the requirements of Dharma, the moral value. This conception of dharma as a regulative principle is stressed by Śrī Kṛṣṇa when he says in the second part of śloka VII.11 : "In beings I am the kāma which is not contrary to dharma, O Arjuna." This approach is relevant to social applications of the Gita, because if self-restraint is applied to kāma by householders, we would see (in developing countries like India) only a modest increase in population.

Another point mentioned in verse 15.5 refers to the inclusion of self-restrained kāma in "śarīrayātrā". This term, occurring in Gita śloka III.8, represents the maintenance of body, both physically and psychologically, or in other words, certain minimum levels of artha and kāma. A modern interpretation of śarīrayātra can be comparable to the basic needs approach, according to which priority should be given to the satisfaction of certain minimum needs of each family (including food, clothing, shelter, health, education, recreation). In that case, lokayātrā would include, besides the preceding items, the basic social needs also, like sanitation, energy and transport infrastructure, clean environment, opportunities for productive employment as well as cultural advancement, and commonly shared values which hold the society together.

१५.६. श्रेयोऽपि लक्ष्यं ज्ञातव्यं न केवलं वैयक्तिकं ।
सर्वमुक्तिरूपेण हि प्राप्तव्यं धर्मकर्मणा ॥

śreyo'pi lakṣyaṁ jñātavyaṁ na kevalaṁ vaiyaktikaṁ
sarvamuktirūpeṇa hi prāptavyaṁ dharmakarmaṇā

Having looked into the conditions which need to be fulfilled in connection with Artha and Kāma—or Preyas for short—we now consider the role of the remaining two Puruṣārthas, that is, Dharma and Mokṣa—or Śreyas for short. In regard to Dharma—meaning moral value—the Gita's emphasis is that this should help orient us to the right actions, also called sāttvika karma—as distinguished from rajas and tamas—and furthermore, to active participation in God's work—called matkarma by Śrī Kṛṣṇa. Finally, the ultimate goal of salvation—Mokṣa—should not be viewed as a narrow, personal bliss but rather as bliss for all—or sarvamukti as envisaged by Śrī Aurobindo, in the attainment of which the performance of duty in accordance with Dharma has a crucial role.[14]

The next verse, affirming that Lokasaṁgraha, or Lokārtha for short—to rhyme with Puruṣārtha—is essential for the completeness of the Puruṣārthas, can be called "Without Lokārtha Incompleteness of Puruṣārthas Declaration".

लोकार्थाद्विना पुरुषार्थानां अपूर्णत्वघोषणा

LOKĀRTHĀDVINĀ PURUṢĀRTHĀNĀṀ APŪRṆATVAGHOṢAṆĀ

१५.७. लोकसंग्रहकर्मणा प्राप्तव्यं श्रेयो नान्यथा ।
तस्मान्न लोकार्थाद्विना पूर्णत्वं पुरुषार्थानाम् ॥
lokasaṁgrahakarmaṇā prāptavyaṁ śreyo nānyathā
tasmānna lokārthādvinā pūrṇatvaṁ puruṣārthānām

The road to the ultimate goal—Śreyas or Mokṣa—goes through Lokasaṁgraha, and not otherwise. Therefore, the completeness of the Puruṣārthas is possible only when they include Lokārtha, that is Lokasaṁgraha, as an integral part thereof.

The unavoidable link between Mokṣa and Lokasaṁgraha has been pointed out by all the prominent leaders of social movements. For example, Swami Vivekananda coined the famous phrase "ātmano mokṣārthaṁ jagaddhitāya ca" which means that individual salvation and universal welfare can be achieved simultaneously by means of the service-oriented programme of the Ramakrishna Mission.[15]

Lokamanya Tilak summarized his Gita-rahasaya by declaring that "The Gita religion proclaims to everybody, though nominally to Arjuna: perform lifelong your several worldly duties according to your respective positions in life, desirelessly, for the universal good. . .because therein lies your happiness in this world and in the next".[16] The same message is contained in Mahatma Gandhi's statement: "For me the road to salvation lies through incessant toil in the service of my country and humanity".[17]

१५.८. धर्मेण हि समन्विताः पुरुषार्थाः लोकार्थश्च ।
धर्मात् प्रेयश्च लोकार्थः श्रेयो लोकहितधर्मात् ॥

dharmeṇa hi samanvitāḥ puruṣārthāḥ lokārthaśca
dharmāt preyaśca lokārthaḥ śreyo lokahitadharmāt

Dharma should be viewed as inclusive of Lokasaṁgraha. With this wider interpretation, Dharma helps harmonize the individual and social goals of life. The complete harmonization can be expressed in three stages. At the first stage, the individual goal—Preyas—is harmonized with Dharma, because both Artha and Kāma become sanctified through Dharma and then they are allotted their rightful place in the philosophy of life. At the second stage, Lokasaṁgraha is harmonized with Dharma in the sense that, as Iyer summarized Gandhi's thoughts:

"Dharma, in his view, has no meaning apart from Lokasaṁgraha, the welfare of the whole world".[18]

At the third stage, the individual goal—Śreyas—and the social goal—Lokasaṁgraha—are harmonized, because, as Vinoba says, both the goals can be achieved simultaneously from the same act of social service if performed in accordance with the teaching of the Gita:

The service that is being rendered to the world through my external actions can itself, viewed from within, be described as spiritual exercise. The service of creation and the development of the spirit do not demand two different courses of action; service and spiritual growth are not different things. For both, the effort made, and the action performed is the same."[19]

CHAPTER SIXTEEN

पारिवारिकसम्बन्धात् दायित्वभावदर्शनम्
PĀRIVĀRIKASAMBANDHĀT DĀYITVABHĀVADARŚANAM

LEARNING ABOUT SOCIAL RESPONSIBILITY FROM FAMILY RELATIONSHIPS

The aim of this book is to convey the Lokasaṁgraha message of the Gita, in a language that can be understood and appreciated by modern readers. An important element in this message is the inculcation of a sense of social responsibility in each individual. On a day-to-day basis, and as a simple checking device, it can be stated that, the more we hear the words "I don't care", the greater the lack of social responsibility. But in the current atmosphere threatened by growing individualism, we need to consider how people's attitudes can be changed so that they care more and more for other members of the society. This is obviously a sort of social education—formal as well as non-formal—and it can partly be given by the use of written materials and of the audio-visual aids. But perhaps the most effective way of learning about social responsibility is the impressions created by family relationships.

However, the families themselves are undergoing changes, because the new wave of individualism, expressed by the words "I don't care", is cutting at the root of family's sense of unity. Too much exposure to television—or dūradarśana in Sanskrit—which busy parents use as a substitute for parental company, is turning children away from healthy recreation, because several of the T.V. programmes are full of violence, sex crimes, and other harmful features. The adolescents—failing to get support and guidance at home—often run the risk of falling prey to "peer pressure", which is described by Ambati and Gomathi Rao as "the catch phrase for the litany of undesirable influences that seemingly have a strangle hold on the school yard".[1] In Sanskrit, we have conveyed this idea by the word 'kusanga' (meaning bad company).

We take the view that, to prevent the disintegration of families is important not only for family welfare and the proper bringing up of children but also because, on the children's part, a feeling of gratefulness towards parents for what they do can help inculcate a sense of social responsibility also.

Busy parents need to take appropriate action before it is too late. One possible way for them is to consider taking help from the family support system—not only the traditional form thereof as represented by a joint family or an extended family but also recent modifications made in it to suit modern conditions and attitudes. The family support system in modified forms is not a joint family arrangement for all matters; rather it seeks a co-ordinated effort for tackling selected, important issues like the care and upbringing of children. How such co-ordination is brought about varies from family to family. A suggestion is made in this chapter as to how the advantage of mutual family support in the proper bringing up of children can still be preserved if individualism is not carried to extremes. Possible benefits from the suggested approach will not only be at the family level, because the practical training in social responsibility imparted thereby can help save the society also from the impending dangers of disintegration. Hopefully, the words "I don't care" will then be heard less and less.

For purposes like the proper bringing up of children, the phrase 'family support system' can also include support groups made up of neighbours, friends, etc.

This chapter might appear to be unnecessary to those who have no memories or appreciation of what is called here "the family support system". It is suggested that such persons may read it as students of social history go through passages applicable to different social systems. In any case, no criticism is implied of those who do not believe in "the family support system"—hoping that they will be able to find other ways of strengthening the notions of mutual care and help, particularly in regard to the proper bringing up of children.

After this brief introduction, a verse-by-verse look into the arguments put forward in this chapter follows.

१६.१. पारिवारिकाः सम्बन्धाः मधुरकटुमिश्रिताः ।
परं तु तेभ्यः प्राप्तव्यं दायित्वभावदर्शनम् ॥

pārivārikāḥ sambandhāḥ madhurakaṭumiśritāḥ
paraṁ tu tebhyaḥ prāptavyaṁ dāyitvabhāvadarśanam

Family relationships are usually a mixture of sweet and bitter elements, but they can still play a useful role in imparting practical training in social responsibility.

१६.२. **देवानां प्रसंगादुक्ता भाषा स्तेनस्य गीतायाम् ।**
तैर्दत्तानप्रदायैभ्यो यो भुंक्ते स्तेन एंव सः ॥
devānāṁ prasaṁgāduktā bhāṣā stenasya gītāyām
tairdattānapradāyaibhyo yo bhuṁkte stena eva saḥ

In ślokas III.11-12, the Gita has defined the term "thief", in the context of an assumed relationship of give-and-take between human beings and gods. The second line of śloka III.12, which is quoted as the second line of the verse 16.2, literally means that one who enjoys what one has received, without giving anything in return, is verily a thief.

The use of the expression 'thief'—or stena in Sanskrit—might appear to some as being too strong. The idea behind it is not to generate controversy or conflict, but rather to draw attention to the inappropriateness of a one-way traffic, that is, of taking advantage but doing nothing in return.

१६.३. **देवतुल्यभावेनैव साहाय्यं मातृपितृभ्याम् ।**
आदौ गृह्णाति संततिः तस्मात् कालेन दायित्वम् ॥
devatulyabhāvenaiva sāhāyyaṁ mātṛpitṛbhyām
ādau gṛhṇāti saṁtatiḥ tasmāt kālena dāyitvam

Just as gods—to continue the idea of the preceding verse—give desired things to human beings, and the Gita advises human beings to give something in return, similarly parents give assistance to children, who should, in return, feel—voluntarily, and not half-heartedly—that they too will have a responsibility towards parents when the appropriate time comes.

The Gita believes that only those actions which are within one's competence and capability, and which are done willingly and voluntarily can be called sāttvika (ślokas XVIII.23-25 and

XVII.20-22). Śrī Kṛṣṇa's final advice to Arjuna was: Having reflected on my words fully, do as thou choosest (śloka XVIII.63). Of course, the Gita does not support the abandonment of one's duty because of improper thinking or on grounds of unwillingness to work hard (ślokas XVIII. 7-9).

१६.४. आयुभेदात् मूल्यभेदात् त्यक्तं तु चेत् तद्दायित्वम् ।
गीताशिक्षानुसारेण ज्ञातव्या स्तेनवृत्तिः सा ॥

āyubhedāt mūlyabhedāt tyaktaṁ tu cet taddāyitvam
gītāśikṣānusāreṇa jñātavyā stenavṛttiḥ sā

In continuation of the preceding statement, if members of the new generation want to forget about their responsibility, on one plea or the other—for example, arguing on the basis of a generation gap or a changed value system—then, according to the Gita, such persons are adopting the attitude of a "thief".

The argument that the parents did for their children and we too are doing for our children, can also be viewed as an excuse for forgetting their responsibility. Similarly about the plea that the parents were guided by what gave them pleasure, and so no responsibility is generated thereby on the part of children.

१६.५. दूरदर्शनात् बालानां कुसंगात्तु युवकानाम् ।
सात्त्विकगुणनाशनं न रुचिः पितृमूल्येषु ॥

dūradarśanāt bālānāṁ kusaṁgāttu yuvakānām
sāttvikaguṇanāśanaṁ na ruciḥ pitṛmūlyeṣu

A plea commonly put forward is that the new generation wants independence or liberty, above everything else, and that, if parents are too busy, then children have to be left with baby sitters—who often take extensive help of television. Adolescents, under similar circumstances, say Ambati and Gomathi Rao "start to stay out late, sport unconventional hairstyles and clothes, disobey their parents, and so on, . . .as if derailed by the wayward influences of 'peer pressure' ".[2] According to us, these are indications of a loss of 'sāttvika virtues', and they show that the younger people have no real interest in the values that appeal to the parents. Therefore, even acts of service that the younger people can do for their parents can only be such as do not infringe on the new generation's liberty. Under these circumstances, it must be recognized that whatever is done half-heartedly, in an atmosphere of conflict, cannot possibly contribute much to the family's happiness.

The disrespect towards the traditional values, shown by the younger generation—without trying to understand the good points thereof—pained Swami Vivekananda. He himself never demanded blind adherence to evil practices in the name of tradition. But he was equally opposed to a blanket denunciation of India's past—because he considered it as a blind imitation of the West. Kulandaival has summarized Swami Vivekananda's views on the pitiable condition of such a blind imitator of the West:

> He laughs at the ancient sages. All Hindu thoughts to him are arrant trash, philosophy, mere childish prattle, and religion, the superstition of fools. He wants to imitate the West in his daily life and in his thought and actions. Anything coming from the West is good to him. This kind of imitation never makes for progress. It is a sign of aweful degradation of man. When a man begins to hate himself and is ashamed of his ancestors, the end has come.[3]

१६.६. अष्टादशायुप्राप्ते चेत् उच्चरेत् पूर्णस्वातंत्र्यम् ।
कर्तव्यविनाधिकारं तस्मात् का दायित्वशिक्षा ॥
aṣṭādaśāyuprāpte cet uccaret pūrṇasvātantryam
kartavyavinādhikāraṁ tasmāt kā dāyitvaśikṣā

The legal age of attaining maturity is, in many societies, eighteen years. If children take the view that, as soon as they are eighteen, they are "independent" in the sense that they have the right to do what they want, they are likely to ignore that they have certain duties and responsibilities also. Social norms are then set aside, and although the newly "mature" persons may feel they are doing all this for their own happiness, the actual results might be quite different. In any case, we should not expect that such an attitude can facilitate any training in social responsibility.

१६.७. लक्ष्यं बालपालनस्य सुपात्रगुणवर्धनम् ।
रक्षणं मादकद्रव्यात् हिंसाशस्त्रवृत्तिस्तु न ॥

lakṣyaṁ bālapālanasya supātraguṇavardhanam
rakṣaṇaṁ mādakadravyāt hiṁsāśastravṛttistu na

The advantages of the family support system are particularly felt when children are growing up. At that time, if both parents are working, the children are likely to remain without proper supervision, and there is a risk that they might fall in bad company that uses drugs or carries weapons. The family support system can help minimize this risk; it can also help inculcate in the children values and qualities that will make them good citizens. These are important gains, not only for the family but also for the society as a whole. It might not be a bad bargain if individualism is partly, and voluntarily, given up in the interest of a proper bringing up of children.

The "success story" of Asian Americans—attributed in large measure to the family support system—was identified by William Peterson in 1966, as symbolized by the following four criteria of success and exemplary behaviour:

(i) high educational attainment levels,
(ii) high median family incomes,
(iii) low crime rates, and
(iv) absence of juvenile delinquency and mental health problems.[4]

१६.८. ऋणभावः चेन्मात्रे च पित्रे सर्ववरेभ्यश्च ।
कर्तव्यभावादेतस्मात् सात्त्विकमूल्यवर्धनम् ।।

ṛṇabhāvaḥ cenmātre ca pitre sarvavarebhyaśca
kartavyabhāvādetasmāt sāttvikamūlyavardhanam

If children grow up with a feeling that they are grateful and indebted to their parents and other members of the family who brought them up, then they are likely to attach as much importance to their duties as they do to their rights. This will help inculcate what we can call 'sāttvika social values' in them—the adjective 'sāttvika' being used to emphasize the high ethical standards of the values that we want the children to grow up with.

As we mentioned in the introductory explanation given in the beginning of chapter fifteen, Hiriyanna finds a close correspondence between 'social values' and 'other-regarding virtues'. Usually, the lists of virtues given in the Gita include both the 'self-regarding' and the 'other-regarding' virtues because they are viewed as inter-connected. For example, ślokas XVI.1-3 list as many as twenty-six virtues under the title "daivī sampat" or divine endowments. Broadly guided by these and other virtues highlighted in the Gita, Lokasaṁgraha-activists, facing challenges of a varied nature, identified in their own way—depending on the urgent needs of the time—virtues or values on a selective basis. For example, Swami Vivekananda emphasized the importance of 'unselfishness', 'fearlessness', and 'spirit of dedicated service to the needy'. Lokamanya Tilak and Śrī Aurobindo, fully recognizing the supreme value of these three virtues, added thereto two more, namely 'respect for the values which have held the society together' and 'willingness to suffer for a just cause'—the latter assuming particular significance in the light of their confrontation with the British Empire.

Mahatma Gandhi did not deny the importance of the virtues identified by his predecessors, but added 'truth' and 'non-violence' to the list—almost placing non-violence on the top. Vinoba Bhave, carrying on the Gandhian approach in the socio-economic field, added 'sharing inspired by a feeling of equality' to the virtues or values highlighted by the Lokasaṁgraha-activists who had come before him.

An important implication of the general approach adopted by the above-mentioned leaders of social action is that selection of the values can, and should, be made to face newer and newer challenges as they come. This means updating the Lokasaṁgraha ideal. Ursula King attaches much significance to such updating. To the original ideal exemplified by King Janaka and Śrī Kṛṣṇa in the Gita, says Ursula King, the modifications made by new interpreters like Gandhi "are a sign of the creativity of Hinduism and of its religious activity, sensitive to the needs of modern man".[5]

The next verse, highlighting the possibility of learning about social responsibility from family relationships, can be called "Social Responsibility Declaration"

दायित्वभावघोषणा
DĀYITVABHĀVAGHOṢAṆĀ

१६.९. न केवलं स्वजनेभ्यः तथैव सर्वलोकाय ।
दायित्वभावः प्राप्तव्यो भूतानां साहाय्यं प्रति ॥
na kevalaṁ svajanebhyaḥ tathaiva sarvalokāya
dāyitvabhāvaḥ prāptavyo bhūtānāṁ sāhāyyaṁ prati

A sense of duty to family members can gradually make one inclined to accept partial responsibility towards the society at large, and particularly towards the weaker sections of the society who need help. If family relationships can thus help promote a sense of social responsibility among family members, it would imply a significant contribution to the good of the society at large.

१६.१०. युवकानां स्वातंत्र्यं च बालपालने साफल्यम् ।
संतुलनं द्विपक्षयोः लोकसंग्रहसाधनम् ॥
yuvakānāṁ svātantryaṁ ca bālapālane sāphalyam
santulanaṁ dvipakṣayoḥ lokasaṁgrahasādhanam

What is needed is a balance between two objectives, namely, young people's desire for independence, on the one hand, and a successful bringing up of children, on the other. Efforts to achieve such a balance can bring in gains, not only at the family level but also for the society as a whole, because of inculcation of a sense of duty to family members, initially, and a sense of responsibility to the needy members of the society, as an extension thereof. The family support system, if properly implemented, can thus contribute to Lokasaṁgraha.

Those who advocate young people's desire for independence donot recognize adequately the need for anyone to ask oneself the question: What will be the impact of my action or inaction on other members of the family or the society? However, the Lokasaṁgraha concept of the Gita starts with the raising of this question. Swami Vivekananda illustrated this by pointing out the 'responsibility' of mothers to ensure that, by leading a 'pure life'—free from drugs, for example—they would give birth to healthy babies. "So long as you live in society", said Vivekananda, "it is your responsibility to prevent the very birth of evil".[6]

Swami Vivekananda also wanted the richer sections of the society to recognize that they are at least partly responsible to help those whose ancestors suffered at the hands of their forefathers. We cannot pretend to ignore history, said Vivekananda, and behave as if we are starting on a clean slate. He outlined the purposes of recalling the past and of rendering service in the present:

> . . . .to struggle unto life and death to bring about a new state of things—sympathy for the poor and bread to their hungry mouths, enlightenment to the people at large, and struggle unto death to make men of them who have been brought to the level of beasts by the tyranny of your forefathers.[7]

CHAPTER SEVENTEEN

अहंकारो रिपुर्महान्
AHAṀKĀRO RIPURMAHĀN

EGOTISM—A GREAT ENEMY OF LOKASAṀGRAHA

In the preceding chapter it was argued that extremes of individualism can come in the way of imparting practical training to the new generation in regard to social responsibility. A comparable theme in the Gita is that egotism is a great enemy of Lokasaṁgraha. The destructive role of "egotism" in relation to "Lokasaṁgraha" is viewed to be as serious as that of "attachment" in relation to "Śreyas". Since Śreyas and Lokasaṁgraha can be identified as the two most important goals of life according to the Gita, a close look into the two respective enemies—attachment and egotism—is obviously necessary. Attachment to the fruits of one's action has received particular attention in the Gita, and the remedy suggested is samatva, or even-mindedness in success or failure after having put in one's best effort. A summary of the main ideas on this topic has been included in this book, for example in the first part of chapter five, and in other places also wherever considered necessary. Egotism has also been referred to, for example in chapter six. Nevertheless, it is felf that, before presenting a brief summary of the whole book (in the next chapter which is also the concluding chapter), a separate chapter should be devoted to egotism. Hence the present chapter.

१७.१. लोकसंग्रहे संलग्नमहंकारो रिपुर्महान् ।
अहंकारविमूढात्मा कर्ताहमिति मन्यते ॥

lokasaṁgrahe saṁlagnamahaṁkāro ripurmahān
ahaṁkāravimūḍhātmā kartāhamiti manyate

The Lokasaṁgraha-teaching is, within the Gita, first given in ślokas III.20-26. And immediately thereafter, that is, in śloka III.27, a warning is given about the damage to Lokasaṁgraha that can be caused by Ahaṁkāra—egotism. The second line of śloka III.27 is quoted here as the second line of the verse 17.1, and its literal translation is: He whose soul is bewildered by ahaṁkāra thinks 'I am the doer'. "A sense of self-importance", says Hiriyanna, "is ruinous", because as soon as it arises in one's mind, one starts expecting gains for oneself in the form of honour, high position, money or other rewards.[1] But this cuts at the very root of what the Gita presents as Lokasaṁgraha—because the Gita's technique is Niṣkāma Karma, that is, no desire for selfish gains. Hence egotism should be recognised as a great enemy of Lokasaṁgraha.

The Gita advice against having a sense of self-importance does not mean giving up self-confidence. The need for guarding against the risk of self-importance is stressed in the Gita, not only in the context of karmayoga, but also—and perhaps more so—for the Jñānins or persons giving primary place to knowledge. For example, Gita ślokas XIII.7-11, which list as many as twenty virtues of a jñānin, place at the head of the list 'amānitvam' meaning humility or freedom from vanity. The same idea is conveyed through the popular saying: vidyā dadāti vinayam (knowledge leads to humility).

While recognizing this, Swami Vivekananda wanted for his movement "men with self-confidence, men who believe in themselves":

> What we want is muscles of iron and nerves of steel. We have wept long enough. No more weeping, but stand on your feet and be men. . . Men, men, these are wanted: everything else will be ready, but strong, vigorous, believing young men, sincere to the backbone, are wanted. A hundred such and the world becomes revolutionized. . .[2]

The next verse, which is based on Gita śloka XVI.18, and which presents a sort of a chain linking Ahaṁkāra to Hatred in society, can be called "From Ahaṁkāra to Hatred Declaration".

अहंकारजनितद्वेषघोषणा
AHAṀKĀRAJANITADVEṢAGHOṢAṆĀ

१७.२. अहंकारं बलं दर्पं कामं क्रोधं च संश्रिताः ।
प्रद्विषन्तः प्राह कृष्णो मामात्मपरदेहेषु ॥

ahaṁkāraṁ balaṁ darpaṁ kāmaṁ krodhaṁ ca saṁśritāḥ
pradviṣantaḥ prāha kṛṣṇo māmātmaparadeheṣu

How does Ahaṁkāra—accepting that egotism is a vice—adversely affect Lokasaṁgraha? An answer to this question is available from śloka XVI.18 of the Gita, most of which is quoted here in verse 17.2—a slight re-arrangement being made here to mention specifically the words "prāha kṛṣṇo" to remind the reader that this was spoken by Śrī Kṛṣṇa. Five vices are put together in a sequence in this verse—starting from egotism, the other four vices being force, insolence, lust and anger. Śrī Kṛsṇa says that, given over to egotism, etc., malicious people despise Me dwelling in the bodies of themselves and others. We feel justified in characterizing this description as a "chain of vices"—starting from egotism, and proceeding through force, insolence, lust and anger, ultimately leading to hatred—dveṣa—between different members of the human society. The same chain of hatred is repeated by Śrī Kṛṣṇa in śloka XVIII.53 with the advice: Get rid of this chain of hatred and be even-minded towards all people—samaḥ sarveṣu bhūteṣu—that is, work for Lokasaṁgraha.

In the introductory part of this chapter, we mentioned that the Gita-remedy for attachment is samatva or even-mindedness in all situations, that is, irrespective of success or failure. Such 'samatva'—also called by us in chapter five as 'samatva of the first category'—leads us to 'Śreyas'. In the closing sentence of the preceding paragraph, we have mentioned the 'second category' of samatva or even-mindedness towards all people. Such 'samatva' or 'sāmya' leads us to Lokasaṁgraha.

We have presented above the harm done to Lokasaṁgraha, by hatred resulting from egotism. This is in line with Mahatma Gandhi's statement: "Had violence, that is, hate, ruled us, we should have become extinct long ago. . . It is no non-violence if we merely love those that love us. It is non-violence only when we love those that hate us. . ."[3]

The "chain of vices"—from egotism to hatred—has, in the Gita, another parallel "chain of vices"—from attachment to unhappiness and destruction. It seems useful to examine why two chains of vices are mentioned rather than one.

The first chain of vices, presented in ślokas II.62-63 of the Gita, is shown below—the chain starting from attachment to objects of pleasure, and ending in unhappiness and destruction:

When a man dwells in his mind on the objects of sense, attachment to them is produced. From attachment springs desire and from desire comes anger. From anger comes delusion, from delusion loss of memory, and from loss of memory, the destruction of intelligence, and from the destruction of intelligence he perishes.

Now we ask the question: Why two chains? A simple answer is that, since Śreyas and Lokasaṁgraha are the two most important goals in the Gita, the first chain is relevant mainly to those whose goal is Śreyas—salvation, while the second chain is relevant mainly to those whose goal is Lokasaṁgraha—the good of the society.

१७.३. अहंकारजनितेन नष्टं सत्कर्म द्वेषेण ।
कर्ता सात्त्विको गीतायां मुक्तसंगोऽनहंवादी
ahaṁkārajanitena naṣṭaṁ satkarma dveṣeṇa
kartā sāttviko gītāyāṁ muktasaṁgo'nahaṁvādī

Once a person comes under the influence of egotism, then the chain of vices mentioned in the preceding verse gets into motion, leading up to hatred between different members of the human society. In such a condition, it becomes practically impossible to perform what the Gita calls "sāttvika karma", that is, ethically correct, unselfish actions for Lokasaṁgraha. That is why the Gita has highlighted two characteristics of a sāttvika worker, first that he or she is free from attachment to the fruits of one's actions, and secondly that he or she is free from egotism.

१७.४. अहंकारं कथं दूरं कुर्यात् लोकहितकर्ता ।
कर्मसमर्पणरूपा दर्शिता विधिः कृष्णेन ॥
ahaṁkāraṁ kathaṁ dūraṁ kuryāt lokahitakartā
karmasamarpaṇarūpā darśitā vidhiḥ kṛṣṇena

Egotism was first specified by Śrī Kṛṣṇa, in śloka III.27, as a great enemy of Lokasaṁgraha. Arjuna naturally would then want to know the right method by which a Lokasaṁgraha-worker could free oneself from egotism. In anticipation of this, Śrī Kṛṣṇa indicated in the Gita a relatively easy way by which one can achieve freedom from egotism. The best method, according to Śrī Kṛṣṇa, of freeing oneself from egotism is "karma-samarpaṇam", that is, to dedicate all actions to God. Śrī Kṛṣṇa refers to this method several times in the Gita—an indication of how important this is considered by Him. The first reference comes in śloka III.30, that is, immediately after egotism is identified in śloka III.27 as a great enemy of Lokasaṁgraha. For ready reference, a translation of śloka III.30 follows:

Dedicating all thy works to me, with thy consciousness fixed in the Self, being free from desire and egotism, fight, delivered from thy fever. (III.30). Perhaps it should be clarified that the expression 'fight' has been used in the Gita (for example, in śloka VIII.7 also) to convey the advice 'do thy duty or svadharma'.

१७.५. यत्करोषि यदश्नासि यज्जुहोषि ददासि यत् ।
यत्तपस्यसि कौन्तेय तत्कुरुष्व मदर्पणम् ॥

yatkaroṣi yadaśnāsi yajjuhoṣi dadāsi yat
yattapasyasi kaunteya tatkuruṣva madarpaṇam

The most well-known śloka of the Gita containing the teaching on karma-samarpaṇam is IX.27 which is quoted here as verse 17.5, and which can be translated as follows:

Whatever thou doest, whatever thou eatest, whatever thou sacrificest, whatever thou givest away, whatever austerities thou dost practice, do that, O Arjuna, as an offering to Me. (IX.27).

The act of dedication is a harmonious combination of karmayoga and bhaktiyoga, and it has several important implications. For one thing, the person becomes free from egotism which is the starting point for the chain of hatred, as already referred to in verse 17.2. An attitude of samarpaṇam makes it easier to give up the desire for selfish gains or mamatva. Another great advantage is that one would feel the urge to do only sāttvika or pure deeds, because how can impure deeds by dedicated to God? This last point is taken up in the next verse.

१७.६. कृष्णार्पणभावकृतं निमित्तमात्रं यत्कर्म ।
अवश्यमेव निष्पापं निःस्वार्थं च जनहिते ॥

kṛṣṇārpaṇabhāvakṛtaṁ nimittamātraṁ yatkarma
avaśyameva niṣpāpaṁ niḥsvārthaṁ ca janahite

When we perform our duty with an attitude of dedication to God, we feel as if we are merely an instrument—nimittamātram—in the hands of God. In fact, karma-samarpaṇam and nimittamātram have been spoken of in the Gita as two terms conveying the same message of dedication to God. Regarding karma-samarpaṇam, the Gita śloka IX.27 has already been quoted above. The nimittamātram terminology is used in the Gita śloka XI.33. Verse 17.6 says that by dedicating our actions to God, we ensure two things. First, that the actions are pure, morally right, because no one would feel like dedicating impure deeds to God. Secondly, the actions would be unselfish and would contribute to the good of the society. As Mahatma Gandhi specified an important condition for resorting to Satyagraha:

"Satyagraha cannot be resorted to for personal gain, but only for the good of others".[4]

In the Gita, the idea of dedicating one's actions to God—karma-samarpaṇam—is extended to what Śrī Aurobindo calls 'surrender without reservations' or 'samarpaṇam of sarvadharmān'. Such complete dedication, according to Aurobindo, leads to 'universal good' or Lokasṁgraha:

The Gita indicates that the surrender must be without reservations; our Yoga, our life, our state of inner being must be determined freely by the living Infinite, not predetermined by our mind's insistence on this or that dharma or any dharma. . .An Almighty Power will take up our virtue and sin, our right and wrong, our strength and our weakness, cast away their tangled figures, sarvadharmān parityajya, and transform all into its transcendent purity and universal good and infallible force. . .[5]

१७.७. यत्रेश्वरार्पितबुद्धिः सात्त्विकरूपं कर्म च ।
कथं न लक्ष्यप्राप्तिर्हि कर्ता चेत् दृढनिश्चयः ॥

yatreśvarārpitabuddhiḥ sāttvikarūpaṁ karma ca

kathaṁ na lakṣyaprāptirhi kartā cet dṛḍhaniścayaḥ

What are the chances of success when Lokasaṁgraha-actions are performed with an attitude of karma-samarpaṇam? A reply is given in verse 17.7, namely, when sāttvika actions are done with an attitude of dedication to God, there should be no doubt about the ultimate achievement of the objective—the good of the society—provided the persons performing those actions have a firm determination.

Mahatma Gandhi's Satyagraha-based non-violent struggle for India's political independence lasted twenty-eight years—from 1919 till 1947—and there were ups and downs, but he maintained all the time, even in the face of stiff opposition, that "there is no such thing as defeat in non-violence; the end of violence is surest defeat".[6]

Some people raise the question: On the one hand, the Gita advises us not to hanker after the fruits of our actions, and on the other hand, Gita-followers have a firm faith in the success of non-violent struggles. Isn't there an element of inconsistency? The answer is "No", and perhaps it is best to refer again to Mahatma Gandhi's explanation as to how the two parts of the statement preceding the specification of the question can be mutually reconciled. Before quoting Gandhi's actual words, it may be clarified that renouncing the fruit does not imply doing the work carelessly or unscientifically; nor does it imply any insistence on throwing away the fruit when it comes as a natural consequence of effort. Now to quote Mahatma Gandhi:

> Renunciation of fruit in no way means indifference to the result. In regard to every action one must know the result that is expected to follow, the means thereto, and the capacity for it. He who, being thus equipped is without desire for the result and is yet wholly engrossed in the due fulfilment of the task before him is said to have renounced the fruits of his action.
>
> Again let no one consider renunciation to mean want of fruit for the renouncer. The Gita reading does not warrant such a meaning. Renunciation means absence of hankering after fruit. As a matter of fact, he who renounces reaps a thousandfold.[7]

The conditions under which non-violent activists maintain faith in the ultimate success of their cause must be clearly understood. Gandhi himself warned against the risk of Satyāgraha turning into durāgraha (evil force):

> Satyāgrahis must not transgress the limits prescribed by wisdom and appreciation of their own capacity. Satyāgraha offered on every occasion, seasonable or otherwise, would be corrupted into durāgraha. And if any one takes to Satyāgraha without having measured his own strength and afterwards sustains defeat, he not only disgraces himself but he also brings the matchless weapon of Satyāgraha into disrepute by his folly.[8]

१७.८. त्यक्ताहंकारः एव यो न तं विद्धि निस्तेजं हि ।
अनहंवादी गीतायां धृत्युत्साहसमन्वितः ॥
tyaktāhaṁkāraḥ ėva yo na taṁ viddhi nistejaṁ hi
anahaṁvādī gītāyāṁ dhṛtyutsāhasamanvitaḥ

This verse refers to the fact that opponents of non-violent struggles often under-estimate the capacity and inner strength of such activists. But a sāttvika doer—according to the Gita śloka XVIII.26 which is partly quoted in this verse—is not only free from egotism but also "full of resolution and zeal".

Mahatma Gandhi often quoted the Hindu Rishi who said that "Violence vanishes before Ahiṁsā".[9] The basis of this statement must have been either the Rishi's own experience or the experience of other Rishis, in facing violence with non-violent means. The more violent the aggressor, the firmer the practice of Ahiṁsā required to bring about an abandonment of violence. Cultivation of the virtue of Ahiṁsā to such an extent may need long practice. Also, a non-violent person is willing to lay down one's life in a an attempt to win over the heart of the aggressor. Hindus read from ancient scriptures the glorious example of the seer Dadhīchi who laid down his life to protect the society, of king Shibi who risked his life to save the life of a dove, of Prahlād and Sudhavnā who went through untold ordeals, and of Muni Nārada who won over a robber by his non-violence. In the middle ages, the history of Vaiṣṇava saints provides many examples of evil appearing on the path of good but melting away by the love of the saints. Śrī Chaitanyadeva, an apostle of Vaiṣṇavism, remained calm and offered his love to the ruffian who violently struck him. Similar instances of the successful use of non-violence, in extremely difficult situations, by great personalities are available from Buddhist and Jain literature also. To underestimate the potential strength of Gita-followers is therefore not justified.

१७.९. निरहंकारभावेन सहयोगसंवर्धनः ।
शक्यं तेनैव भावेन लोकसंग्रहकार्यं हि ॥
nirahaṁkārabhāvena sahayogasaṁvardhanaḥ
śakyaṁ tenaiva bhāvena lokasaṁgrahakāryaṁ hi

Other than the spirit of determination and the faith in success that characterize the Lokasaṁgraha-activists, the fact that they are free from egotism also helps strengthen their attitudes of cooperation and unity amongst themselves. As already stressed in verses 17.2-3, egotism causes hatred amongst different members of the society, so chances of mutual cooperation and unity are relatively greater in the absence of egotism. This obviously contributes to their efficiency in the performance of the tasks that they take in hand to promote Lokasaṁgraha.

CHAPTER EIGHTEEN

उपसंहाररूपेण लोकसंग्रहसप्तकम्
UPASAṀHĀRARŪPEṆA LOKASAṀGRAHASAPTAKAM

CONCLUDING STATEMENT ON LOKASAMGRAHA IN SEVEN VERSES

The purpose of this concluding chapter is to present a seven-verse-summarization of the Lokasaṁgraha message of the Gita in a form that can be understood relatively easily as well as appreciated by modern readers. The first verse of the chapter is of an introductory nature, following which come the seven summarizing verses. The number "seven" in this context has a symbolic significance as well, because the original Lokasaṁgraha message in the Gita has been given in seven ślokas, namely III.20.26. It is worth recalling here what Śrī Aurobindo wrote about these seven verses in his "Essays on the Gita":

> There are few more important passages in the Gita than these seven striking couplets.[1]

१८.१. उपसंहाररूपेण शृण्वन्तु श्रीगीतासारम् ।
धारयन्तं नवरूपं लोकसंग्रहसप्तकम् ॥

upasaṁhārarūpeṇa śrṇvantu śrīgītāsāram
dhārayantaṁ navarūpaṁ lokasaṁgrahasaptakam

Listen, O well-wishers of humanity, we would now like to make a concluding statement so as to summarize the Lokasaṁgraha message of the Gita in seven verses. We have attempted to present this message in a form that can appeal to modern readers, but we must remember that Lokasaṁgraha, according to us, is a potentially dynamic social ideal—and not a static one—because it can be updated from time to time, according to the changing needs of the society. In our opinion, this can be viewed as containing the essence of the Gita-teaching of which the modern society is in the greatest need.

After this introductory statement are presented the seven verses.

लोकसंग्रहसप्तकम्

LOKASAṀGRAHASAPTAKAM

१८.२. त्रस्तजनवर्गरक्षा लोकसंग्रहकार्यं हि ।
तथैव सेवा दीनानां संघर्षो न्यायप्राप्तये ।।
trastajanavargarakṣā lokasaṁgrahakāryaṁ hi
tathaiva sevā dīnānāṁ saṁgharṣo nyāyaprāptaye

In what forms or types of activities have Lokasaṁgraha-oriented tasks found their expression in modern times? We want to draw pointed attention to six such forms. First, the Lokasaṁgraha-activists have tried to protect innocent groups of people from being killed by oppressors under one pretext or the other, such protection being brought about by changing the beliefs of the oppressors.[2] Secondly, they have created voluntary organizations to render selfless service to the poor and the needy.[3] Thirdly, they have organized mass movements to put an end to gross violation of social justice.[4]

१८.३. सात्त्विकतपसाधनं यथाशक्यमहिंसा च ।
स्वलाभात् स्वजनहितात् परं लक्ष्यं सर्वहितम् ॥
sāttvikatapasādhanaṁ yathāśakyamahiṁsā ca
svalābhāt svajanahitāt paraṁ lakṣyaṁ sarvahitam

Fourthly, the Lokasaṁgraha-activists have not only observed 'sāttvika tapas' themselves, but have also inspired, encouraged and trained large numbers of people to do the same, so that they can successfully work for the good of the society as well as for their own salvation.[5] Fifthly, Gita-followers having themselves realized the importance and feasibility of non-violent methods for Lokasaṁgraha activities, they have tried to make Ahiṁsā generally acceptable as the Yuga-dharma so that the society and the world can be saved from the impending dangers of mutual destruction.[6] Sixthly, they have taken in hand the important task of changing the attitudes and values of the people so that their goal in life may be not merely their own gains nor merely narrow family or group gains but the good of the whole society.

The specification of the above-mentioned six Lokasaṁgraha-tasks is based largely on the selective narration of the Gita-applications made in Part Two of this book, for example, one item from each of the five case studies, and the last item representing the common educative attempt of all the five leaders. Obviously, this summarization should be viewed only as illustrative, and by no means a complete listing of the tasks that await the attention of Lokasaṁgraha-activists. For example, this list does not include environmental protection, which according to Arapura, calls for greater support in the years to come.[7] For a more comprehensive list than the one presented here, reference may be made to the author's earlier—but more detailed—book, *The Social Role of the Gita: How and Why.* The following ten aspects of Lokasaṁgraha are discussed there:

(i) Protective aspect
(ii) Productive aspect
(iii) Service aspect
(iv) Stability aspect
(v) Self-help aspect
(vi) Responsibility aspect
(vii) Niṣkāma aspect
(viii) Ethical aspect
(ix) Cohesive aspect
(x) Educative aspect[8]

१८.४. स्वार्थमात्रं तामसिकं स्वजनसीमां राजसम् ।
सात्त्विकं लोकसंग्रहं ज्ञेयं सारं समासतः ॥

svārthamātraṁ tāmasikaṁ svajanasīmāṁ rājasam
sāttvikaṁ lokasaṁgrahaṁ jñeyaṁ sāraṁ samāsataḥ

This verse has been inspired by the favourite Gita technique of using the sattva-rajas-tamas classification to recommend one line of thought and/or action, in preference to one or more alternatives. The thought etc. which is recommended is characterized as "sāttvika" (god or divine), and the alternatives as "tāmasika" (bad or devilish), or "rājasa" (worldly or in between the good and the bad). This threefold classification has been applied in the Gita to as many as twelve concepts (śraddhā, āhāra, yajña, tapas, dānam, tyāga, jñāna, karma, kartā, buddhi, dhṛti, sukham). Obviously, it is not Śrī Kṛṣṇa's intention to restrict this type of threefold classification to these twelve concepts only. Rather the Gita-teaching on "buddhiyoga" means, in the present context, that the same technique of classification should be extended by us to new concepts also, with a view to deciding what is appropriate for us and what is not.

After having given the background, the content of the verse 18.4 can be explained. Since this book deals mainly with issues connected with the good of the society, the attitude of those people who think merely of their own selfish gains can be characterized as tāmasika, that is, most unhelpful to the society at large. Slightly better than this is the attitude of those people who want to benefit svajanam, that is, whom they consider their own people. However, their attitude is still narrow because they make a distinction between own people and others, and so we use the expression rājasa, or worldly, for them. Best of all are those who want to work for Lokasaṁgraha—the good of the whole society—that is, without discriminating between groups or subgroups based on relationships or other divisive considerations. The expression sāttvika, meaning good or divine, can be used for them. The statements made on the basis of verse 18.4 can be considered as containing the essence of the Gita-teaching.

१८.५. श्रेयोऽर्थं नरजीवनं साधनं लोकसंग्रहः ।
लोकसंग्रहे येनैव श्रेयो दृष्टं स दर्शकः ॥

śreyo'rthaṁ narajīvanaṁ sādhanaṁ lokasaṁgrahaḥ
lokasaṁgrahe yenaiva śreyo dṛṣṭaṁ sa darśakaḥ

But what about mokṣa, or salvation, which, according to Hinduism is the ultimate goal of life, and for which the term śreyas has also been used in the Upaniṣads and the Gita? Verse 18.5 says: Yes, śreyas is indeed the ultimate goal of human life, but Lokasaṁgraha—doing good to all—is the means for achieving śreyas. Our concentration should be on the means, that is, Lokasaṁgraha, and having done that, we need not worry about śreyas, because śreyas will automatically follow Lokasaṁgraha. One who uderstands and sees all this clearly can be called a person having the right vision.

Verse 18.5 has been inspired by Swami Vivekananda's famous Sanskrit phrase—ātmano mokṣārthaṁ jagaddhitāya ca—meaning that a monk of the Ramakrishna Order should simultaneously aim at achieving mokṣa for oneself and the good of the world.[9] Swami Vivekananda gave this motto in 1897 when he started the Ramakrishna Mission. A second source of inspiration for verse 18.5 is the following statement of Mahatma Gandhi in which he stressed the importance of sticking to the means—Lokasaṁgraha—and viewing it as the only road leading to mokṣa, or salvation:

> For me the road to salvation lies through incessant toil in the service of my country and humanity. I want to identify myself with everything that lives. I want to live at peace with both friend and foe. So my patriotism is for me a stage on my journey to the land of eternal freedom and peace.[10]

१८.६. लोकसंग्रहो भावैक्यो धर्मलिंगभेदाद्विना ।
भेदभावमुक्तये तु कर्तव्योऽहिंसको यत्नः ॥
lokasaṁgraho bhāvaikyo dharmalingabhedādvinā
bhedabhāvamuktaye tu kartavyo'hiṁsako yatnaḥ

Lokasaṁgraha activists need to focus attention on the most pressing needs of the society. For purposes of this summary statement, we take the view that social disharmony and disunity, aggravated by discrimination, call for urgent action in today's world. So we say in verse 18.6 that unity of thought and purpose—or bhāvaikyaḥ based on Gita ślokas III.11-16—without any discrimination on the basis of sex, religion, race, etc., represents the core of Lokasaṁgraha. We should look for those instances, past as well as present, when such a message of social harmony and unity was given, not only by saints in the form of a teaching, but also by kings or political leaders, for example, Emperor Aśoka in the third century B.C. The lesson to be learnt from this is that social harmony and unity led to all-round development of the country as well as peace, happiness and salvation of individual members of the society. But we have to be realistic enough to recognize that, in spite of all exhortations and appeals based on glorious examples, some problems of discrimination and denial of justice are likely to continue. Lokasaṁgraha activists are advised in this verse to try to find non-violent solutions to such problems, because otherwise the persons suffering from injustice are likely to fall victims to terrorists using violent methods.

१८.७. नवयुक्तिप्रयोगाद्धि सात्त्विकमूल्यवर्धनम् ।
दायित्वभावः प्राप्तव्यः सर्वभूतहितं प्रति ॥
navayuktiprayogāddhi sāttvikamūlyavardhanam
dāyitvabhāvaḥ prāptavyaḥ sarvabhūtahitaṁ prati

This verse stresses, first, the importance of promoting sāttvika social values—or sāttvika mūlya in Sanskrit—so that all the members of the society, and particularly the younger generation, support socially beneficial activities and causes, like mutual respect, caring for one another and sharing joys and sorrows without any discrimination. Lokasaṁgraha activists are called upon to try to evolve newer and newer techniques—or yukti in Sanskrit—so that people's interest in social values can be preserved and further strengthened. The need for new techniques is highlighted because forces of disintegration and extremes of individualism are taking people away from the very concept of social values, and all possible ways of countering these negative trends will have to be thought of.

The second point that is stressed in this verse relates to social responsibility—or dāyitvabhāva in Sanskrit. Every individual needs to have a feeling that, since parents and other members of the society bring up the new generation, they in turn have an obligation to contribute to the proper maintenance of the social order. It is not enough that people care only for themselves and their own families; the good of the whole society—or sarvabhūtahitam in the language of the Gita—also has to be taken into account—and this is the message of Lokasaṁgraha first introduced in chapter three of the Gita entitled "Karmayoga"—and, of course, continued in other chapters thereafter.

The phrase 'sarvabhūtahitam' used in verse 18.7 is intended to recall Gita ślokas V.25 and XII.4 where the longer phrase 'sarvabhūtahite ratāḥ' occurs (meaning those who rejoice in doing good to all creatures).

१८.८. लोकसंग्रहः कर्मणः आधारः आदौ वर्णितः ।
तथैव भक्तौ ज्ञाने च विशिष्टो लोकसंग्रहः ॥

lokasaṁgrahaḥ karmaṇaḥ ādhāraḥ ādau varṇitaḥ
tathaiva bhaktau jñāne ca viśiṣṭo lokasaṁgrahaḥ

The Gita ślokas III.20-26 in which Śrī Kṛṣṇa initially gave the teaching on Lokasaṁgraha are from the Karmayoga chapter. However, let no one think that the Lokasaṁgraha teaching was exhausted thereby—in fact, this teaching, using terms like sarvabhūtahitam, samaḥ sarveṣu bhūteṣu, ātmaupamya, nirmamo nirahaṁkāraḥ, etc., was equally emphasized by Śrī Kṛṣṇa in the chapters dealing with Bhakti as well as Jñāna. This has been explained in Part One of this book, and particularly in chapters five and six. Therefore, we can say that, for all Gita-followers, irrespective of whether they place the primary emphasis on Karma or Bhakti or Jñāna, Śrī Kṛṣṇa's advice is the same, namely, work for Lokasaṁgraha—the good of the society.

NOTES

PART ONE

CHAPTER ONE

1. Klaus K. Klostermaier, A Survey of Hinduism. State University of New York Press, Ablany, New York, 1989, pp. 385-6.
2. Ramesh S. Betai, Gita and Gandhiji. Gujarat Vidyapith Ahmedabad, 1970, pp. 36-45.
3. Nirad C. Chaudhuri, Hinduism. Oxford University Press, Oxford, 1979, pp. 123-4.
4. *Ibid.*, p. 124.
5. Eric J. Sharpe, The Universal Gita: Western Images of the Bhagavad Gita, A Bicentenary Survey. La Salle, Open Court, 1985.
6. Satya P. Agarwal, The Social Role of the Gita: How and Why. Urmila Agarwal, 11293 Ridermark Row, Columbia MD 21044, USA, 1993.

CHAPTER TWO

1. Kashi Nath Upadhyaya, Early Buddhism and the Bhagavad Gita. Motilal Banarsidass, Delhi, 1971, p. 475.
2. Sri Aurobindo, Essays on the Gita. New York edition, 1950, p. 156.
3. S. Radhakrishnan, The Bhagavad Gita. Harper and Row, New York, 1973, p. 96.
4. *Ibid.*, p. 50.
5. *Ibid.*, p. 96.
6. D.S. Sarma, "The Path of Yoga in the Gita". In the Cultural Heritage of India, Vol. III, H. Bhattacharyya, ed. The Ramakrishna Mission Institute of Culture, Calcutta, 1983, pp. 403-4.
7. Vinoba Bhave, Astadasi, Sarva Seva Sangh, Rajghat, Varanasi 1983, Hindi edition, p. 6.
8. Mahadev Desai, The Gospel of Selfless Action or The Gita according to Gandhi. Navajivan, Ahmedabad, 1977, pp.125-34.
9. K.N. Upadhyaya, Early Buddhism and the Bhagavad Gita, *op. cit.*, pp. 472-3.

10. Swami Ranganathananda, The Message of the Upanisads. Bharatiya Vidya Bhavan, Bombay, 1971, p. 150.
11. *Ibid.*, p. 152.
12. K. Klostermaier, A Survey of Hinduism, *op. cit.*, p. 105.
13. Swami Vivekananda, Complete Works (eight volumes). Advaita Ashrama, Calcutta, fourteenth edition, 1972, Vol.IV, p. 110.

CHAPTER THREE

1. P.M. Thomas, Twentieth Century Indian Interpretations of Bhagavad Gita: Tilak, Gandhi and Aurobindo. Indian Society for Promoting Christian Knowledge, Dellhi, 1987, p. 23.
2. B.G. Tilak, Gitarahasya. Tilak Borthers, Poona, sixth edition, 1986, p. 944.
3. S. Radhakrishnan, The Bhagavad Gita, *op. cit.*, p. 383.
4. Swami Vivekananda, Complete Works, *op. cit.*, Vol. III, pp. 142-3.
5. *Ibid.*, Vol. III, pp. 430-3.
6. Mahadev Desai, The Gospel of Selfless Action or the Gita according to Gandhi, *op. cit.*, p. 183.
7. Vinoba Bhave, Talks on the Gita. Sarva Seva Sangh, Varanasi, 1978, pp. 28-32.
8. Swami Vivekananda, Complete Works, *op. cit.*, Vol. I p. 457.
9. *Ibid.*, p. 457.
10. *Ibid.*, p. 457.
11. *Ibid.*, p. 457.
12. Tulsidas, Ramcharitmanas. Gita Press, Gorakhpur, sixty-seventh Hindi edition, 1987, pp. 1, 114, 554, 1047, and many others.
13. Shriman Narayan (ed.), The Selected Works of Mahatma Gandhi (six volumes). Navajivan, Ahmedabad, 1968, Vol. VI, pp. 158-64.
14. B.G. Tilak, Gitarahasya, *op. cit.*, pp. 460-1.
15. *Ibid.*, p. 534.
16. *Ibid.*, pp. 464-5.
17. R.S. Betai, Gita and Gandhiji, *op. cit.*, p. 35.
18. S. Radhakrishnan, The Bhagavad Gita, *op. cit.*, p. 97.

CHAPTER FOUR

1. S. Radhakrishnan, The Bhagavad Gita, *op. cit.*, p. 68.

2. Vinoba Bhave, Talks on the Gita, *op. cit.*, p. 4.
3. B.G. Tilak, Gitarahasya, *op. cit.*, pp. 490-1.
4. *Ibid.*, p. 451.
5. P.T. Raju, The Philosophical Traditions of India. George Allen and Unwin, London, 1971, pp. 215-6.

CHAPTER FIVE

1. B.G. Tilak, Gitarahasya, *op. cit.*, pp. 159-60.
2. Donald H. Bishop (ed.), Indian Thought: An Introduction. John Wiley and Sons, New York, 1975, p. 42.
3. Gita slokas VII.11, XVI.12 and others.
4. S. Radhakrishnan, The Bhagavad Gita, *op. cit.*, p. 119.
5. Mahadev Desai, The Gospel of Selfless Action or the Gita according to Gandhi, *op. cit.*, pp. 131-2.
6. S. Radhakrishnan, The Bhagavad Gita, *op. cit.*, p. 205.
7. Swami Ranganathananda, The Message of the Upanisads, *op. cit.*, p. 109.
8. S. Radhakrishnan, The Bhagavad Gita, *op. cit.*, p. 192.
9. *Ibid.*, p. 182.
10. Swami Chidbhavananda, The Bhagavad Gita. Sri Ramakrishna Tapovanam, Tirupparaitturai, 1975, pp. 366-7.
11. Shriman Narayan (ed.), The Selected Works of Mahatma Gandhi, *op. cit.*, Vol. VI, p. 39.
12. Vinoba Bhave, Talks on the Gita, *op. cit.*, p. 205.
13. Swami Vivekananda, Complete Works, *op. cit.*, Vol.VI, p.504.

CHAPTER SIX

1. Vinoba Bhave, The Steadfast Wisdom. Sarva Seva Sangh, Varanasi, 1985, p. 114.
2. D.S. Sarma, "The Path of Yoga in the Gita", *op. cit.*, p. 403.
3. *Ibid.*, p. 422.
4. *Ibid.*, pp. 422-3.
5. Swami Vivekananda, Complete Works, *op. cit.*, Vol. III, pp. 430-3.
6. Mahadev Desai, The Gospel of Selfless Action or the Gita according to Gandhi, *op. cit.*, pp. 129-31.
7. B.G. Tilak, Writings and Speeches. Ganeshan, Madras, 1922, p. 263.
8. Swami Vivekananda, Complete Works, *op. cit.*, Vol. I, pp. 476-7.

PART TWO

CHAPTER SEVEN

1. Robert N. Bellah, "Epilogue", in Religion and Progress in Modern Asia, ed. by him. Free Press, New York, 1965, p. 215.
2. Quoted by Arvind Sharma (with A. Ray, A Hejib and K. Young), Sati—Histoical and Phenomenological Essays. Motilal Banarsidass, Delhi, 1988, p. 27.
3. Satya P. Agarwal, The Social Role of the Gita: How and Why, *op. cit.*, p. 19.
4. *Ibid.*, p. 22.
5. K. Nag and D. Burman (eds.), The English Works of Raja Rammohun Roy. Sadharan Brahmo Samaj, Calcutta, 1945, p.126.
6. *Ibid.*, p. 116.
7. *Ibid.*, p. 105.
8. *Ibid.*, p. 112.
9. Arvind Sharma (with A. Ray, A. Hejib and K. Young), Sati—Historical and Phenomenological Essays, *op. cit.*, pp. 75-81.
10. Benoy Bhushan Roy, Socio-economic Impact of Sati in Bengal and the Role of Raja Rammohun Roy. Naya Prokash, Calcutta, 1987, pp. 108-9.
11. K. Nag and D. Burman (eds.), The English Works of Raja Rammohun Roy, *op. cit.*, p. 116.
12. *Ibid.*, p. 117.
13. *Ibid.*, p. 125.
14. *Ibid.*, p. 116.
15. *Ibid.*, p. 117.
16. *Ibid.*, p. 120.
17. Arvind Sharma (with A. Ray, A. Hejib and K. Young), Sati—Historical and Phenomenological Essays, *op. cit.*, p. 94.
18. Benoy Bhushan Roy, Socio-economic Impact of Sati in Bengal and the Role of Raja Rammohun Roy, *op. cit.*, p. 117.
19. Arvind Sharma, "The Gita, Suttee and Rammohun Roy", in Indian Economic and Social History Review, Vol. XX, No. 3 (1983), pp. 341-7.
20. Eric J. Sharpe, The Universal Gita, *op. cit.*, p. 14.
21. M.N. Jha, Modern Indian Political Thought: Rammohun Roy to Present-Day. Meenakshi Prakashan, Meerut, 1975, p. 14.

CHAPTER EIGHT

1. Romain Rolland, The Life of Ramakrishna. Advaita Ashrama, Calcutta, eighth eidtion, 1970, p. 222.
2. *Ibid.*, p. 223.
3. R.C. Majumdar, Swami Vivekananda: A Historical Review. General Printers, Calcutta, 1965, p. 13.
4. Ainslie T. Embree (ed.), The Hindu Tradition. Random House, New York, 1972, p. 302.
5. Romain Rolland, The Life of Ramakrishna, *op. cit.*, p. 85.
6. *Ibid.*, p. 230.
7. *Ibid.*, p. 231.
8. R.C. Majumdar, Swami Vivekananda: A Historical Review, *op. cit.*, pp. 18-9.
9. D.S. Sarma, The Renaissance of Hinduism. Banaras Hindu University, 1994, p. 265.
10. Swami Vivekananda, Complete Works, *op. cit.*, Vol. III, p. 301.
11. *Ibid.*, Vol. VI, p. 504.
12. Swami Nikhilananda, Vivekananda: A Biography. Advaita Ashrama Mayavati, third edition, 1975, p. 244.
13. *Ibid.*, p. 246.
14. *Ibid.*, pp. 246-7.
15. Life of Swami Vivekananda by his Eastern and Western Disciples. Advaita Ashrama, Calcutta, fifth edition, 1981, Vol. II. p. 328.
16. R.C. Majumdar, Swami Vivekananda: A Historical Review, *op. cit.*, p. 72.
17. Romain Rolland, The Life of Vivekananda and the Universal Gospel. Advaita Ashrama, Calcutta, seventh impression, 1970, p. 285.
18. Swami Vivekananda, Complete Works, *op. cit.*, Vol. III, p. 142.
19. *Ibid.*, Vol. III, pp. 213-27.
20. *Ibid.*, Vol. I, p. 4 and p. 18.
21. *Ibid.*, Vol. III, pp. 142-3.
22. *Ibid.*, Vol. V, p. 441.
23. R.C. Majumdar, Swami Vivekananda: A Historical Review, *op. cit.*, p. 41.

CHAPTER NINE

1. Stanley A. Wolpert, Tilak and Gokhale: Revolution and Reform in the Making of Modern India. University of

California Press, 1962, p. 2.

2. D.V. Tahmankar. Lokamanya Tilak: Father of Indian Unrest and Maker of Modern India. John Murray, London, 1956, p. 24.
3. *Ibid.*, p. 253.
4. *Ibid.*, p. 242.
5. D.S. Sarma, The Renaissance of Hinduism, *op. cit.*, p. 143.
6. K.M. Panikkar, The Foundations of New India. Allen and Unwin, London, 1963, p. 36.
7. B.G. Tilak, Gitarahasya, *op. cit.*, p. ix.
8. V. Subramaniam, "Karmayoga and the Rise of the Indian Middle Class", In the Journal of Arts and Ideas, Nos. 14-5, pp. 137-9.
9. K. Damodaran, Indian Thought: A Critical Survey. Asia Publishing House, Bombay, 1967, p. 394.
10. P. M. Thomas, Twentieth Century Indian Interpretations of Bhagavad Gita: Tilak, Gandhi and Arubindo, *op. cit.*, p. 73.
11. K. M. Panikkar, The Foundations of New India, *op. cit.*, p. 36.
12. D.P. Karmarkar, Bal Gangadhar Tilak: A Study. Popular Book Depot, Bombay, 1956, pp. 107-8.
13. D.V. Tahmankar, Lokamanya Tilak: Father of Indian Unrest and Maker of Modern India, *op. cit.*, Prelude.
14. D.S. Sarma, The Renaissance of Hinduism, *op. cit.*, pp. 143-4.
15. B.G. Tilak, Gitarahasya, *op. cit.*, pp. 464-5.
16. *Ibid.*, p. 534.
17. T.V. Parvate, Bal Gangadhar Tilak. Navajivan, Ahmedabad, 1958, p. 213.
18. *Ibid.*, p. 477.
19. B.G. Tilak, Gitarahasya, *op. cit.*, p. 554.
20. *Ibid.*, p. ix.

CHAPTER TEN

1. Karan Singh, Prophet of Indian Nationalism. George Allen and Unwin, London, 1963, p. 155.
2. R.C. Majumdar, History of the Freedom Movement in India. Mukhopadhyay, Calcutta, 1963, Vol. I, p. 423.
3. Karan Singh, Prophet of Indian Nationalism, *op. cit.*, p. 42.
4. *Ibid.*, p. 138.
5. *Ibid.*, p. 136.
6. T.V. Parvate, Bal Gangadhar Tilak, *op. cit.*, p. 530.

7. Karan Singh, Prophet of Indian Nationalism, *op. cit.*, pp. 143-44.
8. D.S. Sarma, The Renaissance of Hinduism, *op. cit.*, p. 338.
9. R.C. Majumdar, History of the Freedom Movement in India, *op. cit.*, Vol. II, p. 176.
10. Kishor Gandhi, Social Philosophy of Sri Aurobindo and The New Age. Sri Aurobindo Ashram, Pondicherry, second edition, 1991, p. 8.
11. Karan Singh, Prophet of Indian Nationalism, *op. cit.*, p. 138.
12. Sri Aurobindo, Essays on the Gita, New York edition, 1950, p. 499.
13. *Ibid.*, p. 122.
14. Sri Aurobindo, Essays on the Gita (second Series). Arya Publishing House, Calcutta, 1949, p. 407.
15. Sri Aurobindo, The Doctrine of Passive Resistance. Pondicherry, 1952, p. 78.
16. *Ibid.*, pp. 77-8.
17. Ursula King " Who is the Ideal Karmayogin? The Meaning of a Hindu Religious Symbol". In Religion, Vol. X, Spring 1980, p. 50.
18. V. Madhusudan Reddy, Seven Studies in Sri Aurobindo. Institute of Human Study, Hyderabad, 1989, p. 32.
19. Basant Kumar Lal, Contemporary Indian Philosophy. Motilal Banarsidass, Delhi, 1987, p. 220.
20. Karan Singh, Prophet of Indian Nationalism, *op. cit.*, p. 68.
21. *Ibid.*, p. 68.
22. T.V. Parvate, Bal Gangadhar Tilak, *op. cit.*, p. 529.
23. *Ibid.*, p. 530.
24. Karan Singh, Prophet of Indian Nationalism, *op. cit.*, pp.155-6.
25. Sri Aurobindo, Essays on the Gita (First Series). Arya Publishing House, Calcutta, 1949, p. 168.
26. K.M. Panikkar, The Foundations of New India, *op. cit.*, p. 45.
27. S. Radhakrishnan and C.A. Moore (eds.), A Sourcebook in Indian Philosophy. Princeton University Press, 1957, p. 577.
28. V. Madhusudan Reddy, Seven Studies in Sri Aurobindo. *op. cit.*, p. 32.
29. D.S. Sarma, The Renaissance of Hinduism, *op. cit.*, p. 338.

CHAPTER ELEVEN

1. M.K. Gandhi, The Story of My Experiments with Truth.

Beacon Press, Boston, 1957, p. 33.
2. *Ibid.*, p. 72.
3. D.S. Sarma, The Renaissance of Hinduism, *op. cit.*, p. 441.
4. *Ibid.*, p. 440.
5. V.P. Verma, The Political Philosophy of Mahatma Gandhi and Sarvodaya. Laxmi Narain, Agra, 1959, p. 59.
6. M.M. Verma, Gandhi's Technique of Mass Mobilization. R.K. Gupta, New Delhi, 1990, p. 124.
7. Mahadev Desai, The Gospel of Selfless Action or The Gita according to Gandhi, *op. cit.*, p. 127.
8. Quoted by M.M. Verma, Gandhi's Techinque of Mass Mobilization, *op. cit.*, p. 207.
9. Ramesh S. Betai, Gita and Gandhiji, *op. cit.*, p. 156.
10. Quoted by V.P. Verma, The Political Philosophy of Mahatma Gandhi and Sarvodaya, *op. cit.*, p. 72.
11. Mahadev Desai, The Gospel of Selfless Action or The Gita according to Gandhi, *op. cit.*, p. 128.
12. Harijan, 7th April, 1946, quoted by V.P. Verma, The Political Philsosophy of Mahatma Gandhi and Sarvodaya, *op. cit.*, p.31.
13. V.P. Verma, The Political Philosophy of Mahatma Gandhi and Sarvodaya, *op. cit.*, pp. 160-1.
14. S. Radhakrishnan, The Bhagavad Gita, *op. cit.*, pp. 101-2.
15. *Ibid.*, p. 205.
16. Romesh S. Betai, Gita and Gandhiji, *op. cit.*, p. 196.
17. Quoted by M.M. Verma, Gandhi's Techinque of Mass Mobilization, *op. cit.*, p. 207.
18. Ramesh S. Betai, Gita and Gandhiji, *op. cit.*, p. 155.
19. D.S. Sarma, The Renaissance of Hinduism, *op. cit.*, p. 436.
20. Raghavan Iyer, The Moral and Political Thought of Mahatma Gandhi. Oxford University Press, New York, 1978, p. 275.
21. K.M. Panikkar, The Foundations of New India, *op. cit.*, p. 44.

PART THREE

CHAPTER TWELVE

1. Jawaharlal Nehru, The Discovery of India. Oxford University Press, New Delhi, third impression, 1983, pp. 93-6.

2. Swami Vivekananda, Complete Works, *op. cit.*, Vol. III, pp. 430-3.
3. Sissela Bok, "Toward a Practical Ethic of Non-violence", and Devaki Jain, "Gandhian Contributions towards a Feminist ethic". In Speaking of Truth, Diana Eck and Devaki Jain (eds.), New Society Publishers, 1987, p. 256 and pp. 290-1.
4. Shriman Narayan (ed.), The Selected Works of Mahatma Ghandi, *op. cit.*, Vol. VI, pp. 160-3.
5. Martin Luther King, Strength to Love. Fount Paperbacks, UK, fourteenth impression, 1982, pp. 150-5.
6. Shriman Narayan (ed.), The Selected Works of Mahatma Gandhi, *op. cit.*, Vol. VI, p. 163.
7. S. Radhakrishnan, The Bhagavad Gita, *op. cit.*, p. 96.
8. Swami Vivekananda, Complete Works, *op. cit.*, Vol. I, p. 478.
9. S. Radhakrishnan, The Bhagavad Gita, *op. cit.*, p. 199.
10. Sri Aurobindo, Essays on the Gita, *op. cit.*, New York edition, 1950, pp. 200-1.
11. B.G. Tilak, Gitarahasya, *op. cit.*, pp. 464-5.
12. Raghavan Iyer, The Moral and Political Thought of Mahatma Gandhi, *op. cit.*, p. 326.

CHAPTER THIRTEEN

1. B.G. Tilak, Gitarahasya, *op. cit.*, pp. 400-7.
2. Mahadev Desai, The Gospel of Selfless Action or The Gita according to Gandhi, *op. cit.*, p. 133.
3. K.N. Upadhyaya, Early Buddhism and the Bhagavad Gita, *op. cit.*, p. 488.
4. Mahadev Desai, the Gospel of Selfless Action or The Gita according to Gandhi, *op. cit.*, p. 176.
5. B.G. Tilak, Gitarahasya, *op. cit.*, p. 958.
6. *Ibid.*, p. 407.
7. Swami Chinmayananda, The Holy Geeta. Central Chinmaya Mission Trust, Bombay, no date, p. 173.
8. J.G. Arapura, Personal Discussion at McMaster University, August 1990.
9. Shriman Narayan (ed.), The Selected Works of Mahatma Gandhi, *op. cit.*, Vol. IV, pp. 344-6.
10. Vinoba Bhave, Talks on the Gita, *op. cit.*, pp. 202-3.
11. *Ibid.*, pp. 203-4.
12. M.K. Gandhi, The Bhagavad Gita, Orient Paperbacks, New

Delhi, no date, pp. 79-80.
13. *Ibid.*, pp. 79-80.
14. Sri Aurobindo, The Doctrine of Passive Resistance. Pondicherry, 1952, pp. 77-8.
15. Sri Aurobindo, Essays on the Gita, *op. cit.*, pp. 112-3.
16. S. Radhakrishnan, The Bhagavad Gita, *op. cit.*, p. 135.
17. B.G. Tilak, Gitarahasya, *op. cit.*, p. 407.

CHAPTER FOURTEEN

1. Balkoba Bhave, Gita Tattva Bodh (Hindi edition). Sarva Seva Sangh, Varanasi, 1981, p. 130.
2. Vinoba Bhave, Talks on the Gita, *op. cit.*, p. 203.
3. *Ibid.*, p. 203.
4. J. G. Arapura, "Sociological Alienation and Gandhian Philosophy", in Panchshila, Vol. I, No. 4, 1956, p. 24.
5. Swami Vivekananda, Complete Works, *op. cit.*, Vol. I, p. 77.
6. Raghavan Iyer, The Moral and Political Thought of Mahatma Gandhi, *op. cit.*, p. 282.
7. Swami Chidbhavanda, The Bhagavad Gita, *op. cit.*, p. 827.
8. Raghavan Iyer, The Moral and Political Thought of Mahatma Gandhi, *op. cit.*, pp. 275-83.
9. Sri Aurobindo, Essays on the Gita, *op. cit.*, pp. 435-6.
10. D.S. Sarma, The Renaissance of Hinduism, *op. cit.*, p. 340.
11. S. Radhakrishnan and C.A. Moore (eds.), A Sourcebook in Indian Philosophy, *op. cit.*, p. 577.

CHAPTER FIFTEEN

1. Swami Ranganathananda, Science of Human Uniqueness: Vikram Sarabhai Memorial Lecture. Ahmedabad, 1991, pp. 54-5.
2. K. Mishra, "Indian Value System and Social Development": Paper presented at the Annual Conference of the Association of Asian Studies at Laval University, Quebec, 1989, pp. 1-3.
3. M. Hiriyanna, "Philosophy of Values". In The Cultural Heritage of India, Vol. III, H. Bhattacharyya, ed. The Ramakrishna Mission Institute of Culture, Calcutta, 1983, pp. 645-54.
4. B.G. Tilak, Gitarahasya, *op. cit.*, p. 90.
5. M. Hiriyanna," Philosophy of Values", *op. cit.*, pp. 647-8.
6. B.G. Tilak, Gitarahasya, *op. cit.*, p. 456.

7. K. Mishra, "Indian Value System and Social Development", *op. cit.*, pp. 1-3.
8. Romain Rolland, The Life of Vivekananda and the Universal Gospel, *op. cit.*, p. 286.
9. Indira Patel, Vivekananda's Approach to Social Work. Sri Ramakrishna Math, Madras, 1987, p. 91.
10. Indira Rothermund, "Discussion", in Tradition and Modernity in India, ed. by A.B. Shah and C.R. M. Rao Manaktalas, Bombay, 1965, p. 125.
11. M.M. Verma, Gandhi's Technique of Mass Mobilization, *op. cit.*, p. 125.
12. S. Radhakrishnan, The Bhagavad Gita, *op. cit.*, p. 383.
13. M. Hiriyanna, "Philosophy of Values", *op. cit.*, p. 648.
14. B.K. Lal, Contemporary Indian Philosophy, *op. cit.*, pp. 219-20.
15. Swami Vivekananda, Complete Works, *op. cit.*, Vol. VI, p.504.
16. B.G. Tilak, Gitarahasya, *op. cit.*, p. 713.
17. Quoted by V.P. Verma, The Political Philosophy of Mahatma Gandhi and Sarvodaya, *op. cit.*, p. 72.
18. Raghavan Iyer, The Moral and Political Thought of Mahatma Gandhi, *op. cit.*, p. 67.
19. Vinoba Bhave, Talks on the Gita, *op. cit.*, p. 205.

CHAPTER SIXTEEN

1. Ambati Rao and Gomathi S. Rao, "Helping Kids Overcome Peer Pressure", in India Abroad Weekly Paper, New York, 25 November, 1994, p. 3.
2. *Ibid.*, p. 3.
3. Seminar on Swami Vivekananda's Teaching. Sri Ramakrishna Vidyalaya, Coimbatore, 1964, p. 98.
4. William Peterson, "Success Story: Japanese American Style", in New York Times Magazine, 9 January, 1966.
5. Ursula King, "Who is the Ideal Karmayogin? The Meaning of a Hindu Religious Symbol", *op. cit.*, pp. 52-3.
6. Swami Vivekananda, Our Women. Advaita Ashrama, Calcutta, 1990, p. 43.
7. Quoted by Swami Ranganathananda, The Message of Kanyakumari. Vivekananda Kendra, Madras, 1981, p. 9.

CHAPTER SEVENTEEN

1. M. Hiriyanna, The Essentials of Indian Philosophy. Macmillan,

New York, 1949, pp. 54-6.
2. Swami Vivekananda, Complete Works, *op. cit.*, Vol. III, pp. 223-4.
3. Shriman Narayan (ed.), The Selected Works of Mahatma Gandhi, *op. cit.*, Vol. VI, pp. 155-60.
4. Quoted by Raghavan Iyer, The Moral and Political Thought of Mahatma Gandhi, *op. cit.*, pp. 311-2.
5. Sri Aurobindo, Essays on the Gita, *op. cit.*, pp. 498-9.
6. Raghavan Iyer, The Moral and Political Thought of Mahatma Gandhi, *op. cit.*, p. 194.
7. Mahadev Desai, The Gospel of Selfless Action or The Gita according to Gandhi, *op. cit.*, p. 131.
8. M.K. Gandhi, Satyagraha in South Africa. Navajivan, 1950, p. 206.
9. Shriman Narayan (ed.), The Selected Works of Mahatma Gandhi, *op. cit.*, Vol. VI, p. 169.

CHAPTER EIGHTEEN

1. Sri Aurobindo, Essays on the Gita, *op. cit.*, p. 122.
2. For details, please see Chapter Seven.
3. For details, please see Chapter Eight.
4. For details, please see Chapter Nine.
5. For details, please see Chapter Ten.
6. For details, please see Chapter Eleven.
7. J.G. Arapura, Personal Discussion at McMaster University, August 1990.
8. For details, please see Satya P. Agarwal, The Social Role of the Gita: How and Why, *op. cit.*, Chapter Eleven.
9. Swami Vivekananda, Complete Works, *op. cit.*, Vol. VI, p. 504.
10. Quoted by V.P. Verma, The Political Philosophy of Mahatma Gandhi and Sarvodaya, *op. cit.*, p. 72.

INDEX

Numbers refer to pages except that a number following the letters fn denotes a footnote